THE POWER OF BEAUTY

On the Aesthetics of Homer, Plato, and Cicero

THE POWER OF BEAUTY

On the Aesthetics of Homer, Plato, and Cicero

BY INGA R. GAMMEL

Aarhus University Press |

THE POWER OF BEAUTY
– On the Aesthetics of Homer, Plato, and Cicero
© The author and Aarhus University Press 2015
Layout: Anette Ryevad, www.ryevadgrafisk.dk
Cover: Idea, Inga R. Gammel. Design, Jørgen Sparre
The book is typeset in Adobe Garamond Pro
Printing: Narayana Press, Denmark

ISBN 978 87 7124 771 8

Aarhus University Press
Langelandsgade 177
DK – 8200 Aarhus N
www.unipress.dk

International distributors:
Gazelle Book Services Ltd.
White Cross Mills
Hightown, Lancaster, LA1 4XS
United Kingdom
www.gazellebookservices.co.uk

ISD
70 Enterprise Drive, Suite 2
Bristol, CT 06010
USA
www.isdistribution.com

Published with the financial support of

The Carlsberg Foundation
The VELUX Foundation
The Carlsen-Lange Foundation

CONTENTS

PREFACE   9

GENERAL INTRODUCTION   11

The Spell of Beauty   11

The Arrogance of Modernity   13

The Greek-Roman Beginnings of Aesthetics   14

Methodical Approach   17

PART I

THE BEAUTIFUL AND THE UGLY   21

The Mythic Worldview of Homer   21

Introduction: Myth and Beauty   21

1. The Order of the Homeric World   22
   The Relationship between Zeus, Poseidon, and Hades   23
   A Strange Friendship: Hades and Helios   25
   A Holistic Worldview   26

2. Shining Olympos   27
   The Divine Residences and Their Inhabitants   28

3. The Underworld   29
   The God Hades   30
   The Underworld from a Human Perspective   32
   Erebos, the Dark as the Image of Ultimate Horror   35

4. Earth and "the Sweetness of Life"   36
   Sunrise   36
   The Quality of Shining   37
   Remote Places   38
   The Spirit of Life   39

5. Shining Beauty as Destiny   39
   The Magnetism of Physical Beauty   40
   To be Godlike   41

Divine Tricks of Beautification and De-Beautification 42
Old Age and Care of the Dead Body 44

6. The Embellishment of Life 46
The Allure of Smiles, Courtesy, and Seduction 46
The Shining Artefacts 49
Shining Purple 52
The Marriage of Aphrodite and Hephaistos 54

7. The Ugly 54
The Ugly Ones: Ugliness and Lack of Intelligence 55
The Ambiguity of the Ugly: Monsters 56

8. Beyond the Ugly: War and Destruction 58
War as a Pastime for the Gods 59
The Meadow of Skamandros as War-Theater 60
The Prize of Glory 61

9. The Legacy: The Infinite Beauty of the World 63
The Hierarchy: The Beautiful versus the Ugly 63
Living Beauty versus Artificial Beauty 65
The Epiphany of Beauty 65

PART II

THE BEAUTIFUL, THE GOOD, AND THE TRUE 67

Plato's Philosophy of Beauty 67

Introduction: Philosophy and Beauty 67

1. The Question 67

2. The Passion for Beauty 68
Eros, the Daemon 69
The Dynamics of Beauty 71

3. Passion, Beauty, and Education 72

4. The Myth of Beauty 74
Beauty Itself 77

5. Myth and Philosophy 78
Philosophical Myths 79
On Why Philosophers Must Surrender To Myths 79

6. The Myth of Beauty Continued: Beauty, and the Myth of Soul 81
Under the Plane Tree 81
The Palinode, or the Myth of Soul 83

7. Beauty and Rhetoric   87

8. The Beauty of Cosmos   88
   Cosmos as Beautiful Order   *90*
   The Beauty of Living Beings   *91*

9. The Ugly as a Border Concept   92
   The Ugliness of Socrates   *95*

10. Paideia and Beauty   97
    The Lawgiver   *98*
    Laws as Magic Songs   *99*
    Sing and Dance   *100*
    The Golden Mean   *101*
    Eudaimonia   *103*

11. The Legacy: Beauty as the Bond between Man and the Divine   104
    To Elaborate on Tradition   *104*
    The Metaphysics of Beauty   *104*
    Beauty as the Shining Bond between Man and the Divine   *105*

PART III

DECORUM   107

Cicero's Ideas of Beauty in Everyday Life   107

Introduction: Beauty in Everyday Life   107

1. Cicero, a Man of the World   107
   Being a Man of Letters   *108*
   Vocation and Grand Ambitions   *110*

2. The Mission   110
   Cicero's Approach to Philosophy   *111*
   The Rural Greeks and the Urban Romans   *112*
   Tradition   *113*

3. Eloquence   114
   Rhetoric   *116*
   The Rhetorician   *116*

4. Details of Beauty   118
   Style   *119*
   Proper Wording   *120*
   On Charm, Wit, and Humor   *121*

5. Decorum as the Great Concept for *the Art of Rhetoric* and *the Art of Life*   122
  The Beauty of Decorum   124
  Lack of Decorum: Ugliness and Evil   124

6. The Origin of Beauty   126
  Natural Aesthetics   128
  On the Ugly   129

7. Tusculum: The Art of Civilized Living   131
  The Beauty of the Environment   132
  Dress, Polite Manners, and Hospitality   134
  Libraries   136
  Humanitas   137

8. Dignity   137
  Vita Activa and Vita Contemplativa   138
  Otium cum Dignitate   139

9. The Legacy: The Civilizing Effect of Beauty   140
  Education   141
  Decorum: An All-Embracing Aesthetics   142
  Common Sense   142

PART IV

THE MODERN EXILE OF BEAUTY   145

  Repercussions from the Collapse of a Philosophical Tradition   145

1. Aesthetic Theory in the Twentieth Century   145

2. Aesthetics as the Philosophy of Art   148

3. Wrestling with Plato   150

4. The Concept of Beauty in Modern Receptions of Antiquity   154

5. Historians of Ancient Aesthetics   159

6. The Importance of Reconsidering Beauty   162

REFERENCES   167
INDEX OF NAMES   171
INDEX LOCORUM   175

PREFACE

When I started many years ago to carry out research on the idea of beauty, it came as a surprise that the philosophical and theoretical traditions on this very concept had collapsed. How could such a prominent idea become outdated? I turned to the history of aesthetics for an answer and studied the collapse of classical tradition leading to the contemporary exile of the concept of beauty.

The phenomena that were the center of interest to the ancient authors such as, for example, sunrise, glittering colors, the countless number of forms, the lucidity of style, etc. are still part of our contemporary world, but these phenomena are being neglected in terms of philosophy and theory. Therefore, I moved further to the ancient authors in whose footsteps we still walk. Here I found a rich, varied, and profound discourse, showing many aspects of the beautiful and the ugly. Throughout Antiquity the idea of beauty is interlaced in almost every topic from cosmology down to questions such as: how should I organize my life, and what belongs to the good life. In brief, the ancient authors have something to say about the power of beauty.

The present study is an attempt to illuminate the aesthetics of Antiquity and to show how much we still owe to these traditions in terms of our approach to life in general. Also, in our imagery, and in the vocabulary we use, the ancients are with us. In a period of time in history where the idea of beauty has been abandoned as a proper subject for philosophical and theoretical investigation, it is crucial to reconsider this classical legacy.

I would like to thank for funding, which, looking back, made this work possible. In this regard my sincere gratitude goes to the Carlsberg Foundation in Denmark from which I was privileged in 1996 to obtain a two-year research grant with study space at the University of Aarhus. Following this, from 1998 to 1999 I held the Carlsberg-Clare Hall Visiting Fellowship at the University of Cambridge. These periods allowed me to study the dawn of ancient aesthetics, which over the years gave rise to a number of publications, activities, and engagements in research programs in Denmark and abroad. This book is one of the results of this very rewarding period of my life.

In addition, I am indebted to Her Majesty Queen Ingrid's Foundation for funding in association with Accademia di Danimarca, Rome.

Aarhus, June 2015
Inga R. Gammel

When the ancients speak, they do not merely tell us about themselves. They tell about us. They do that in every case in which they can be made to speak, because they tell us who we are.

Bernard Williams

GENERAL INTRODUCTION

The Spell of Beauty

The fascination of beauty is universal. Archaic man was puzzled by the beautiful, and evidence is abundant. The sense of beauty can be traced even further back in pre-historic times where a variety of images, artefacts, burial customs etc. bear witness to man's appreciation of beauty. The careful beautification of the body, of tools and utensils, and of surroundings appears to be a universal phenomenon, and we simply do not know of cultures, pre-historic, ancient, or present that do not in one way or another pay attention to beauty, whether it appears in the form of order and structure or in the forms of pattern, decoration, color, etc.

Reflections on beauty were put into words by myth long before the idea of beauty ever became the subject of philosophical investigation. Archaic man associated creation and the becoming of the world with the divine and the beautiful. Thus the archaic mind combined the very essence of life, or *being,* with the idea of the beautiful, the good and the true, a profound view that was to captivate and puzzle the human mind for centuries, and still does.

As a phenomenon beauty calls attention to itself in a captivating and enchanting way. The beautiful emerges with a certain sovereignty and presence. It has been argued that the Greek term *to kalon* might have been derived from *kalein,* or *kelein,* both meaning "to call."[1] Then, phenomena of beauty seem to serve as landmarks that might focus man's orientation in the direction of life sustaining forces and thus fight the feeling of alienation. The beautiful might be stunning, or exotic, but it is in principle never daemonic. Rather, it embodies an aphrodisiac tenor. Then, the encounter with beauty produces energy in the human soul and supports feelings of being at home in the world, and for a moment the world is set free from feelings

---

[1] Arthur Hilary Armstrong (Ed.): *Classical Mediterranean Spirituality.* Egyptian, Greek, Roman. Vol. 15 of World Spirituality. An Encyclopedic History of Religious Quest. London 1986, p. 307.

of estrangement. Other considerations to the term *to kalon* are, that its meaning is mingled with a range of positive values such as good, strong, just, healthy, whole, and powerful. Ancient man strongly believed in the beautiful and the good as an entity, and this principle, articulated by the Greeks as *kalon kagathon,* dwells at the roots of Western aesthetics.

While beauty is considered essential to life itself as a life sustaining force, this very experience at the same time calls attention to the opposite, namely lack of beauty, or even the ugly. In a deep sense the ugly is believed to be antagonistic to life itself, and, therefore, the ugly becomes associated with evil and with life threatening forces. Hence, man's perception is influenced by what he thinks may be good for him, and at the bottom of man's likes and dislikes aesthetic theory has to face some very fundamental issues, namely the question: what supports life, and what does not? As we shall see, the ancient authors are somehow reluctant to offer too much energy to discuss the ugly. As a matter of fact, it is only in recent times that the extensive discussion of the ugly has gained ground in the history of aesthetics. An example of this is Karl Rosenkranz' work *Ästhetik des Hässlichen,* written in the nineteenth century.

The aesthetics of Antiquity has had a huge impact on European culture. The Greek-Roman poets, philosophers, and rhetoricians developed a rich and fertile text corpus that has provided generation after generation with images, words, phrases, and ideas of the beautiful and the ugly. This legacy has to a major degree shaped our way of thinking and given rise to a sophisticated aesthetic vocabulary. The use of ancient mythology and philosophy as points of reference manifests itself in the humanities, but also in areas such as advertising and natural science. Although the world of Antiquity is often addressed and treated in a superficial way by the use of names, symbols, images, and vocabulary, any reference to this legacy is, nevertheless, supposed to ennoble the area to which it is attached. Also, in the language of everyday life as for example in colloquial speech, the terms from the aesthetic vocabulary developed by Antiquity have come to rank almost as natural terms. One of the more conspicuous examples is the word *cosmos*, still used by modern scientists. The very word *cosmos* is a word that was used to describe something which appeared as beautiful order. Although modern cosmologists can inform us that *cosmos* is not only about order, order does indeed still prevail over chaos.[2]

---

2   For at more detailed discussion, see chapter 7: "Epiphany. The Dawn of Cosmology with Focus on Empedocles" in Inga R. Gammel: *The Passion for Order.* Myth and Beauty in the Writings of Plato, Heisenberg, Pauli, Jung, John D. Barrow, and Others. Münchener Schriften zur Design Science, Band 3. Shaker Verlag. Aachen 2015.

Today, however, we face a huge gap between the experience of beauty and contemporary aesthetic theory. If we look at the theoretical landscape, produced by Modernity, it is hardly possible to find any theories of beauty. Contemporary aesthetics is all about art. For various reasons the philosophy of beauty, in which art is only one of the areas where beauty may be found, has collapsed. Modernity has disqualified the myths and the philosophies of the past, and thus the idea of beauty has slowly become obsolete. In brief, the concept of beauty has become exiled from contemporary aesthetic theory. Nevertheless, beauty is a concern to everybody, and the term ranks among other vital terms.

The Arrogance of Modernity

While the pre-modern epochs found that the concept of beauty was needed like other essential concepts such as, for example, soul, the good, truth, the divine, and quality in order to understand reality and human life, the modern approach to beauty has become one of skepticism and contempt. Scholars in general are hostile towards the idea of beauty, and they also consider the concept of the beautiful and the good – the *kalon kagathon* – as a primitive and unconscious response to the world. Thus the modern emergence of historical consciousness has resulted in a paradox; the more we know about the past the more the past becomes reduced to a field we struggle to describe, but one to which we take no interest in real dialogue. The arrogant denial of the actuality of pre-modern aesthetics has left modern aesthetics with a totally alienated approach to fundamental philosophical problems such as the importance of beauty to human life.

In addition, the separation of aesthetics and ethics has turned out to become a major problem. According to Susan Sontag, Modernity is characterized by a tendency to compartmentalization, resulting in a razor sharp distinction between the beautiful, the good, and the true. This, Sontag considers to be a Western confusion triggered by historical condition. According to her it is not possible to make a clean cut between the aesthetic and the ethical. The aesthetical as well as the ethical dimension are both at work, whether we respond to beauty, to art, or to events in life as such.[3] In a similar way, Heinz Meyer has called attention to the fact that the precise division between the beautiful, the artificial, and the aesthetical forces upon reality the act of Procrustes – his favorite game having been that of shortening, or stretching whatever came his way so that it fitted to the size of his bed. These different concepts, says Meyer, refer to almost the same.[4]

---

3   See Susan Sontag's essay "On Style" in *Partisan Review,* 4/1965. Vol. XXXII. 1965.
4   See Heinz Meyer: *Das Ästhetische Urteil.* Zürich. New York 1990, p. 94 ff.

In effect, contemporary aesthetics suffers from the lack of philosophical and theoretical awareness of the broader scope of beauty, and the breakdown of the concept of beauty as an all-inclusive concept has had some very negative consequences. Modernity has put a theoretical taboo on the concept of beauty, and the repercussions from the collapse of the philosophies of beauty can be observed in the humanities and in the social and natural sciences as well. Today, the philosophical and academic neglect of the concept of beauty has reached a point where the modern approach turns out to be misleading. Thus, the need to reconsider the pre-modern aesthetical traditions springs from Modernity itself. Historical development does in no way transgress or outdate the function of aesthetic categories, which have their origin in epochs prior to ours. Despite the philosophies of beauty having slowly collapsed during the nineteenth and twentieth centuries, aesthetics is, to a large extent, a field where images, terms, and concepts are recycled, the latter under slightly different labels. Therefore, as suggested by the German historian and philosopher, Wilhelm Perpeet, it makes sense to study again the history of the idea of beauty.

The Greek-Roman Beginnings of Aesthetics

A number of pre-modern epochs might serve as ground for a study on beauty. But some epochs are more conspicuous than others. In a European context the aesthetics of Antiquity is of special interest as this epoch, in particular, contains the beginnings of articulated and philosophically reflected writings on beauty. The ancient reflections on beauty show that beauty is naturally linked with matters such as cosmology, the general education of man, and the art of living. In addition, the attempt to understand the nature of beauty is in any case an exercise in searching for an adequate interpretation of reality itself. Hence, the main purpose of my study is to illuminate the origin of the images and ideas of beauty developed and refined through a long and arduous process, the beginnings of which are to be found in Greek mythology and philosophy. Cornerstones in this tradition are the Homeric epic and the philosophy of Plato. Later, Greek tradition comes to play an important role in the establishment of Roman rhetoric. Cicero translates the Greek texts into Latin in order to educate the Roman people, and the inspiration from Greek philosophy flows into Cicero's own ideas of applied aesthetics. Thus the reason for choosing Homeric epic, Plato's philosophy, and Cicero's rhetoric is the simple fact that these three areas *together* hold the key to what became a long-standing tradition upon which generation after generation has thrived. Although the works of Homer, Plato, and Cicero are disparate in time and in genres, the theme of beauty runs through these works. Thus Plato flourishes on the achievements of Homeric mythology, and Cicero brings further the rich inspiration from Greek culture. Each of them in their own fashion reflects on beauty and aspires to grasp the *ratio* of the world. Another equally strong motivating force, which furthers the development of an aesthetic vocabulary, is their urgent felt need to educate and improve mankind. The entanglement of beauty and *paideia*, that is, education in a broad sense, is a feature that is equally shared by Homer, Plato, and Cicero. And last, but not least, as we shall see, with the development of aesthetic reflection the issue of beauty spreads to every facet of human life.

Another crucial feature, which links together Homer, Plato, and Cicero, is the fact that their reflections take their departure first and foremost from the beauty of living beings, and from the beauty of the natural world. By consequence, the beauty of cosmos, the beauty of the natural world, and the beauty of living beings prevail over the beauty of any man-made artificial object. Over time this outlook generates two different paths in European aesthetic tradition, namely the philosophy of beauty, and the philosophy of art. The founding father of the philosophy of art is Aristotle. He focuses on art and not on the philosophy of beauty. In his *Metaphysics (XIII, iii 8 iv)* Aristotle points out that the main examples of beauty are to be found in the field of mathematics as orderly arrangement, proportion, and definiteness. He announces that he will return to this topic later, but we have no evidence that he ever did. Hence, Aristotle's contribution was to the philosophy of art, and not to the philosophy of beauty. Among those who later contributed greatly to the philosophy of beauty were Plotinus and Saint Augustine, but as I have chosen to focus on the very beginnings of a tradition, my analyses are exclusively reserved to Homeric mythology, Plato's philosophical reflections, and to Cicero's writings on applied aesthetics.

It is a recurring phenomenon among scholars and scientists who have studied Antiquity to be fascinated and deeply moved by the abundance of fair counseling and wisdom stored in the ancient sources. Scientists such as Carl Gustav Jung, Wolfgang Pauli, Werner Heisenberg[5] and Erwin Schrödinger were deeply impressed by Plato's philosophy. In his book *What is Life?* Schrödinger asks the following question: "what has endowed Plato's life-work with such unsurpassed distinction that it shines in undiminished splendour after more than two thousands years?"[6] According to Schrödinger, Plato's fame is due to his theory of the forms, or ideas. This sort of reverence for Plato gave rise to the following witty remark made by Alfred North

---

5   For approaches to the authorship of Plato by scientists such as Werner Heisenberg, Wolfgang Pauli, and Carl Gustav Jung, see Inga R. Gammel: *The Passion for Order*. Shaker Verlag. Aachen 2015.

6   Erwin Schrödinger: *What is Life?* Cambridge University Press 2001, p. 141ff.

Whitehead: "the safest general characterization of the European philosophical tradition is that it consists of a series of footnotes to Plato."[7]

Indeed, it has been and still is a much discussed topic as to how Greece, in particular, could in a relatively short span of time produce such an abundance of geniuses whose works just still shine. In his essay *The Value of Greece to the Future of the World* Gilbert Murrey has considered this question. Although Murrey's essay was written in 1921, it is not out of date. On the contrary, it nails down some very crucial facts, which illuminate why it is still worth studying Antiquity. In terms of general knowledge, scientific knowledge and technical skill, we have got far beyond Antiquity, but we cannot in spite of all our progress get beyond the human values or topics that are dealt with in, for example, the works of Homer or Aeschylus. Murrey says: "but hardly any sensible person ever imagines that he has got beyond their essential quality, the quality that has made them great."[8] What Murrey hints at is this: we may be modern, but in regard to our values and emotional life we have not changed dramatically. Therefore, the significance of such phenomena as sunrise, love, war etc. to human life remains. Also, Murrey's characterization of Greek philosophy and poetry is of interest. He writes: "Greek philosophy speaks straight to any human being who is willing to think simply, Greek art and poetry to any one who can use his imagination and enjoy beauty. He has not to put on the fetters and the blinkers of any new system in order to understand them; he has only to get rid of his own – a much more profitable and less troublesome task."[9]

I myself have also found it a great privilege to study authors such as Homer, Plato and Cicero who laid the building blocks for some of the most cherished values in Western culture. It has been a journey full of surprise. If one should ever forget to notice the beauty, the greatness, and the splendor of life, Homeric epic can guide one's attention back to basics. As for Plato, one must admire the profound tenor of his thinking and his ability to illuminate the quality of beauty, manifesting itself throughout the whole of cosmos down to the single seed. And, finally, with Cicero, sound counseling concerning of all sorts of everyday life, vitality, elegance, and humor flow in abundance. We may think that mankind has changed dramatically in the course of time, but in terms of human life and its basic values we are pretty much concerned with the same issues as our ancestors. We are still engrossed more,

---

7   Alfred North Whitehead is quoted from Harry A. Wolfson: "Extradeical and Intradeical Interpretations of Platonic Ideas" in *Journal of the History of Ideas*. April-June 1961. Vol. XXII, Number 1, p. 3.

8   Gilbert Murrey: "The Value of Greece to the Future of the World" in *The Legacy of Greece*. Ed. by R. W. Livingstone. The Clarendon Press. Oxford 1928 p. 5.

9   Gilbert Murrey 1928, p. 17.

or less, in the same great questions about life and death, beauty and the ugly, and how to find the proper formula for how to live a decent life. According to Bernard Williams, whose viewpoint I have chosen as a motto for my study, the ancients not only tell about themselves. They also tell about us.

Methodical Approach

Finally, I want to make a few comments as to the approach that has been guiding my work. First, it must be emphasized that this study is in no way a philological project. As noticed by the Polish philosopher and writer of the history of aesthetics, Wladyslaw Tatarkiewicz, it is not always advantageous to restrict the limits of the research of beauty to the very words.[10] Homer, for example, does not employ the word *kalos* when the old men of Troy describe the outstanding appearance of Helen. But Homeric epic is, nevertheless, teeming with descriptions of the beautiful, including the beauty of Helen that became the cause of the Trojan War.[11] Then, my aim has been to throw light upon the many and diverse features in which beauty appears in ancient myths, in Greek philosophy, and in Roman rhetoric. The texts differ according to genre and content, but the reflections on beauty are their recurring concern.

Second, as my main objective is to introduce the emergence of a tradition I have chosen to focus on the variety of examples and, for the most part, to abstain from referring to discussions of problems and specific issues in the overwhelming academic literature on Homeric epic, Platonic tradition, and Roman rhetoric. My aim is rather to show how the images and ideas of beauty over time become elaborated in terms of philosophical depth and during this process flow into various areas of life. Accordingly, I do not address, for example, the popular anecdote claiming that Homer was blind, and I do not address "the Homeric Question" either, that is, the standing dispute on whether the *Iliad* and the *Odyssey* were indeed composed by the same author. As to the question of authorship, I am in agreement with Richmond Lattimore whose translations I have used. Lattimore and others acknowledge the unity in the Homeric epic. Among other things Lattimore emphasizes the important observation that the main characters in the *Iliad* and the *Odyssey* do not

---

10   In *Geschichte der Ästhetik* Tatarkiewicz has articulated his strategy as follows: "Wer die Entwicklung des menschlichen Denkens über das Schöne darstellen will, darf sich nicht an das Wort (das Schöne) klammern, denn diese Gedanken traten in mannigfach verschiedener Terminologie auf, nicht selten sogar, ohne dass dieses Wort vorkommt." *Geschichte der Ästhetik*, Erster Band. *Die Ästhetik der Antike*. Basel/Stuttgart 1979, p. 23.

11   See Wladyslaw Tatarkiewics: *Geschicte der Ästhetik, Band I*, pp. 56-57.

differ in terms of personality and psychology.[12] Also concerning Plato, biographic data is sparse, and there are standing scholarly debates as to whether, for example, a dialogue such as *Greater Hippias* was indeed written by Plato. However, for my purpose it is sufficient that the dialogue is included in the *Plato. Complete Works* and introduced by John M. Cooper with the remark that "its philosophical content seems genuinely Platonic."[13]

In the case of Cicero we are faced with a totally different situation. Cicero wrote extensively about the development of his own authorship; he also wrote about his life and work, and about his family, friends, and contemporaries. And they wrote about Cicero. As luck would have it, the greater bulk of all this information was saved for posterity. Hence, Cicero is the one person from Antiquity about whom we are really well informed. As biographic data is a genuine part of Cicero's authorship, it comes naturally to use this information.

To the best of my belief there will in principle always be an inner connection between the personal life of an individual and his works, or theoretical outlook. But in many cases we must forgo further proof because of the lack of suitable material. In this way my analyses of Homer, Plato, and Cicero reflect the very nature of each individual authorship rather than complying with rigid schemata.

Third, to give systematic and detailed analyses of Homeric epic, Platonic philosophy, and the rhetoric of Cicero are beyond the scope of this study. I nurture no ambition to have touched upon all the disparate questions that could be asked in relation to the texts that I deal with. Instead, I have followed the strategy, which was commonly used by the ancients themselves, that is, the method of eclecticism. Quintilian is said to have phrased this strategy as a matter of selecting the best from every source.[14] Then, facing such a rich and overwhelming body of texts, the principle of selecting the most appropriate examples for analyses seems like a sensible approach. My sole purpose has been to focus on the idea of beauty in order to show how this theme develops through the very beginnings of ancient aesthetics. Here, namely, were laid down the building blocks to what is usually addressed as the classical tradition.

Fourth, the analyses are based on a body of texts that for some readers may count as new ground, or something yet unexplored. Therefore, I have found it crucial to provide my analyses with plenty of quotations so that the reader may get a sense of the charm, greatness, and dignity of these texts. Each Part of the book can be read

---

12 For a brief discussion of "the Homeric Question," see the Introductions in Richmond Lattimore's translations of *The Iliad of Homer*, p. 29 ff, and *The Odyssey of Homer*, p.18 ff.

13 See *Plato. Complete Works*. Edited, with Introduction and Notes, by John M. Cooper, p. 899.

14 See for example Quintilian: *The Orator's Education*, Book 8, Prooemium § 3, and Book 10.2.25-26.

exclusively in its own right. However, read as a whole – Part I, Part II, and Part III – describes how the theme of beauty gradually expands to cover almost every facet of human life. Through this process the images of beauty increase in number and depth, and the ideas of beauty become refined to become building blocks in our cultural heritage.

Nevertheless, the concept of beauty has been abandoned in modern aesthetics. In the final section – Part IV – I delineate a few aspects of the historical background resulting in the collapse of the philosophy of beauty. The repercussions from the collapse of the philosophies of beauty have had a heavy impact on academic scholarship and have come to thwart the very heart of ancient aesthetics. In particular, the tendency to isolate the aesthetic from the ethic goes against the spirit of ancient thought. Further, under influence of Hegelian philosophy it is generally concluded that the aesthetics of Antiquity is not aesthetics in a proper sense. Not only is the very reception of Antiquity somewhat hampered by this situation; also our understanding of reality suffers from negligence of the idea of beauty. Indeed, the flavor of life is linked with the beautiful.

PART I

THE BEAUTIFUL AND THE UGLY
The Mythic Worldview of Homer

Introduction: Myth and Beauty

The celebration of the world and the sheer fact that it is there in front of us is to be found in almost all mythological accounts dealing with the very beginning and the glorious past. Feelings of marvel and awe over the natural world and the universe are equally shared by storytellers, singers, poets, and later, also by philosophers to a certain degree. Hence, the tendency to ponder upon things and embellish the events of beginnings seems to be universal.

In a Western context Greek mythology elaborated a rich and refined attempt to understand the world. In particular, Homeric epic stands out. Not only does Homeric epic deal with the beginning of the world, but it also becomes the starting point, or genesis, of a long-standing European aesthetic tradition in which the beautiful and the ugly are the main concepts.

Homeric epic is a cornucopia of aesthetic images and vocabulary. Homer entertains us with a huge variety of examples of the beautiful and the ugly some of which are highly impressive and outstanding even to this day. Although mythic tales to a modern mind may seem an exercise in caprice, Homer, time and again, shows that he has a profound understanding of human life as such. In particular, he is aware of the importance of being able to differentiate between the beautiful and the ugly. As we shall see, Homer approaches the world with wonder. As wonder is a real eye-opener to Homer, he indulges himself in listing and describing the beauty of the world. In the end, this approach leads to a celebration of being. Still, Homer is never really carried away; he knows of evil and the ugly too. Indeed, these factors add to the profound knowledge of human life that Homer has left to the world through his mythological narratives.

1. The Order of the Homeric World

Above all Homer's concern is to celebrate life. To Homer life is "sweet," and to be alive is described as partaking in "the sweetness of life." (See, e.g., *Il.* 10.495) But he also takes an interest in elaborating the order of the world, an enterprise that is carried out in surprising ways. Compared to Hesiod who in the *Theogony* devotes his energy to elaborating how order came into the world to become an enduring structure, guaranteed by the Olympians, Homer's view of how the world came into being is revealed through bits and pieces of information, distributed throughout the whole *oeuvre* of Homeric epic. But putting together these hints reveals a rather exquisite order. To be more precise, they set the background on which the stories of gods and heroes unfold. Though Homer's main concern is man, the life of humans is, nevertheless, part of a larger setting, namely the life of nature gods, semi-divine beings, and the Olympian gods. Then, man is not a lone being in the Homeric world, but his Destiny is interwoven into a grand, divine pattern, which, more or less, is obscure to man, and, at times, even to the gods. The Olympians count as the ruling clan, but even they are occasionally subject to laws not of their own making.

Like Hesiod, Homer also holds that order was absent from the very beginning of the world. But due to change and revolutions within the divine race together with an increase of divine wisdom, order emerges out of disorder, and Zeus becomes head of the Olympian clan.[1] He, together with his two brothers, bestows order upon the world and guarantees the duration of it. The establishment of this delicate order, being the marriage of destiny and noble agreements among the three brothers, represents a covenant to which both gods and men refer when taking an oath. (See *Od.* 5.184 ff.) As will be discussed below, the covenant represents a special type of sophisticated order among others.

From the Olympos to the Underworld order is found to pervade almost every dominion. It could be held that Homer's ambition to depict the order of the world is only tentative and, therefore, by consequence contains blind spots and contradictions. If measured by strict philosophical terms we must agree with G. S. Kirk, when he concludes, "there is almost nothing in Homer that can reasonably be construed as specifically cosmogonical or cosmological in content."[2] But Homer is not a philosopher interested in precise concepts, but a storyteller, or a *mytho-*

---

1   In the spelling of Homeric names I follow the practice of Richmond Lattimore from whose translations I quote.

2   G. S. Kirk and J. E. Raven: *The Presocratic Philosophers*. A Critical History with a Selection of Texts. Cambridge University Press. Cambridge 1957, p. 16.

logos.[3] Therefore, it should not escape our awareness that the Homeric worldview is indeed permeated by an unmistakable order, which contains elements of both cosmogony and cosmology. In elaborating a coherent and unified view of the world Homer only touches slightly upon cosmogonical matters and more directly on the cosmological structure of the world. In the following, we shall analyze with which persistent concern Homer actually voices the splendor of the world order.

It is a common feature of mythological worldviews as such that they include a mapping of space. Also the Homeric universe is characterized by a certain spatial and geographical order. On the periphery Homer locates the waters of Okeanos, the river encircling the earth, from which the first generation of gods emerged. (See *Il.* 14.200 ff.) As to the spatial structure of the Homeric universe this is stated by Zeus in the *Iliad*, Book 8. The earth is believed to be a flat disk over which the Heavens arch. Further, it is claimed that Olympos counts as the highest region on earth and that the Underworld is to be found equally far beneath the surface as Olympos is above. Zeus even lists one more scale of order, namely that Tartaros, the deep abyss underneath the Underworld, is situated in the same remote distance from the surface of the earth, as the starry Heaven is above. (See *Il.* 8.13-16) In this way, the Homeric worldview contains a general and simple, but symmetric and balanced structure. How this structure has in fact come into being is not touched upon. The question is by far overshadowed by an interest for elaborating how order is established within this frame. Hence, the account of the very beginning has an inferior place in Homer's epic. The establishment of the Olympian order, on the other hand, is elaborated in detail. That Homeric mythology focuses on cosmological order rather than on cosmogonical questions may be seen as a consequence of the fact that the ordered world functions as the theater in which the Destiny of man and his fated relationship with the gods takes place.

The Relationship between Zeus, Poseidon, and Hades

The first generations of gods are of minor interest to Homer, but the victorious generation, who manages to stay in power, is more interesting because it represents a stable order. The upheavals from the shifting generations of gods and semi-gods, their tribal wars and power struggles come to an end when the three brothers Zeus, Poseidon, and Hades force their way into power, showing their superiority by wise decision instead of continuing warfare. Their wisdom and the fact that they are equal in powers make them agree on throwing dices in order to mark out their dominions. Thus agreement joined by Fate becomes the factor that catapults Zeus to

---

3   See Fritz Graf: *Griechische Mythologie*. Eine Einführung. München und Zürich 1991, p. 7.

stardom, his lot being ruler of the Sky and head of the Olympian clan who resides on Olympos. Poseidon and Hades attain rank as chthonic gods, Poseidon's dominion being the seas and the deep, and Hades' that of the Underworld where the souls of the dead are to dwell. Then, the prevailing order of the Homeric universe is based on a subtle balance of power among three brothers.

Certain events, however, reveal that the Destiny of Zeus, putting him into the most glorious and conspicuous position, encourages him to bullying behavior; the tensions between Zeus and Poseidon are especially outspoken. In general, man is in danger and suffers when the gods quarrel, but the hostility between Zeus and Poseidon rises to the point where their controversy becomes a threat to the established world order. However, in moments of confrontation Zeus does in fact realize that his powers are not any stronger than those of his brothers. Therefore, he resorts to weak argumentation by referring to his status as being the eldest, that is, first-born. By this trick Zeus tries to divert attention from the crucial point, stated in Poseidon's self-defense, in which the latter recalls the equal division of authority. So Poseidon utters, "earth and high Olympos are common to all three." (*Il.* 15.193) Zeus is considered to be wiser than Poseidon (see *Il.* 13.355), while the latter is stronger than the former. But on several occasions sheer force is on its way to win over wisdom. Romping among the conspirators and planning to revolt against Zeus, Poseidon becomes a real threat. (See *Il.* 1.400) But as referred to at the beginning of the *Iliad,* Thetis and the Giant Briareus finally prevent the upheaval. Later, Poseidon turns to more subtle ways of warfare against his elder brother. In fact, his sons, the beautiful twins, Otos and Ephialtes, carry on the project, which their father gave up on. They try to invade the Heavens, but do not succeed either; Apollo, the son of Zeus, kills them. (See *Od.* 11.305-320)

While the maintenance of the Homeric universe is under some strain from the conflicts between Zeus and Poseidon, the bonds between Zeus and his brother, Hades, king of the Dark, are surprisingly harmonious. In the *Iliad* Homer reminds us that Hades is indeed as dignified as are the other gods. A sign of this is the episode in which Hades is wounded by Herakles. Hades, then, for refuge spontaneously takes to his former home, Olympos, where he is received by his clan and healed from his wounds. (See *Il.* 5.394 ff.) Another episode, referred to in *The Homeric Hymns,* also echoes the mutual friendship between Zeus and Hades. When Hades kidnaps Persephone, the young daughter of Demeter, to make her his wife and queen of the Underworld, the misdeed turns out to have been agreed upon by Zeus. In despair Demeter travels the surface of the earth searching for her daughter, but finds her nowhere. Finally, for advice, she seeks Helios, he who sees all things, and listens to all things. (See *Il.* 3.277, *Od.* 8.271, *Od.* 11.109, and *Hymn to Demeter,* 62 ff.) And with Helios a strange conversation takes place. Feeling pity for Demeter, Helios reveals the co-operation between the two brothers, Zeus and Hades, and now tells the mother, how Persephone, against her will, was forced down into the kingdom of Hades. After having revealed his knowledge, Helios tries to console Demeter by referring to the noble descent of the god of the dead. Hades, says Helios, is not an evil god as he is honored by being the ruler over one–third of the world. (See *Hymn to Demeter*, 75-87)

A Strange Friendship: Hades and Helios

The unity of the Homeric world is even further substantiated by the friendly relationship between Helios and Hades. To our surprise we learn that they are on very good terms. When Odysseus' men kill and eat the cattle belonging to Helios, the god gets very upset as the demolition of his property shows contempt for his power. However, when complaining to Zeus over the misdeed, Helios does not refer to the obvious reasons but to the fact, that he took *delight* in looking upon his cattle. As a matter of fact he is referring to the aesthetical aspect of the loss. These – "the handsome broad-faced horn-curved oxen" (*Od.* 12.354) – were the first to catch his sight at dawn when setting out on his journey, and in the evening the cattle constituted the last sight to dwell upon before his nocturnal journey. Hence, the god Helios is a passionate lover of beauty, and the angry Sun god utters a shocking threat to Zeus, the Sky-ruler. Helios says: "Unless these [Odysseus' men] are made to give me just recompense for my cattle, I will go down to Hades' and give my light to the dead men." (*Od.* 12.381-383) So the strange alliance and the friendship between Helios and Hades becomes yet one more element that emphasizes the holistic character of the Homeric universe.

Then, between Helios, son of the Titan Hyperion, and the Olympian gods a kind of sympathetic friendship seems to prevail, a friendship tested only once by the dispute over the cattle. Though only a singular event, Heilos' threat does nevertheless air an uncanny sense of doom. While Poseidon seems to be the only real competitor to Zeus and potentially embodying a new kind of order, the warning uttered by the nature god, Helios, is in fact a more serious one. The idea that Helios might prefer not to rise, but instead dwell in his nocturnal sphere, represents the real eschatological perspective in the Homeric universe. In comparison, the threats from Poseidon and the three Titans, imprisoned in Tartaros, are minor ones. Of course, a change of powers could set the world back into an unpleasant state of upheaval and disorder. But Helios' ominous utterance is worse, and it may count as the closest the Homeric universe comes to an image of eschatology. A world with no sun in it would be a threat to gods as well as to human beings.

A Holistic Worldview

In conclusion, the friendly relationships between Zeus and Hades, and between Helios and Hades emphasize the image of a unified cosmos. The image of a unified cosmos is even further substantiated by a number of minor hints. The Sky is associated with precious metal. (See *Od.* 3.2) And quite unexpectedly, we also find that precious metal is used for the making of the entrance to Tartaros where there are "gates of iron and a brazen doorstone." (*Il.* 8.15) The notion of iron, of course, stresses the idea of a fortified dungeon while the doorstone made of bronze seems to be a phenomenon of extravagance. Tartaros is the worst of places, where only a few have been imprisoned to suffer the utmost punishment. While Homer allows for some faint sources of light in the Underworld, the condition of which is a prevailing twilight, Tartaros, on the contrary, is a place into which not even the slightest rays of light have access. Iapetos and Kronos "have no shining of the sun god Hyperion to delight them nor wind's delight, but Tartaros stands deeply about them." (*Il.* 8.480-81) It means that the culprits themselves have no possibility of enjoying the radiance from the precious metal. But since this awful location serves as a dungeon for divine beings, and further represents a location belonging to a god, namely Hades, it must necessarily array some sort of splendor.

Hence, the order of the Homeric universe is based on a subtle balance of power, and none of the gods or goddesses is granted absolute power. Olympic gods are not omnipotent beings. They too are subject to Destiny, or Necessity. For example, immortal Night has power to suppress Zeus from acting against her will. (See *Il.* 14.259) Rather than being omnipotent each divinity has been appointed a certain area of life, in which he, or she, performs his/her particular essence. Overstepping their appointed powers leads to trouble and is not accepted. When Aphrodite flings herself into warfare issues, she is immediately hurt by an arrow. Zeus lovingly reminds her to stay out of the war games and to concentrate on her appointed dominion, namely inspiring living beings to courtship and lovemaking. (See *Il.* 5.426-30) Hence, no god in the Homeric universe is granted the power of omnipotence, and no god is without some kind of shortcomings. Even Aphrodite, who is a mighty force, becomes subject to a trick, when Zeus makes her fall in love with a human. (See The *Homeric Hymns, To Aphrodite*, verses 45-60 ff.) Another funny paradox is Helios who is repeatedly referred to as the god seeing and hearing all things. But he too, like other divine beings, occasionally falls victim to tricks played upon him. So Helios fails to witness the love scene between Zeus and Hera on mount Ida as Zeus creates a golden cloud to cover the dwelling place. (See *Il.* 14.342-345) Also, there seems to be places on earth not accessible to the Sun god, one of these places being the cave in which Hephaistos was hidden and saved. (See *Il.* 18.403-405) Usually, Helios sticks to his daily routine of crossing the firmament, but from time to time also this habit is made subject to slight changes due to requests from the goddesses

Athene and Hera. (See *Od.* 23.241-246 and *Il.* 18.239-41) Delaying sunrise, or demanding a speeding up of sunset are of course minor alterations, and in no cases we hear about a radical revolution in respect of Nature deities. In general, Nature deities, Titanic in origin, are co-operative and attentive to orders and requests from members of the Olympic clan.

The Homeric world order is conditioned by the achievement of immortality, and the divine race is said to be immortal. But there are some contradictions and confusion in Homer's account on the immortality of the Olympic clan and their defeat of the first generations of gods. In fact, some of the latter are still around, being immortal like the Olympians themselves. While the bestial stock of this breed is imprisoned in Tartaros, others do enjoy great honor as, for example, the Nature deities like Okeanos and Gaia. The Titans and the Giants might have been defeated, but they are not necessarily dead all of them. As mentioned already, Helios has a genealogy that traces his origin to being the son of a Titan, namely Hyperion. Also Eos, that is, the goddess of Dawn, and Selene, goddess of the Moon, are of Titanic origin; in fact, Eos, Selene and the Sun-god are siblings.

On closer examination the triumph of the Olympic clan might not really be the reason why they have become immortal. Hence, the establishment of the Olympic order seems to produce some strange consequences, namely that of the reduction of fertility among the Olympic gods themselves. After the children of Hera and Zeus had been born, only Aphrodite and Ares produce a child. Instead, the divine Olympic race turns part of their emotional life towards semi-gods, the element gods, and, in particular, to human beings with whom they generate offspring, that is, the race of heroes and heroines. As Poseidon says to Tyro after having seduced her: "For the couplings of the immortals are not without issue." (*Od.* 11. 249-50) Then, the guarantee that the world will stay in order is based on the specific constitution of the Olympian family. Each member has been appointed ruler of each their own domain of life. If new members were to show up, it would, by consequence, mean renewed upheaval of the prevailing order.

2. Shining Olympos

As mentioned above, Homer employs the idea of symmetry concerning the location of Olympos and the Underworld, held to be equal in distance to the earth. But while the spatial symmetry is in place, the very narrative of these two opposed locations, on the other hand, lacks in symmetry. Strangely enough, the image of Olympos and also the image of the *Elysian Field* are elaborated with just few, but very pleasant details. No human beings have ever returned from these regions. In comparison, both Herakles and Odysseus return from their visit to the Underworld, which are events, as will be discussed later, that stand out with a lot of horrible and depressing details.

Olympos, the dwelling place of the gods, surpasses the *Elysian Field* in splendor being a privileged area never to suffer from the fury of the elements. So the weather on Olympos is compared to a bright summer's day, neither too hot, nor too cold, with no storms, no heavy rain and no snow but always with "shining bright air" and "white light." (*Od.* 6.44-45) As master of the weather Zeus can make "a golden wonderful cloud" from which "glimmering dew" descends, if needed. (*Il.* 14.350-51)

The Divine Residences and Their Inhabitants

The divine court and its interior is built and designed by Hephaistos. Each of the Olympian clan has his or her own residence, and most conspicuous of these are Hephaistos' own house and that of his mother. The residences are made by precious metal, and the pavement is of gold. (See *Il.* 14.173) Tools and household goods are "a wonder to look at." The exquisite architecture and refined artificial objects, created by Hephaistos, all share the same aesthetic quality: they shine.

In describing Olympos Homer turns to the use of comparison. So Olympos is compared to a human court, namely that of Menelaos, experienced through the eyes of Telemachos: "Only look at the gleaming of the bronze all through these echoing mansions, and the gleaming of gold and amber, of silver and of ivory. The court of Zeus on Olympos must be like this on the inside, such abundance of everything. Wonder takes me as I look on it." (*Od.* 4.71-75) The interior of Menelaos' earthly residence shines with a quality compared to the golden light of the Sun and to the pale silvery light of the Moon. (See *Od.* 4.45) Smooth-polished bathtubs, shining oil, refined clothing, furniture, plenty of food and wine, and an abundance of household objects being made of polished gold, or silver, are all great pleasures to the human eye. Hence, the court of the Olympic clan must be something in that style.

While the climate on Olympos is gentle, the emotional storms and quarrels among the gods are fierce. The immortality of the gods is paired with the image of a passionate race forever entertaining themselves by way of a turbulent emotional life. They laugh excessively, cry, fight, foster intrigues, hatch strategies, and are carried away by love affairs. Highlights of Olympic life are the assemblies, banquets, and feasts. To celebrate and feast seems to be their favorite sport. In the *Iliad,* Book 1, we are introduced to their passion for partying. When Zeus pays a visit to the Aitheopeans, who are giving a feast in his honor, all the other gods go with him. (See *Il.* 1.423-25) On their return to Olympos they feast again. The feast, at which they gather, indicates that feasting is a daily activity, including food, wine, music, songs, and laughter. Wedding feasts in particular are favored by gods as well as by human beings. (See *The Homeric Hymns, To Aphrodite*, verses 141-42) Thus the wedding of the goddess, Thetis, to a human, namely Peleus, symbolizes the bond between the gods and humans. (See *Il.* 24.60-64)

A more gloomy aspect of how the gods enjoy entertainment is that they take pleasure in watching the human war-theater. Achilleus says: "Such is the way the gods spun life for unfortunate mortals, that we live in unhappiness, but the gods themselves have no sorrows." (*Il.* 24.525-26) As immortals they do not die, but from time to time they do in fact suffer emotional pain because of their bonds to humans, especially when their favorites must die. By Athene it is suggested that Apollo would go so far as to "undergo much, and wallow before our father Zeus" (*Il.* 22.220-21) in order to save Hektor from early death. But despite Zeus himself showing compassion for Hektor, he cannot change Hektor's Destiny, which is to die. Also among the divine who suffer because of a human being is Thetis, the mother of Achilleus.

Besides being anthropomorphized the gods are above all endowed with a *shining* quality. Their eternal beauty does not fade. When making themselves known to man the divine race radiates a shining appearance. And, likewise, when bestowing their gifts and support to man, a shining quality radiates from the objects, the deeds, the actions, or the events. Finally, when gods decide to approach humans, they seem to favor among humans those who in character are very much like themselves. So Odysseus, who is known for his taste and skill for cunning tricks, is the favorite of Athene, famous for exactly the same disposition.

Then, the divine race is a race of beauty lovers, and, as will be discussed later, most of the semi-divine beings such as nymphs, cyclops, and monsters participate in the celebration of beauty from time to time. However, they all seem to be less attracted towards their own race than to the race of humans for whom they show a fatal attraction. Human beauty has strong influence on the gods, but the humans themselves are in trouble and even danger when they attract the love of a god. Another characteristic trait of the Olympian clan is that, some more than others, do have an uncanny taste for metamorphoses. As gods they possess the faculty of being able to change their appearance. The talent of metamorphosis is a divine skill, which gives way to fascination, but also to fear. Later, when the Greek philosophers put the issue of metamorphosis on the agenda, the phenomenon is not appreciated. From a philosophical point of view beings, or phenomena, oscillating between several states of identity are no longer subject to fear, or fascination, but become subject to contempt and devaluation.

3. The Underworld

Conspicuous to Greek thought is a tendency to find a location for everything. Dreams, for example, are located in "the country of dreams" (*Od.* 24.12-13), and close to this strange region the Underworld is situated. Similar to Olympos, this chthonic region is also a well-ordered place, characterized by a certain compartmentalization. While Zeus and Hera reside at Olympos, so the Underworld is ruled by a king and a queen, that is, Hades and his queen, Persephone.

The description of the Underworld naturally stands as opposed to the description of Olympos. But the symmetric picture, slightly disturbed in a number of ways, focuses on the surroundings, and not on the very centre of the Underworld. As we shall see, Odysseus and his men actually never enter into the House of the Dead; instead they tarry outside at a specific location, identified to them by Circe. We shall discuss this in a moment. Beneath Hades' region is yet one more compartment of the Underworld, Tartaros, where former gods are imprisoned. When bullying the other Olympians to follow his command Zeus warns that rebels might get thrown into Tartaros: "I shall take him and dash him to the murk of Tartaros, far below, where the uttermost depth of the pit lies under earth, where there are gates of iron and a brazen doorstone, as far beneath the house of Hades as from earth the sky lies." (*Il.* 8.13-16) As mentioned already, according to the mapping of the Homeric universe, Tartaros is "the undermost limits of earth and sea" (*Il.* 8.478-79), and by Zeus described as the essence of a negative place. (See *Il.* 8.480-481) Then, the Underworld, including Tartaros, is indeed part of a unified whole, characterized by a symmetrical structure. The symmetrical structure is regarded as a divine order, and therefore, to our surprise, Homer ascribes some dignified images even to the Underworld, a place that stands out with a kind of gloomy beauty. In a strange way, this feature even adds to the buoyant worldview of Homer.

The God Hades

The image of Hades is a subtle one, oscillating between descriptions of a dignified, beauty-loving Olympic god and his ghastly task and gloomy residence. As has been emphasized, Homer is cautious not to question the virtues of Hades, and, in fact, shows Hades as a lover of beauty. When the gods finally are licensed to participate in the war between the Greeks and the Trojans with full power, the fight is echoed as far as into the Underworld. Thunder and earthquakes, the languages of Zeus and Poseidon, are on the breaking point to reveal to the whole world the ugliness of the Underworld. Hades reacts as follows: "Aïdoneus, lord of the dead below, was in terror and sprang from his throne and screamed aloud, for fear that above him he who circles the land, Poseidon, might break the earth open and the houses of the dead lie open to men and immortals, ghastly and mouldering, so the very gods shudder before them; for such was the crash that sounded as the gods came driving together in wrath." (*Il.* 20.61-67) By his worried concern that the ugliness of his kingdom should become visible, Hades reveals his divine character. As an Olympic god he loves beauty. Therefore, he is embarrassed that the ugly features of his kingdom should be made visible though he himself is forced by Destiny to bear the sight of the ugly.

To Homer gods are lovers of beauty, and Hades is no exception. Destiny has put him in a hard environment, but when it comes to his personal belongings they are not without some aesthetic splendor. To Homer a god living in a habitat totally void of any beauty is a contradiction in terms, and thus Homer shows how Hades is surrounded with attributes of luxury and perfection. The immortal horses pulling his golden chariot are perfectly black, his scepter is of gold, and his throne of ebony. Also rituals concerning the god Hades are to be performed with no less care than rituals to other gods. Animals sacrificed to Hades must not lack in beauty, being always the very best and perfectly black. (See *Od.* 11.32-33) That gods and divine beings are beauty-lovers is an image to win a long-standing reputation. For example, as we shall discuss in Part II, the semi-god in Plato's cosmology, that is, the Demiurge, who puts the cosmos in order, is too a beauty-loving daemon.

Especially on one occasion, when choosing young Persephone as his bride, Hades displays a refined taste for beauty together with an ingenious sense for affinity. At the outset, he does not take action to pursue his plan before Zeus has given his consent. First then he pursues the goal, and that is by trickery. However, just by chance, Persephone happens to meet him halfway, symbolically revealed by the remote location, in which she has chosen to play with the daughters of Okeanos. To attract her attention Hades orders Gaia, the earth, to grow a narcissus:

> *A lure it was, wondrous and radiant, and a marvel to be seen*
> *by immortal gods and mortal men.*
> *A hundred stems of sweet-smelling blossoms*
> *grew from its roots. The wide sky above*
> *and the whole earth and the briny swell of the sea laughed.*
> *She was dazzled and reached out with both hands at once*
> *to take the pretty bauble.* (*The Homeric Hymns: To Demeter*, verses 10-16)

Using tricks to court a human being is the privilege of the gods. Compared to the many tricks performed by his divine family as, for example, that of transforming themselves into the bodily shape of other beings, Hades' trick seems a modest one, and even elegant.

Later, when Hermes by request of the Olympian assembly, is send to the Palace of Hades to negotiate the release of Persephone that she may visit her mother, Hades gently allows the new arrangement and acts with a dignity not inferior to that of his brother. Hades himself provides for the golden chariot and the dark horses, so Hermes can bring back Persephone but only for some time. The covenant between Zeus and Hades is unbroken. Before Persephone departs, Hades exercises yet one more of his many magical tricks by serving her one sweet tasting seed from a pomegranate, which is meant to intensify the bonds between him and his queen. Forever, Persephone has to return after her visit among the living. Indeed, for Homer the Underworld cannot be without a queen.

It should also be emphasized that the harsher aspects of the physical decaying corpses is a process not to take place in the centre of Underworld, but rather on the periphery and visible to everybody. Only once, when performing his job of collecting the souls of the dead, Hades is viewed directly in contact with corpses. Standing among a pile of corpses, he is hit by an arrow from Herakles. (See *Il.* 5.394-97)

The total picture of Hades is a subtle one. Being a dark figure, he is nevertheless a noble god and a just character too. His unpleasant task, bestowed upon him by Destiny, demands that he must take care to keep away the sight of the ugly from the immortals and from the living. In more than one sense Hades is the Gatekeeper. As mentioned already, Homeric epic is cautious not to question his divine status. Hades is a god, and as such he is a lover of beauty like his Olympian family. However, among humans Hades and his region do indeed have a bad reputation. Though not an evil god he is, nevertheless, says Homer, "pitiless and therefore he among all the gods is most hateful to mortals."(*Il.* 9.159) Then, from an Olympic point of view Hades is a god in his own right. But to humans Hades and his region is associated with gloom, sadness, and an atmosphere of eternal grief as life under his sovereignty is imagined to be a life without the glow and excitement of real life. For humans life in the kingdom of Hades is nothing but dedicated to an endless memorizing of former events and the emotional situations which characterized the situations shortly before death, or even causing death itself.

The gods are said to communicate in a special elevated poetic language. Thus the river, by humans called Skamandros, is called Xanthos by the divinities. Likewise their perspective on life differs from that of humans. In the following we shall examine how Homer tries to advocate a double perspective of Hades in which the Olympic view is mixed with a human perspective of Hades' kingdom.

The Underworld from a Human Perspective

From a divine point of view the Underworld is just one part of a perfect grand system, and the aesthetics involved so far is one of order and dignity. But as Homer also gives voice to the pain of the human heart and the emotional sufferings of the souls of the dead when confronted with Hades' kingdom, new dimensions are added to the ideas about what is considered beautiful and what is considered ugly. Though ruled by an Olympic god whose virtues are beyond doubt, the image of the Underworld is one of ambiguity; here dignified splendor blends with utter estrangement, touching upon the ugly and the horrible. The Underworld is a most discouraging place to those alive, but also to the souls of the dead. In the following we shall examine these other strands of Homeric aesthetics, that is, the images of the ugly.

The Underworld is described with details which echo the atmosphere of an immense sadness and grief. In spite of its dignified order, the region of Hades is "hard for the living to look on." (*Od.* 11.156) When Odysseus arrives in the Underworld, the images of the ugly are elaborated in more detail. Told that he has to undertake a journey to the kingdom of Hades to get information on his destiny, Odysseus cries bitterly. Embarking on this journey both he and his crew are struck by despair "weeping big tears." (*Od.* 11.5) The House of the Dead has to be reached by crossing the waters of Okeanos. The paths, leading to the Underworld, run from the foggy banks of Okeanos, and dusk prevails. At the very border between the world of the living and the world of the dead are the gates of the Sun: "There lie the community and city of Kimmerian people, hidden in fog and cloud, nor does Helios, the radiant sun, ever break through the dark, to illuminate them with his shining, neither when he climbs up into the starry heaven, nor when he wheels to return again from heaven to earth, but always a glum night is spread over wretched mortals." (*Od.* 11.14-19) Though the Sun is said to pass through this area, rising and setting here, the inhabitants never experience its vitalizing forces, their existence therefore lingering in a state of insubstantiality. In this ominous atmosphere human emotions become weak and fluctuating, and the spirit of life itself gets hampered.

Hence, for the living, in this case Odysseus and his crew, the experience, accompanying the journey to the Underworld, is one of sorrow and fear. But also the souls of the dead become overwhelmed by similar sensations when approaching this environment. When, for example, Hermes guides the suitors, killed by Odysseus on their way to the Underworld, Homer says: "And as when bats in the depth of an awful cave flitter and gibber, when one of them has fallen out of his place in the chain that the bats have formed by holding one on another; so, gibbering, they went their way together, and Hermes the kindly healer led them along down moldering pathways." (*Od.* 24.6-10) The dead, in a state of disorientation and bewilderment, are reduced to timid beings. Though deprived the bodily senses, sensation as such has not totally left them. Hence, they are still responsive to environmental change. All colors have vanished, leaving the environment in a *claire obscur*, but with enough light so as to notice the unfamiliar and ugly vegetation, among which are the asphodels with thick leafs and white and yellow flowers with an unpleasant smell. Even in the state of being dead aesthetics has not lost its power.

Even after having arrived at their final destination the souls of the dead continue to be sensitive to the environment. The souls of the dead are said to dwell "in the meadow of asphodel." (*Od.* 24.13) In front of Hades and Persephone's residence are the groves of Persephone with "tall black poplars" and "fruit-perishing willows." (*Od.* 10.510) Of major importance is, however, the lack of warm sunlight, and the prevailing twilight adds an atmosphere of immense sadness to their situation. Though Hades as a god enjoys some pleasures, the dead do not.

Having poured the drink offers, including the blood, Odysseus is instantly surrounded by the dead, making themselves present by visual appearance similar to their former physical bodies and by sound too. Though speechless, an "inhuman clamor" (*Od.* 11.43) is heard from the assembly of the dead. This is the overwhelming cry for life. The world of the dead is not a world without activity, but without life. The souls of the dead dwell in a state of eternally memorializing life on earth, that is, their former lives and deeds. Though deprived the feeling of life and the experience of sunlight, activity prevails in some sense, but leads to nothing. The waste of energy, or the impotence and emptiness of all actions, is symbolically signified by the fruit-perishing willows and also from the fact that the relation between Hades and Persephone is characterized by lack of offspring. Thus alive in some way, the souls of the dead, each encapsulated in his or her individual history and sorrow, seem to repeat some of their former activities, but to no avail and therefore also without any pleasure. For example, Orion, who was a great hunter, chases and kills the same prey he killed when alive. Also, the souls of the dead show a tendency to focus on the sad and unjust aspects of their individual destinies that catapulted them to this place, often before old age.

Now, facing the possibility for dialogue the hunger for life becomes almost inhuman. A number of the dead, among which are Elpenor and Teiresias, Achilleus, and Odysseus' mother, recognize Odysseus even before having sipped from the blood. Correspondingly, Odysseus recognizes the visual appearances of the dead as they have not shed their former features. However, the forms meeting the eye are not stable, nor do they represent substantiality. Three times Odysseus tries to embrace his mother, but in vain. Also the soul of Agamemnon tries to embrace Odysseus. But the living cannot embrace the dead, and vice versa. On both sides of the great divide the pains of the heart remain for the living as well as for the dead. From the conversation between Odysseus and Achilleus, the latter now appointed king of the souls of the dead, we learn of the desperate longing for life. Achilleus says: "O shining Odysseus, never try to console me for dying. I would rather follow the plow as trall to another man, one with no land allotted him and not much to live on, than be a king over all the perished dead." (*Od.* 11.488-491) The longing for life and bright sunshine is repeated also by Herakles. (See *Od.* 11.619 ff.) Though almost senseless the dead are still subject to an immense sadness and grief, haunted too with a longing for their dear ones. Achilleus, for example, is happy to hear the good news of his son. Though the Underworld is ordered by divine providence, both those alive and those dead suffer equally when confronted with its crystallizing order. Movements in the Underworld are minimized to repetition, the epitome of which is Sisyphos whose actions are restricted and fixed into a frame of eternal repetition, but of no avail.

Even worse than actually being a dead soul in the Underworld is to be dead and unburied. As unburied, the soul of the dead is excluded from the community of the living and of the dead as well. Thus Patroklos, approaching Achilleus in a dream, begs: "Bury me as quickly as may be, let me pass through the gates of Hades. The souls, the images of the dead men, hold me at a distance, and will not let me cross the river and mingle among them, but I wander as I am by Hades' house of the wide gates." (*Il.* 23.70-74) Also the suitors, killed by Odysseus, are unburied, but they are guided by Hermes and go straight to Hades. To Homer the idea of not belonging is considered to be even worse than having in fact crossed the final borders to the Underworld.

Erebos, the Dark as the Image of Ultimate Horror

When Odysseus arrived in the Underworld, the dead teemed out from Erebos, being the very centre of Hades' kingdom, and having finished their conversations with Odysseus, they again disappear into Erebos. Then, in the Homeric universe Erebos seems to manifest the image of the utmost ugly and desolate. In fact, the centre of the Underworld becomes even worse than Tartaros from where some of its divine inhabitants occasionally are allowed to take leave. Indeed, the souls of the dead are facing an even harder fate than that of the unfortunate gods, imprisoned in Tartaros. The limit of the Homeric universe and therefore the absolute ugly is identified as Erebos, the Dark, which is not subject to further elaboration. Then, Erebos, the Dark, becomes a border image in which hides the absolute negative. This episode calls attention to Homer's general distinction between the beautiful and the ugly, being associated with light versus darkness.

The intention behind the grand order of the Homeric universe is to give the impression of symmetrical perfection. As mentioned already, the door stone at the entrance to Tartaros mirrors the shining interiors of the Heavens and is made from shiny metal. And when taking an oath even the gods themselves swear by the gods of the Underworld, and thus acknowledge its peculiar and sacred status. Also Kalypso's oath is a confirmation of a unified cosmos: "Earth be my witness in this, and the wide heaven above us, and the dripping water of the Styx, which oath is the biggest and most formidable oath among the blessed immortals." (*Od.* 5.184-86) Then, order in the Homeric universe is an issue of major concern embracing everything although not everything is equally described.

4. Earth and "the Sweetness of Life"

The surface of the earth is the shining region in which life unfolds. Here, in this zone everything comes together, earth being the playground for Nature's deities, the Olympic clan, semi-divine beings and monsters, and for man himself. In this grand theater, which is Homer's main concern, life unfolds in a diversity of forms, counting among them the wonder of dawn, the splendor of Nature, and the joys of human beings. Here, in this region, the experience of beauty unfolds, and here can be tasted "the sweetness of life." Homeric epic depicts a huge scale of fundamental human conditions and the emotional life evoked by it. Sunrise, bathing the world in a rose-colored light, encourages man to set out on audacious adventures and gain new experiences. But the images of buoyancy, of joy, of excitement, and of the zest for life, are mixed with harsh experiences too. Homer also describes the destruction of beauty, the horrors of war, sorrow, despair, suffering, and death, all images which, by sheer contrast, somehow intensify "the sweetness of life."

Sunrise

The glory of dawn, sunrise, and to a minor degree sunset are favorite issues to Homer. The recurring phenomenon of sunrise is described in the manner of a festive procession to which is added a courtly note as well. The arrival of the sun is heralded, first by the Morning Star, then in turn by Eos. (See *Il.* 23.226) Eos, the goddess of Dawn, arises from her love nest with Tithonos to herald that the Sun god is now about to set out on his glorious journey across the firmament. (See *Il.* 11.1-2) Zeus, Head of the Olympic clan, is the first to receive the information about sunrise. (See *Il.* 2.48-49) This very moment displaying itself as a grand show is treasured and celebrated by Nature's deities, by the immortals, and by mortals too. First Eos covers the earth in gleaming colors, revealing a fan moving from pale light to rosy, from rosy to saffron, and, finally, to shining brightness. First then, the Sun with his fierce rays of light, brilliance, and heat starts his journey across the firmament.

Among the deities of Nature, Helios is the one to attract most attention. Although he belongs to the older clan of gods, the Titans, he, nevertheless, gives rise to the most admired aesthetic quality in the Homeric universe, namely the quality of *shining*. In a true sense, Helios is a joy to the world, the very force on whose benevolence all beings depend, including gods and man. Therefore, Helios' threat that he might choose to descend to the Underworld in order to shine for the dead is a most serious one. Both gods and mortal beings suffer when darkness prevails. Though Night, like all phenomena of Nature in general, is perceived as sacred, she is nevertheless an overwhelming, ominous force that subdues the spirits of both gods and mortals. (See *Il.* 14.259) Indeed, to shine like the Sun then becomes the most cherished aesthetic quality throughout the Homeric epic. To shine, of which the

Sun is the great paradigm, is used as a term to describe the spectacular appearance of everything from the appearances of the divine race to the conspicuous fringes of Achilleus' helmet, made by Hephaistos, and the robes of the heroines. In the following we shall examine a number of examples.

The Quality of Shining

Like the Sun, beautifying the sky in daytime, so the stars adorn the night-sky. (See *Il.* 8.46) Admired too for its shining radiance is the Moon.[4] However, the light from the Moon and the stars is of a different quality, compared to the light from the Sun. While the light from the Moon is pale and fair, the stars shine with a sparkling light. Especially the evening star, Hesper (See *Il.* 22.318), and the autumn star, Orion's Dog [Sirius], are conspicuous for their glow and brightness, the latter "beyond all stars rises bathed in the ocean stream to glitter in brilliance." (See *Il.* 5.5-6) Unfortunately, Orion's Dog is also a sign of evil as this star shows in a season which brings with it fever and death upon man. However, in a number of cases there seems to be no real interest in distinguishing between the shine, produced by the Sun, or the shine from the Moon, or the stars. As mentioned earlier, the shining interior at the house of Menelaos was compared to the shining of the Sun, *or* the Moon.

A most remarkable description of the shine produced by the Moon and the stars, is elaborated by Homer in a comparison which is part of the description of the war-theater. When, at night-time the Trojan army camps are awaiting yet another day of battle, they encourage themselves by making watch-fires. Homer compares the thousand fires at the Trojans camp to a moonlit night when seen from afar: "As when in the sky the stars about the moon's shining are seen in all their glory, when the air has fallen to stillness, and all the high places of the hills are clear, and the shoulders out-jutting, and the deep ravines, as endless bright air spills from the heavens and all the stars are seen, to make glad the heart of the shepherd." (*Il.* 8.555-559) The comparison is, of course, meant to magnify the impressive sight of the enemy's camp, but at the same time it also stresses a note of sorrow, combining the shining splendor of Nature with the harsh reality of war and the destruction of lives. The mixture of splendor and sorrow in Homer's description is of unsurpassed beauty, and in a way, it may be argued, emphasizes the main concern of Homeric epic, namely the celebration of life itself, shining forth in an abundance of forms in spite of the harsh realities. Homer's ultimate credo is this: "Life is sweet," and he also knows that life is so fragile and so easy to destroy. To walk "under the light of the sun" (see *Od.* 11.498) is the essence of being alive. As mentioned already,

---

4   For the glittering quality of light, see the *Homeric Hymns: To Selene*, 3-13, and *Cratylus*, 409a-b.

the experience of warm sunlight is referred to by the soul of dead Achilleus, and Odysseus and his men weep when they unwillingly are sent on a mission to the Underworld.

Remote Places

Yet, a final indication that the Homeric worldview tends towards a holistic perception may be highlighted by the ambiguous status of remote regions and their inhabitants. In most cases outcasts living in such godforsaken areas are indeed, more often than not, related to the gods, and in many cases by family bonds. As divine, or semi-divine in origin they, therefore, do enjoy some divine protection. Accordingly, the regions they inhabit are of a fertile, or conspicuous kind. Of remote places on earth the *Elysian Field* enjoys a special status. From Proteus, the Old Man of the Sea, we learn that this place is located at "the limits of the earth, where fair-haired Rhadamanthys is, and where there is made the easiest life for mortals, for there is no snow, nor much winter there, nor is there ever rain, but always the stream of the Ocean sends up breezes of the West Wind blowing briskly for the refreshments of mortals." (*Od.* 4.563-568) Only the very favored such as Menelaos, for example, goes to the *Elysian Field*, not because he is a hero but because he is the husband of Helen and thus the son-in-law of Zeus.

Since the inhabitants of remote regions usually are of divine descent they do in fact show some sense of beauty as well. That they are lovers of beauty may show from the very location in which they have chosen to dwell. Homer describes to us the beautiful location of Kalypso's cave around which are black poplars, fragrant cypresses, and "meadows grown soft with parsley and violets" and, says Homer, "even a god who came into that place would have admired what he saw, the heart delighted within him." (*Od.* 5.73-74) Sometimes the love of beauty will also shine forth in their activities such as singing, weaving, running a well-ordered household etc.

Homeric cosmology represents a high degree of structure, but being mythological it also allows for inconsistency and blind spots. Within the grand order there are hidden places of which even the Olympian gods do not know. And yet, Homer knows of these places! Of such a remote place is the cave, where Hephaistos was brought up by the daughters of Okeanos: "No other among the gods or among mortal men knew about us except Eurynome and Thetis," says Hephaistos. (*Il.* 18.403-405) Of the remote places, mentioned by Homer, only a few are described as being unpleasant and horrifying such as, for example, the Kimmerian country which is a sad and damp location with no sunlight.

The Spirit of Life

The Homeric epic's charm and vitality is due to its complex blend of bold imagery, life experience, and a heart felt concern for human life. In a multifarious number of episodes Homer, time and again, shows his deep sense of what heightens the zest for life, and he knows too about the destruction of these vital forces. When Odysseus and his men find rescue and hospitality on Circe's island, their spirit of life has been hampered from endless suffering. To help their recovery, therefore, Circe demands a special treatment: "But come now, eat your food and drink your wine, until you gather back again into your chests that kind of spirit you had in you when first you left the land of your fathers on rugged Ithaka. Now you are all dried out, dispirited from the constant thought of your hard wandering, nor is there any spirit in your festivity, because of so much suffering." (*Od.* 10.460-465) Homer knows in minute detail about sorrow and suffering and of its influence on the human soul, undermining the courage to face life again. But the human heart can somehow be healed in time. Homer also knows about the time-scale of healing. The goddess, namely, keeps Odysseus and his men for a year.

5. Shining Beauty as Destiny

Homeric epic parades a diversity of beauty of different sorts and on different levels, but to attract fascination above all is physical beauty. The sight of physical beauty stirs the emotions of gods and humans to extremes, the effects of which are love-making, procreation, joy, admiration, praise, and hymns, but also envy, competition, kidnapping, suffering, destruction, war, and death. Physical beauty, one way or the other, becomes part of how to cope with existence. For example, from time to time mankind becomes the target of the affections of the gods and their caprices. The gods fall in love with humans, they envy them, cheat and punish them, in some cases they will expose themselves to suffering because of love for a human, and they even care for their favorite ones when they die. In other words: physical beauty, or lack thereof, becomes Destiny.

The gods kidnap quite a number of mortals. So Ganymedes, who was "the loveliest born of the race of mortals," (*Il.* 20.233) is stolen by the gods and carried off to Olympos. Also Kleitos and Persephone become targets of the affections of the gods, a dangerous situation, to which there are many strange endings, from gaining immortality to being crowned as queen of the House of the Dead. Though strongly attracted to humans the gods avoid ugly persons, their favorites always belonging to the beautiful set. Except for a few persons, among which are Thersites, Dolon, and Iros, really ugly people are non-existent in the Homeric universe. All those, neither beautiful, nor ugly, enjoy hardly any attention. Then, gods and man share strong passions for beautiful appearances. In this way, appearance becomes an issue loaded with Destiny.

The Magnetism of Physical Beauty

Among the gods the issue of beauty gives rise to disorder, quarrels, competition, and strife, and even to inflicting war on humans. Thus physical beauty becomes the very trigger of strife which in the end causes humans to wage war against each other. So Paris, forced to judge the beauty contest among the divine ladies, Hera, Athene, and Aphrodite, is asked to do an impossible job. No matter the choice of his, the hopeless situation fates him to stir trouble anyway. When promised to marry a woman who would look like the Love goddess herself, Paris gives the prize to Aphrodite, an act, which later becomes the cause of war. (See *Il.* 24.28-30) Paradoxically, from the affection for beauty arises war and destruction. In unpredictable ways humans unwillingly become victims of divine caprices and their interest in beauty. But the episode also shows that humans share exactly the same strong passion for beauty. In fact, Paris shares his love of beauty with his protector, Aphrodite. Therefore, theoretically, he himself would have been able to initiate the kidnapping of Helen just because of sheer love of beauty.

Though physical beauty may cause turmoil, upheavals, kidnapping, and even war, it is still an omen of good luck, or at least of some glorious destiny. On the dangerous journey to bring back his dead son from Achilleus' camp, Priam is attended by Hermes, disguised as a handsome, young man. The pleasant features of the young man are interpreted by Priam as "an omen of good, for such you are by your form, your admired beauty and the wisdom in your mind. Your parents are fortunate in you." (*Il.* 24.375-77) Visual beauty is spontaneosly perceived as a reliable sign of excellence. The example is just one among many which suggests that a beautiful appearance is usually linked with other qualities as well, in this case with wisdom.

Homer distributes beauty according to rank, the gods and semi-gods being the most beautiful of races. Each member of the divine race embodies an individual character and special powers, but all of them possess a shining quality in their way of appearance. In general, humans do not meet the divine race face to face, and those who do, are in trouble. To mingle with the divine is a dangerous game for human beings. Accordingly, more often than not gods do in fact show up in disguise. But even in disguise, their shining appearances cannot be totally suppressed. So Poseidon in disguise is recognized because of his imposing way of striding along. (See *Il.* 13.71-72) Also Aphrodite's transformation is incomplete. Though approaching Helen in the shape of an old woman, she is, nevertheless, recognized because of her refined stature and especially because of her shining eyes. (See *Il.* 3.396-97) Yet, another conspicuous way of an entry in disguise is Athene, making her appearance on the war-theater in the shape of a glittering shooting star. (See *Il.* 4.76-79)

To be godlike, therefore, is to emanate an aura of shining. This quality, Homer also applies to the race of heroes and heroines and thereby indicating that heroes and heroines are descendants of the gods. In several cases it turns out that there are even close family bonds between gods and their favorite ones. The observation slightly touches upon the idea that human beings *in toto* may be descendants of the gods, but Homer is not explicit on this point. The emphasis of the bonds between gods and man and the presumption that the same tends to love the same are ideas that will become powerful *topoi* in Greek culture. As we shall see later the idea of the same loving the same is a crucial topos in Plato's philosophy.

To be Godlike

Helen, daughter of Zeus, Penelope, and Nausikaa are all of them by appearance compared to immortal goddesses. (See *Il.* 3.158, *Od.* 19.53-54, and *Od.* 6.15-18) Though being the cause of war Helen's outstanding beauty is praised. Even the old men of Troy, suffering from the acts of war because of her, find her beauty superior, when they watch her as she hurries to the wall to view the fight between Paris and Menelaos: "Surely there is no blame on Trojans and strong-greaved Achaians if for long time they suffer hardship for a woman like this one. Terrible is the likeness of her face to immortal goddesses. Still, though she be such, let her go away in the ships, lest she be left behind, a grief to us and our children." (*Il.* 3.156-160) By bodily structure and beauty also Nausikaa is compared to the goddesses, while the lesser beauty of her maids owe their kind of beauty to the Graces. Thus Nausikaa's outstanding beauty is further emphasized by the fact that the maids surrounding her, are each of them a beauty in their own right. Hence, beauty is enhanced by beauty. And, as always in Homeric epic, beauty radiates a shining quality. Hektor's son, for example, is compared to the beauty of "a star shining." (*Il.* 6.401)

Also the beauty of Odysseus is elevated by comparison with other handsome fellows. While Nausikaa by beauty, skills, and wisdom simply outshines her maids, Odysseus is compared not to his servants, but to Agamemnon and Menelaos ranking above him which, of course, calls for a more detailed and subtle description. By wisdom Odysseus is claimed to be comparable even to Zeus. (See *Il.* 2.169, 407, 636) But also in terms of appearance he is a stately fellow, and when occasionally beautified by Pallas Athene, he becomes godlike. Homer illuminates Odysseus' beauty in many interesting ways. In the following we shall examine the characteristics by which Odysseus is qualified, making him the most attractive male hero in Homer's universe. Though not the most handsome by appearance, Odysseus is, however, the one, desired by both mortal and immortal women. The charm of Odysseus is something that Homer pays great attention to convey.

With Helen at his side Priam, standing on the walls of Troy, is inspecting the Greek warriors. As Helen identifies the warriors to Priam, he comments on their appearance as if he were the judge at a male beauty contest. Being a king himself,

Priam is destined first to catch sight of the leader of the enemy, king Agamemnon. This is the principle of the same searching the same. As to height, Agamemnon is not conspicuous, but to Priam he is by far the most handsome: "Though in truth there are others taller by a head than he is, yet these eyes have never yet looked on a man so splendid nor so lordly as this: such a man might well be royal." (*Il.* 3.168-170) Next in line to catch the eye is Odysseus, who is of minor height but "broader, it would seem, in the chest and across the shoulders,"(*Il.* 3.194) inspiring Priam to compare Odysseus to a deep-fleeced ram. Earlier, in Book 2, the appearance of Agamemnon was pinpointed in the picture of a bull, proudly showing its sovereignty among the cattle. Then, both men expose power, strength, and self-confidence. However, the difference between a bull, pasturing safely among its own members, and the ram, always alert and prepared to make its way into unknown and foreign territories, mirrors symbolically the fact that Agamemnon is the bigger landowner of the two. So far Agamemnon has the prize just by his good looks and by convention. But with the image of the ram Priam has become aware of a special aura and vitality of Odysseus, difficult to define. And now a third person joins the evaluation to attest in more detail what Priam just sensed. The episode, in which Odysseus and Menelaos are sent on a diplomatic mission to Troy, is being recalled. At a first glance Menelaos seems to be taller and more impressive in appearance than Odysseus, and he delivers a remarkable, rhetoric performance "rapidly, in few words but exceedingly lucid." (*Od.* 3.213-14) Though being the younger of the two, Menelaos makes a fine speech with no points to be criticized. As a dramatic hint that Menelaos soon will be outshone by Odysseus, we are told that the audience is puzzled by the manner in which Odysseus enters the scene, almost taking Odysseus for a simpleton. For a few moments the audience is left in the dark, having no idea of what to expect: "Yes, you would call him a sullen man, and a fool likewise. But when he let the great voice go from his chest, and the words came drifting down like the winter snows, then no other mortal man beside could stand up against Odysseus. Then we wondered less beholding Odysseus' outward appearance." (*Il.* 3.220-224) Although Menelaos was clear in his rhetoric with no unnecessary or redundant words, Odysseus' performance is sharp, distinct, and shining. The elegant point of this encounter is, of course, that Odysseus himself represents the ideal, his beauty being a fine balance of outer appearance, a clever mind, and above all courage and stamina. Then, the shining quality of Odysseus is actually first fully recognized when he is experienced in action.

Divine Tricks of Beautification and De-Beautification

During his wanderings Odysseus is subject to divine beautification as well as to strategic de-beautification, both of them strategic acts by Athene in support of her favorite. However, it is crucial to notice that these transformations do not change the fundamental beauty and charm of Odysseus. In a number of episodes Athene suffuses Odysseus with a magical radiance. Of these examples Odysseus' encounter with Nausikaa and his reunion with Penelope and Telemachos are the most conspicuous.

Shipwrecked, his skin damaged by sea water, and naked with just a branch to cover him, Odysseus finds himself in an embarrassing situation when meeting Nausikaa at the beach. In this situation he wisely takes to rhetoric instead of physically approaching her. Complimenting first on her beauty and then behaving very decently he wins her confidence. Though looking ghastly because of his hardship, it is noticed that Odysseus has broad shoulders. After having bathed and treated his skin with oil from the golden bottle he gets dressed properly; finally his natural beauty is further enhanced by divine intervention: "Then Athene, daughter of Zeus, made him seem taller for the eye to behold, and thicker, and on his head she arranged the curling locks that hung down like hyacinthine petals. And as when a master craftsman overlays gold on silver, and he is one who was taught by Hephaistos and Pallas Athene in art complete, and grace is on every work he finishes, so Athene gilded with grace his head and his shoulders, and he went a little aside and sat by himself on the seashore, radiant in grace and good looks; and the girl admired him." (*Od.* 6.229-37) Odysseus is made even more attractive than before, but the expression "gold on silver" indeed emphasizes his natural beauty founded in his bodily features and in his just character. Athene just puts the finishing touch on his whole being.

A similar, divine beautification of Odysseus takes place on his homecoming. Meeting again with Telemachos, Athene with her golden wand enhances the beauty of Odysseus: "She increased his strength and stature. His dark color came back to him again, his jaws firmed, and the beard that grew about his chin turned black." (*Od.* 16.174-76) During the grim act of killing the suitors Odysseus seems to regain his former fine appearance, which, as we shall see below, has never been totally taken away from him anyway. Before his reunion with Penelope and after the usual procedure of bathing, anointing the skin with olive oil and getting dressed in fine clothes, Athene accomplishes his grooming: "and over his head Athene suffused great beauty, to make him taller to behold and thicker, and on his head she arranged the curling locks that hung down like hyacinthine petals. And as when a master craftsman overlays gold on silver, and he is one who was taught by Hephaistos and Pallas Athene in art complete, and grace is on every work he finishes; so Athene gilded with grace his head and shoulders. Then, looking like an immortal, he strode forth from the bath." (*Od.* 23.156-163) Here, the form of wording is repeated, and, in particular, the expression, "gold upon silver" must be noticed. To the genuine quality of silver is added the warm glow of gold, adding an extra dimension of erotic allure and charm to Odysseus.

Athene also beautifies Penelope: "First, for her beauty's sake, she freshened all her fine features with ambrosia, such as fair-garlanded Kythereia uses for salve, whenever she joins the lovely dance of the Graces. She made her taller for the eye to behold, and thicker, and she made her whiter than sawn ivory." (*Od.* 18.192-96) Again, beautification is applied to the original beauty and quality of character that has been present from the outset.

Odysseus is also subject to de-beautification, but for strategic reasons. The hero is transformed into the appearance of a beggar. Besides the ragged and dirty clothes Athene also takes away the radiant look of his, leaving him with a lifeless glance in his eyes, his skin wrinkled, and his dark hair spoiled. (See *Od.* 13.398 ff.) But in spite of hardship and being subject to Athene's tricks of de-beautification his metamorphoses are never complete ones. Even in his state of transformation the noble features of Odysseus' stature and his composure are recognized. He is like a king and a lord in appearance. (See *Od.* 20.194) Though transformed by a stroke from Pallas Athene's golden wand Odysseus' body does not lose its characteristic features, including his scar, which works as a sign of identification to those close to him. Other signs of identification are his hands and feet, together with the quality of his voice. Always being able to maintain a sense of inner self, which makes him loyal to his plans, Odysseus never totally loses his particular beauty. Behind all the changes Odysseus remains the same, which in the Homeric universe is highly valued. As we shall see, this feature is later much celebrated in Greek philosophy, and above all in the philosophy of Plato. In this way, by holding on to his inner self, or inner idea of himself, Odysseus shows his true nobility. As the goddess Athene says to Odysseus: "Always you are the same." (*Od.* 13.330) Outer appearance may be subject to damage and hardship due to unhappy circumstances, just as Odysseus' fine dog that has been ill treated, but which still shows that essence, or quality, will, in a deep sense, somehow come through. Then, physical beauty is an issue of attraction and of high value in the Homeric universe, but as mentioned already, physical beauty is also causing worry and trouble. So, for example, when realizing his true identity, Penelope does not fall immediately into the arms of Odysseus. Instead, she puts him to yet one more test in order to make sure that she is not subject to divine trickery. By testing his knowledge of the marriage bed, Penelope plays a trick on the trickster which, of course, brings about the wanted result; Odysseus immediately reveals that it was indeed he who had with his own hands made and decorated the fine marriage bed. (See *Od.* 23, 181 ff.)

Old Age and Care of the Dead Body

Beauty may fade due to hardship, fate, or just from ageing, but real beauty will always stand its ground, no matter how bad the situation and the circumstances. Through Athene's de-beautification of Odysseus we become exposed to all the signs of poverty and hardship, under which the signs of ageing become even more outspoken. Argos, Odysseus' dog, dying shortly after it has recognized and greeted Odysseus, still possesses some features of its former strength and beauty. (See *Od.* 17.306-23) Likewise, the father of Odysseus, suffering and grieving for years over the uncertain situation of his son, still exhibits a somewhat dignified appearance when finally he and Odysseus meet in the orchard. Although Laertes is old, dirty, and wears ragged clothes he nevertheless looks like one who is "royal" because of "stature and beauty." (*Od.* 24.252-55) When, finally, Laertes has been groomed, Athene again turns to her magical trick and beautifies old Laertes so that when appearing to celebrate their reunion, Laertes looks like "one of the immortal gods." (*Od.* 24.371)

To the very end the beautiful body, alive or dead, is subject to care and admiration. Indeed, care of the beautiful body goes beyond death and is of concern to humans as well as to the gods. For Priam, the possibility that he might fall victim to the enemy, stirs him to imagine that he might end up lying unburied and naked, being prey for the dogs. The real pain, to Priam, in this horrible scenario is to face the fact that his fading physical beauty would then be exposed to the world. The young hero, on the other hand, will always be a beautiful sight, even in death. (See *Il.* 22.71-76) For example, the body of dead Hektor, robbed of armour and left lying naked on the ground is admired by the enemy: "[They] gazed upon the stature and on the imposing beauty of Hektor." (*Il.* 22.371-72) However, the spirit of war is mightier than the beauty of dead Hektor; the enemies mutilate his body, each of them stabbing the corpse.

To the gods the care of loved ones also includes taking care of the dead body, protecting it against assaults, decay, and ugliness. Just as the dead body of Patroklos is protected by Thetis, pouring nectar into the nostrils of the corpse, (see *Il.* 19.37-39) the dead Hektor is cared for in a similar way by Aphrodite and Apollo: "But the dogs did not deal with Hektor, for Aphrodite, daughter of Zeus, drove the dogs back from him by day and night, and anointed him with rosy immortal oil, so Achilleus, when he dragged him about, might not tear him. And Phoibos Apollo brought down a darkening mist about him from the sky to the plain, and covered with it all the space that was taken by the dead man, to keep the force of the sun from coming first, and wither his body away by limbs and sinews." (*Il.* 23.184-91) Later, when Achilleus keeps on repeating his wicked treatment of the corpse of Hektor, Apollo again takes action: "But Apollo had pity on him, though he was only a dead man, and guarded the body from all ugliness, and hid all of it under the golden aegis so that it might not be torn when Achilleus dragged it." (*Il.* 24.18-21)

The Greek adoration of human beauty has caused Alfred Baeumler to emphasize that Western aesthetics originally was fuelled by the sight of natural beauties, and not by the sight of art. Among living beauties man has a prominent position. To Homer, human beauty is a phenomenon of great importance.

6. The Embellishment of Life

The manufacturing of artificial objects, whether clothes, jewelry, weapons, household goods, or fine architecture all contribute to a festive atmosphere and to the celebration of life. Even more so does pleasant human conduct. Finally, skilled and aesthetically pleasing performances such as, for example, singing or delivering a speech also add to the embellishment of life.

All these things, pleasant conduct as well as artefacts, share one particular feature, namely that they somehow radiate *a shining quality*. As we shall see, only at random Homer specifies the actual shade of the shining. Though describing the shining in no great detail, but rather in terms of generality, we still get a strong impression of the objects and the acts of performance, which Homer shows. In the following, we shall touch upon some examples.

The Allure of Smiles, Courtesy, and Seduction

Next to the fascination of natural physical beauty stands the admiration for ingenious performance and creativity, manifesting itself in a number of ways among which are courtesy and seduction, love-making, singing, playing music, dancing, story-telling, rhetoric, hunting, sport games, and, to some extent, warfare.

Charming behavior, courtesy, and seduction are considered as a stroke of genius and, therefore, almost always associated with the beautiful. Already in the *Iliad*, Book 1, Homer demonstrates to us the magic effects of a smile. A dispute between Zeus and Hera has built up considerable tension, threatening the domestic harmony among the gods. Anger, outbursts of violence, and resentment are spoiling the festive spirit of their banquet. To console his mother, Hephaistos courageously intervenes, suggesting to Hera to lay strife behind her. After having put forth his suggestion three times in succession "the goddess of the white arms Hera smiled at him, and smiling she accepted the goblet out of her son's hand." (*Il.* 1.595-96) Hera's smile gives rise to a sudden turn of events. Harmony is regained, the gods enjoy themselves until sunset with food, nectar, music, and endless laughter.

From time to time even Zeus smiles graciously. Especially, Aphrodite and her affairs usually calls forth a smile upon his face. (See *Il.* 5.426-27) Aphrodite, the love goddess herself, according to both Hesiod and Homer, is a "lover of smiles." Hence, Homer is well aware of the psychological fact that a smile has the magic power to change the atmosphere or a situation from being ugly to being beautiful. Another image, which connects smile and laughter with wellbeing, buoyancy, and the beautiful, can be noticed in Hades' cunning plan to seduce Persephone. When Hades orders Gaia, the earth, to grow a narcissus, the result is so wonderful that the whole world rejoices: "The wide sky above and the whole earth and the briny swell of the sea laughed." (*The Homeric Hymns, To Demeter*, verses 10-14) As we shall see later, Homer will repeat the impressive image of the whole world laughing with joy and wellbeing.

A magnificent scene of energy, female allure, and gallant manners is unveiled when the goddess, Iris, messenger of the gods, hurries to Thrace in order to console Achilleus by getting help from the Winds to light the funeral pyre of Patroklos. Here, in the house of Zephyros, the Winds are assembled and partying. But when their eyes catch sight of the goddess, standing by the door-sill they "sprang to their feet and each one asked her to sit beside him." (*Il.* 23.203) The Winds, though boisterous and noisy, are not untouched by female attraction and suddenly know how to conduct themselves. Her request is immediately met with delight: "And they with immortal clamour rose up, and swept the clouds in confusion before them. They came with a sudden blast upon the sea, and the waves rose under the whistling wind. They came to generous Troad and hit the pyre, and a huge inhuman blaze rose, roaring. Nightlong they piled the flames on the funeral pyre together and blew with a screaming blast." (*Il.* 23.212-218) Through this action the Winds show their essential nature, being that of energy and turbulence. But on this background, it becomes still more conspicuous that the lure of female beauty had the power to produce in these rough nature gods an outburst of fine and gentle manners.

The main scene of seduction in Homeric epic is, however, the pastoral scene on Olympos in which Hera seduces her own husband, Zeus. Homer meticulously states the various steps as to how Hera beautifies herself before taking action. For soap Hera uses ambrosia, for lotion sweet olive oil, and when the goddess uses her scent, the fragrance is emitted "forever forth, on earth and in heaven." (*Il.* 14.174) Further, she combs her hair, arranges a special curly hair-style, then dresses herself in a finery made by Athene, and decorated with a golden brooch and a belt with a hundred tassels, earrings with triple drops in mulberry clusters, a veil "glimmering pale like the sunlight", and finally a pair of fair sandals.

Yet, Hera's own physical beauty, "an adorable body" and "shining feet", careful grooming of the body and plenty of adornment, is not enough to succeed. Physical beauty and artificial adornment must be coupled with personal grace, charm, and desire, radiating from the seducer. This special gift can only be provided for by Aphrodite, the goddess of Love, who holds the power to play with life and "to overwhelm mortal men, and all the immortals." (*Il.* 14.199) Though a goddess herself Hera must, nevertheless, beg Aphrodite to bestow upon her the gift of attractiveness and grace that she may be desired. Aphrodite lends Hera a special band, on which is depicted all the images of passion, desire, and sweet words to make Zeus fall under the spell of his own wife. In this witty and spectacular episode, a fundamental feature of Greek aesthetics is present, namely that of emphasizing the superiority of living beauty to artificial beauty. Embellishment by means of luxurious artefacts is important, but still more so, is the special charm and energy, which mysteriously links with the essence of life, being alive and present.

Odysseus' reunion with his wife, Penelope, which takes place through a highly artful succession of steps heeded by strategy on both sides, represents another fine example of Homeric knowledge of the nature of attraction, seduction, and strong, but delicate emotions. On his return to Ithaka, Odysseus shows up in the disguise of an old begger. The recognition of Odysseus enters through various steps. Argos, Odysseus' dog, is the first to recognize him just by the sound of his voice. Old, sick, and not being able to stand on its feet the dog greets Odysseus by rising its head and ears, and wagging its tail. Odysseus is in tears but has to hide his emotions. Then, his old nurse notices the begger's resemblance to Odysseus. When finally meeting with Penelope, Odysseus is still disguised as a beggar. At this first encounter Penelope is somehow prediposed in favor of the beggar as he may have information about her husband. A swineherd further fuels her hopes stating that he himself has already been captivated by the charm of the beggar, who is compared to a singer. (See *Od.* 17.518-19) Then, their encounter takes place on grounds of mutual attraction and interest. Transformed into the appearance of an old man, Penelope does not recognize her husband. But she is indeed aware of his personal integrity, decent manners, and dignity.

Instead of answering her opening question, the disguised Odysseus starts complimenting her for her fame being the lady of the house. Hence, the very first words spoken to his wife after twenty years of separation are molded into a compliment. (See *Od.* 19.107 ff.) In this way confidence is established, and Penelope now starts telling her story, revealing her desperate longing for Odysseus. Next, Odysseus changes strategy in order to make up the story of having met with Odysseus. And by listening to the beggar Penelope gives in to twenty years of accumulated grief that has crystallized her feelings into dullness, leaving her to only sorrow. She suddenly experiences the burning longing for Odysseus: "As she listened her tears ran and her body was melted, as the snow melts along the high places of the mountains, when the West Wind has piled it there, but the south Wind melts it, and as it melts the rivers run full flood. It was even so that her beautiful cheeks were streaming tears, as Penelope wept for her man, who was sitting there by her side." (*Od.* 19.204-209) But like before, when meeting with his dog, Odysseus performs a stern self-control in order to hide his stirred emotions. Therefore, in order to avoid the slightest inkling of showing loving affection through his gaze, he knows he must not allow his eyes to dwell upon his wife: "But his eyes stayed, as if they were made of horn or iron, steady under his lids. He hid his tears and deceived her." (*Od.* 19.211-12)

When Penelope continues to test the beggar further on his knowledge of her husband, Odysseus proceeds complimenting her indirectly by referring to the sumptuous attire of the hero. Thus among Odysseus' equipment the begger has noticed "a woolen mantle of purple with two folds," a golden pin, and a tunic, made from delicate material, resembling "the dried-out skin of an onion" and "shining bright as the sun shines." (*Od.* 19.225-34) The point is this: it was in fact Penelope who provided for these items, and in her heart she keeps the fine sight of Odysseus leaving for Troy, dressed in purple and shining gold. So by compliments and by wise rhetoric Odysseus wins her confidence to the extent that she begins to project the image of an aged Odysseus to the beggar. In particular, she notices his hands and feet. Eurykleia's observations adds to the confusion; she has already noticed the likeness between the beggar and Odysseus in respect of voice and appearance. The whole situation leaves Penelope in a state of emotional turmoil from which springs yet another sensation. During night-time she is awakened by a dream: "For on this very night there was one who lay by me, like him as he was when he went with the army, so that my own heart was happy. I thought it was no dream, but a waking vision." (*Od.* 20.88-90) Odysseus, in a similar fashion, is stirred by their meeting and by the sound of her crying in the night. But both of them show their capacity for self-control. However, when they finally embrace they are in tears. (See *Od.* 23.205-07 and 23.231-32) But the embrace after twenty years of separation is mainly describing the emotional storms of Penelope. (See *Od.* 23.233-240) Realizing that her husband has returned and that the man in front of her is indeed her husband, Penelope gives in to her emotions: "But then she burst into tears and ran straight to him, throwing her arms around the neck of Odysseus, and kissed his head." (*Od.* 23.207-208) Thus the reunion of Penelope and Odysseus, meeting again after twenty years of separation, displays a number of sophisticated strategies in which strong emotions are molded into the frame of delicate and wise courtesy. The reunion signifies fierce passions too. In fact, Odysseus is offered the possibility of being immortal, but prefers Penelope to the goddess Kalypso. But choosing a life together with Penelope is also to accept death. Hence, once again Odysseus' character is manifested through strong will-power to follow his preconceived plan, guided by his passions.

The reunion between a married couple that have been apart for twenty years surprisingly turns out to contain a wise and refined *canon* of courtesy, concerning both male and female behavior. This point becomes even more impressive considering the fact that Penelope and Odysseus reunite under very troubled circumstances in which the whole atmosphere is contaminated with disorder, suspicion, disguise, and danger. Hence, Homer's epic depicts a number of magnificent images of both erotic allure and of fine courtesy.

The Shining Artefacts

To the embellishment of life also belong artificial objects like clothes, jewelry, weapons, households goods, interior designs, and architecture. While Aphrodite owns the capacity to bestow erotic allure to life, the limping smith-god, her consort, is the prime maker of beautiful artifice to enhance life. But his love of beauty is not restricted to material things only. His creative activity has a further purpose, namely that of making people happy and thus to elevate the whole spirit of life. In spite of a harsh upbringing, Hephaistos appears to be a gentle and loving character. Abandoned by his mother, Hera, the orphan is rescued and raised by the daughters of Okeanos with whom he lives for nine years. Because of his wish to please the nymphs Hephaistos starts to make jewelry for them. His excellence in this skill brings him back among the Olympians. As discussed earlier it is indeed Hephaistos who restors domestic harmony on Olympos. Thus Hephaistos does not only show excellence in manufacturing things, but it is also he who consoles the goddesses in moments of grief. When Achilleus has lost his armor to the enemy, his mother, Thetis, hurries to the palace of Hephaistos to ask for new equipment for Achilleus. As a goddess she knows that her son is soon going to die, and she is in great pain. Hephaistos immediately meets the plea of the goddess, and while touching her hand and calling her by name, Hephaistos does all he can to ease the pain of the goddess. (See *Il.* 18.423-427, and 462-467) Besides being the maker of his own palace, which Homer describes as being of outstanding beauty, he is also the maker and interior designer of the residences on Olympos, and for his mother he makes a secret lock. In conclusion, he is the maker of a great number of things from the metal walls and the golden pavement on Olympos to Zeus' golden scales.

Materials for Hephaistos' artefacts are for the most part metals and precious stones, and among their qualities the *shining* effect is always emphasized: they shine like the Sun. (See *Il.* 19.398) Especially Achilleus' armour is described in detail, e.g., the lustre from his famous shield is compared to fire and to the light from the moon. (Se *Il.* 19.374) Achilleus' helmet, matching his glowing eyes "shone like a star, the golden fringes were shaken about it which Hephaistos had driven close along the horn of the helmet." (*Il.* 19.382-83) Finally, Achilleus stands "shining in all his armour like the sun." (*Il.* 19.398) Later, on the plains in front of Ilion, Achilleus' armour is compared to the brightest of the stars, namely Orion's Dog. Further, Achilleus is described as a star moving among stars, and his armor is compared to "Hesper, who is the fairest star who stands in the sky, such was the shining from the pointed spear." (Il. 22.317-319) In conclusion, artefacts by humans and, in particular, artefacts made by Hephaistos, own the special quality of *shining*. When the Achaians in the morning prepare for yet another encounter with the enemy, arming themselves with helmets, corselets, shields, swords and spears, of which Hephaistos has made several pieces, the lustre from their gear becomes spectacular: "The shining swept to the sky and all earth was laughing about them under the glitter of bronze." (*Il.* 19.362-63) Despite the shining armor made by Hephaistos is much admired, Homer is not totally carried away. He does in fact ridicule Nastes. Nastes is a Trojan war hero who arrives at the war-theater dressed like a girl "in golden raiment," (*Il.* 2.872) an attire that does not help against the enemy. Nastes is killed, and Achilleus takes possession of all his golden finery. Here, Homer suddenly reveals knowledge of balance, or *decorum*.

A number of the artefacts made by the limping smith-god is handed down to the race of heroes as gifts. Most famous is the schield of Achilleus. Agamemnon's scepter is another example of which it is stated that Hephaistos was the maker. (*Il.* 2.101-09)[5] All of them share one and the same aesthetic quality: they shine. Yet, another sign of Hephaistos' expertise, is that many of these works look real although they are artificial. Thus the golden attendants, which Hephaistos makes to support himself as he is limping, look like "living young women. There is intelligence in their hearts, and there is speech in them and strength." (*Il.* 18.416-420) Also, the decoration of Achilleus' shield depicts scenes from everyday life with stunning detail. The earth on the painting looks like real earth "that has been ploughed though it was gold. Such was the wonder of the shield's forging." (*Il.* 18.548-49)

In the Homeric universe Hephaistos is he who sets a shining example as maker of beautiful artefacts. But Homer also dwells on the luxurious robes of the goddesses. Homer gives a charming description of how Kalypso at dawn dresses "in a gleaming white robe fine-woven and delightful, and around her waist she fastened a handsome belt of gold, and on her head was a wimple." (*Od.* 5.230-32) It is further given by Fate that Odysseus must also embrace the goddess Circe, and she happens to dress in exactly the same manner. (See *Od.* 10.543-45)

Homeric epic is also brimming with descriptions of artefacts made by humans. Fine goods such as beautiful clothes, jewelry, exquisite household goods, and weapons, often richly adorned seem to accumulate in the life of heroes and heroines. In particular, Homer is fond of describing the apparel of heroes in full gear down to the minutest detail. Fine clothing is a sign of nobility and good fortune, while wretched clothes are the Destiny of the poor. Helen's costumes are "light robes" (*Od.* 4.305) of which she owns a rich collection. As for a wedding gown for the future wife of Telemachos, she selects from her own collection a particularly beautiful dress, shining "like a star." (*Od.* 15.108) When appearing before the suitors Penelope wears a "shining veil." (*Od.* 18.210) Besides a fine robe the suitors also bring Penelope exquisite jewelry made of gold, pearls, and amber "bright as sunshine." (*Od.* 18.296) Penelope, having been forced to complete her piece of weaving washes it before dis-

---

5   Peter Jones has noticed that objects of high significance typically are subject to long digressions like Odysseus' bow, which in former times belonged to Apollo. See Peter Jones: *Homer's Odyssey*. A Companion to the English Translation of Richmond Lattimore. London 1998. For the pedigree of the bow, see p. 195, note 14.

playing it, and it is said that it "shone like the sun or the moon." (*Od.* 24.148) Some of the gifts for Penelope, are made, for example, by a skilled manufacturer, called Ikmalios. He makes a chair for Penelope which is adorned with "ivory and silver." (*Od.* 19.56) The marriage bed of Penelope and Odysseus, made by the hero himself, is even more splendid, adorned with "gold and silver and ivory." (*Od.* 23. 200)

Luxurious goods are a major concern in the Homeric world. Plenty of fine goods are the signs of a good life where nothing is missing. According to Homer, beautiful objects enhance people, environment, and events. The collection of artefacts might be bestowed to the heroes and heroines as heritage, or gifts, or may simply stem from booty. So Odysseus returns to Ithaka, loaded with gifts of bronze, gold in abundance, and clothing. (See *Od.* 23.341) A lot of goods are displayed in order to add a note of grandeur to the house to which it belongs. The gifts for Achilleus, chosen by Priam, in exchange for the corpse of Hektor, are described as follows: "Twelve robes surpassingly lovely and twelve mantles to be worn single, as many blankets, as many great white cloaks, also the same number of tunics. He weighed and carried out ten full talents of gold, and brought forth two shining tripods, and four cauldrons, and brought out a goblet of surpassing loveliness that the men of Trace had given him." (*Il.* 24.229-34) Artificial objects are made to serve various purposes, but they are pleasures to the eye too, many of them "a wonder to look at." While serving their function in an optimal way, the *shining* artefacts at the same time add an atmosphere of celebration and festivity to everyday life. Artefacts, mentioned by Homer, always expose features that add splendor, dignity, and importance to the situation in which they occur.

Shining Purple

The most distinguished word Homer can come up with concerning aesthetic quality is the word *shining*. This word is applied to the shining appearance of the gods and goddesses and to the appearances, acts, and deeds of humans. It further applies to phenomena and objects of outstanding quality. Together with the term *shining* there is one color, in particular, that attracts attention. Among colors in the Homeric universe the color purple stands out. Purple is described in a variety of shades from fiery red, scarlet, and reddish blue to auburn. Homer associates the main image of purple to the sparkling color of red wine, an image that also lends its hues from views of the sea, oscillating between "wine-dark," or "wine-blue." From the fascination of liquid, radiating a fan of glittering shades of purple, Homer's awareness of purple expands to further examples of the natural occurrence of colors close to the color of wine. For example, the cattle are perceived as "wine-coloured." (*Od.* 13.32) The nymphs of the wells on Ithaka weave "sea-purple webs, a wonder to look on." (*Od.* 13.108) Finery, belonging to gods, or to the nobility, is distinguished by being dyed purple. In *The*

Homeric Hymns Dionysos is wearing "a purple cloak," the linen in Circe's household is dyed purple, (*Od.* 10.352) and the heroes setting out on their audacious journeys wear woolen mantles dyed purple. (See *Od.* 4.115, 154, and *Od.* 8.84-85)

Most conspicuous is the splendid sight of Odysseus, leaving Ithaka for warfare against Troy, dressed in a "woolen mantle of purple, with two folds, but the pin to it was golden and fashioned with double sheathes." (*Od.* 19.225-27) Underneath, Odysseus was wearing a tunic, shining like "the dried-out skin of an onion, so sheer it was and soft, and shining bright as the sun shines." (*Od.* 19.233-34) This attire, together with the adornment, serves as one of the proofs as to the identity of Odysseus and is recognized by Penelope: "For I myself gave him this clothing, as you describe it. I folded it in my chamber, and I too attached the shining pin, to be his adornment." (*Od.* 19.255-57) But also for other reasons Odysseus' attire is conspicuous in comparison to the heroines. The heroines usually do not wear purple, but they make all the purple linen and wool. (See *Il.* 3.126, *Od.* 6.306, and *Od.* 19.255-56) As has already been discussed the robes of the goddesses and heroines have the shining quality of either the sun, the moon, or the stars. Thus Odysseus' apparel combines in fact the splendor from both male and female dress.

The heroines produce all the fine materials, dyed with purple, and these products are signs of the noble status of their households. So coverlets, on which the heroes and heroines are seated, are purple, and so are all their bed linen and blankets. And when Penelope, as mentioed already, plays a trick on the trickster, Odysseus reveals that he used an oxhide "dyed bright with purple" (*Od.* 23.201) for the bottom of the ostentatious marriage bed. Also, leaving for war does not mean the absence of luxurious living, as the heroes take fine household goods with them to the battlefield. Here, too, in the war camp, purple blankets add a sense of dignity to the tent of Achilleus. (See *Il.* 9.200)

However, there are a few extraordinary features of purple, in which splendor indeed blends with sorrow. As a celestial phenomenon the purple rainbow attracts fascination and praise, but also ascribed to it is an atmosphere of ominous events to come. When Zeus decides to send people off to Hades, a special kind of dew will emerge from the sky "dripping blood." (*Il.* 11.54) Purple rain, or the purple sky, then becomes an omen of war; also the rainbow as a sign of climatic change to severe wintry conditions with hard frost contains the color of purple. (See (*Il.* 17.547-51) Finally, the golden casket, containing the cremated remains of Hektor, is wrapped with "soft robes of purple." (*Il.* 24.796)

At the very end of the fan of colors stands black, associated with death and grief. In general the goddesses are wearing "light robes," but when Thetis is called to Olympos concerning her son who is going to die in the near future, she leaves her silvery cave dressed in a black veil, "and there is no darker garment." (*Il.* 24.94) From examples, discussed earlier, black is not without a certain solemn dignity. Like other colors black attracts the eye, but it does not radiate any shine and is therefore the appropriate color for animals sacrificed to Hades.

The Marriage of Aphrodite and Hephaistos

It is a stroke of mythological genius to claim the beautiful love goddess, Aphrodite is indeed married to the sweating and limping smith-god, Hephaistos, the maker of artificial wonders. Together, Aphrodite and Hephaistos symbolize beauty and embellishment so that life on earth can prosper.

However, to the marriage of Hephaistos there are two traditions. In the *Odyssey* it is told that Hephaistos is married to Aphrodite, while the *Iliad* claims his wife to be Charis. Though there is a difference in power between Aphrodite and Charis, Hephaistos as consort in both traditions is described as in love with beauty. His marriage with Charis, a personification of grace, is harmonious, while the marriage with Aphrodite, the goddess of love and beauty, is turbulent and dramatic. But together they provide for the embellisment of life. By marrying the very symbol of life, energy, erotic allure, and beauty, namely Aphrodite, with Hephaistos, the master of making all the beautiful objects, Homer's aesthetics embraces almost everything. There are, of course many minor aspects, with which we cannot deal here, such as the Muses, other gods and goddesses, nymphs etc. who from time to time will provide help as to the beautification and enbetterment of the world as a whole. The Winds, the messengers, the Muses singing at Patroklos' funeral pyre etc., all help in one way, or another to beautify the world.

The marrying of the love goddess Aphrodite/Charis to the limping-smith god, Hephaistos, is a mythological image that contains a profound knowledge of the importance of beauty in all aspects of life. At the same time the mythological wisdom is deep and very clear about the hierarchy between different levels of order and beauty. While Zeus, of course, is the symbol of order as such, Aphrodite and Hephaistos are symbolizing the multifarious aspects of living beauty. Though Homer admires all kinds of shining artefacts with which Hephaistos beautifies the environment of gods, heroes, and heroines, he does also reveal his knowledge of erotic allure, and this cannot be obtained by means of artifice. Rather, the glow of erotic attractiveness origins from another source, which according to Homer, belongs to the domain of Aphrodite. Hence, in Homeric aesthetics living beauty always ranks above artificial beauty. But for the embellisment of life, as such, both forces are needed.

7. The Ugly

Both gods and humans take a passionate interest in beauty, and thus beauty becomes entangled with Destiny. Lack of beauty also creates Destiny, but of a different kind.

Those in the Homeric world, who happen to be ugly, suffer a grim fate. While Homer shows no pity for those unfortunates, he does indeed air quite sophisticated views concerning the blend of the beautiful and the ugly when dealing with the divine monsters.

The Ugly Ones: Ugliness and Lack of Intelligence

In the *Iliad* we meet two of the unfortunates, lacking in both beauty and intelligence. Thersites and Dolon are favored by no one, not even by Homer. Thersites has the bad luck to be "the ugliest man" of the whole army, and Dolon, a skilled runner and a scout, is ugly to look upon having an unpleasant appearance with a jailbird's face.

The description of Thersites exposes him to ridicule, being "bandy-legged" and "lame of one foot, with shoulders stooped and drawn together over his chest, and above this his skull went up to a point with the wool grown sparsely upon it." (*Il.* 2.217-219) This unpleasant appearance of his is further emphasized by a lack of good character and decent behavior. To prevent him from exerting any influence on the other soldiers, he is punished by Odysseus and ends up crying cowardly, a behavior for which he becomes the target of contempt. His bad reputation was to be long–standing. In Plato's dialogue, the *Republic,* it is said that his soul in its next life chose to reincarnate in the shape of a monkey. (See *Rep.* 620 c) While Thersites, due to lack of physical beauty, and, especially, due to his own stupidity, suffers the Fate of being ridiculed in front of the whole army and beaten by Odysseus, so likewise everybody betrays Dolon, the Trojan scout. He even betrays himself as he does not realize the kind of action he voluntarily sets out to fulfill, a task which, he imagines, will put him in the position to take over Achilleus' horses and chariot. Instead, he falls into an ambush and is killed by Diomedes.

In the *Odyssey* the issue of ugliness is perceived with more subtle, and complicated overtones. Here a beautiful appearance does not necessarily match with the real essence of a person. Odysseus' controversy with Euryalos highlights what the idea of ideal beauty is about, perceived as a combination of outer appearance and inner virtue and grace. Being a guest at Alkinoos' court, Odysseus is challenged by the Phaiakian hothead Euryalos, breaking the rules of courtesy against a guest. The insult provokes Odysseus to air the following view: "So it is that the gods do not bestow graces in all ways on men, neither in stature nor yet in brains or eloquence; for there is a certain kind of man, less noted for beauty, but the gods put comeliness on his words, and they who look toward him are filled with joy at the sight, and he speaks to them without faltering in winning modesty, and shines among those who are gathered, and people look on him as on a god when he walks in the city. Another again in his appearance is like the immortals, but upon his words there is no grace distilled, as in your case the appearance is conspicuous, and not a god even would make it otherwise, and yet the mind there is worthless." (*Od.* 8.167-177) In these remarks is aired a rather sophisticated approach, according to which the storyteller is able to differentiate between different levels of beauty and their contents. Beauty may, or may not, be totally due to outer appearance. The elegant point of this encounter is this: Odysseus, himself being the archetype of male beauty, is he who gives voice to the Homeric image of ideal beauty by claiming it to be a balance between outer appearance and inner character. As such, sheer physical beauty does not really count.

However, the Phaiakians are descendants from the gods and therefore godlike. Euryalos made a *faux pas* because of young age, but reprimanded by Alkinoos he makes up for his rudeness, excusing his behavior. Hence, the image of the godlike and refined is restored. Euryalos, conspicuous in appearance, does in fact finally act with grace too. But the episode leaves for further investigation the notion that people may exceed in good looks and even so being worthy of nothing, when it comes to a more holistic and substantial estimation of them.

Also Antinoos belongs to the flawed breed of the ugly ones. Antinoos is one of the leading suitors of Penelope; he is conspicuous in good looks and holds some nobility in his character. But his evil attitudes predominate. "Shame," says Odysseus to Antinoos, "the wits in you, it is clear, do not match you outward beauty." (*Od.* 17.454-55) Then, Antinoos becomes yet one more example where beauty occurs, but without no shining quality to it. Also, the expectations, cheered by the eye, are disappointed in the case of Iros, huge and famous for his capacity to eat and drink, but who is nevertheless weak. (See *Od.* 18.1-10) Like beauty creates Destiny in the Homeric world, so does lack of beauty.

The Ambiguity of the Ugly: Monsters

Among the many achievements of ancient myth is also that of giving form to the horrible, and the unknown. Only when caught in some form, it becomes possible to the mind to cope with the horrible. But to lend imagination to the horrible has unforeseen consequences. The process of interpreting reality and giving form to the unknown starts a series of steps which, in the passage of time, results in a certain beautification of what was in the beginning horror beyond human imagination. In the case of Homer this tendency shows in the ambiguity with which he describes the monsters where aspects of beauty mingle with the ugly as is the case with the Cyclops, blinded by Odysseus.

In the Homeric world monsters dwell in remote places, or at the edge of world. Only when man happens to pass by their dwelling places, do monsters become a threat to humans. The monster, Polyphemos, lives on an island, and from a human perspective he is ugly looking because of only having his one eye, and because of his gigantic size of which he brags, claiming himself to be stronger than the Olympian gods. (See *Od.* 9.276) Though mostly on his own, he is always trying to hatch evil actions. All in all, he is a brute. But he is also the son of Poseidon and therefore godlike, a marvel to look upon, says Homer. Though a monster Polyphemos is, nevertheless, a divine being, and as such he does indeed have some affinity with beauty. Despite his eating half of Odysseus' crew, these horrible scenes are combined with other, so to speak, more decent aspects of his character. Polyphemos proves himself to be an excellent shepherd taking good care of his animals. His dwelling place is well–ordered, and he speaks kind words to his favorite animal, the beautiful black ram.

It has been prophesied to Polyphemos that he is to lose his sight at the hands of Odysseus. After the prophecy has come true, and Odysseus is safe back on his ship, the latter identifies himself to the Cyclops by shouting the true name of his. Odysseus' cunning trick was to introduce himself as *Nobody*. Though furious and in great pain Polyphemos is taken by surprise when hearing his slayer was indeed Odysseus: "But always I was on the outlook for a man handsome and tall, with great endowment of strength on him, to come here; but now the end of it is that a little man, niddering, feeble, has taken away the sight of my eye." (*Od.* 9.513-16) As a matter of fact, his expectations are accomplished on a level which Polyphemos does not understand, uncultivated as he is. Odysseus is, according to Homer, an exceedingly handsome fellow desired by mortal women, by the nymphs Kalypso and Circe, and favored by Pallas Athene too. Then, Polyphemos is primitive, uncivilized, and ugly, but the description of him is, nevertheless, diffused with glimpses of beauty. As a divine being Polyphemos is a lover of beauty, although he behaves barbaric. He expected that Odysseus would be handsome, he likes order, and he admires the beauty of his black ram.

The pedigree of monsters usually links back in time to some divine origin. Therefore, monsters, according to Homer, are included in the world of beauty, and they in various ways possess, or show some affinities to beauty. Also, being of divine origin, monsters are cared for by the gods. Hence, Poseidon later takes revenge on behalf of Polyphemos, his son, for whom he shows paternal affection.

Other monsters, or monster-like beings, in the Homeric world are the Laistrygones. In appearrance they show some resemblance to the former race of gods, namely the Giants, (See *Od.* 10.120) The Laistrygones are cannibals, but live in a somewhat civilized society with palaces and fine roads. The female monsters, the Sirens, who by their singing enchant man to draw close to listen to their irresistible knowledge of the past, the present and the future, dwell in a "flowery meadow." (*Od.* 12.159) But in spite of the beauty of their singing with "honey-sweet" voices and the beauty of the enviroment they cause the death of man. (See *Od.* 12.39-46 and 184 ff.) Also Skylla, another female monster, inhabits a location on the edge of world, facing the deep and Erebos; thus already her dwelling place has an uncanny ring to it. Circe warns Odysseus that Skylla is ugly to look at. "No one,", says Circe, "not even a god encountering her, could be glad at that sight." (*Od.* 12.87-88) Skylla is insect–like with six heads, twelve ugly looking feet, etc. In addition, her ugliness is paired with evil. She is an evil, cannibalistic monster. Then, in the Homeric world, Skylla comes to represent the utmost limit of ugliness. Although she is of divine origin, not even the beauty-loving gods, who excel in having a broader sense of beauty than that of humans, can be appeased at the sight. The only positive aspect about Skylla is that she can be put out of action by her own mother. Circe advises Odysseus to call Krataiis, the mother of Skylla, in order to calm things down, but when he becomes the target of Skylla's rage, he strangely enough does not make use of this advice.

In conclusion, Homer holds the view that there is a difference between the aesthetic preferences of the gods and those of man, the former being a sort of grand–scale aesthetics, while the taste of man is adapted to more natural features. Skylla is a bordercase, an immortal monster whose ugliness paired with evil is such that no soothing dimensions can be found, neither on the divine, nor human level. But Skylla is an exception, and Circe tells Odysseus that Skylla is born as a punishment to humans. Skylla is immortal, but even so she is a "mischief immortal." (*Od.* 12.118) The ugly as such, therefore, becomes a marginal phenomenon on the periphery of both divine and human existence.

8. Beyond the Ugly: War and Destruction

Until now we have discussed how Homer, in almost every aspect of life, highlights dimensions of order, splendor and beauty. Homer shows us the abundance of forms in which "the sweetness of life" itself radiates. And to some extent Homer is even able to detect the dimensions of beauty entangled with various forms of the ugly. Therefore, to witness the destruction of life and beauty represents the deepest level of despair and grief, experienced by humans. And in a certain sense, destruction of life and beauty goes beyond the ugly – and beyond description. And, yet, Homer gives voice to the unspeakable pain and sorrow.

As mentioned already, Homer describes the divine race as lovers of beauty, but he also unfolds a darker and more uncanny aspect of their nature. While the grand cosmological order of beauty is provided for by divine intervention, the fragile beauty, belonging to the physical world of humans suffers from the gods taste for play, change, events, and entertainment, which occasionally leads to the destruction of beauty. Though Ilion, Priam's beautiful city, counts as Zeus' favorite among cities on the earth, and the Trojans are dear to him, he nevertheless sacrifices the city and its citizens in order to uphold domestic harmony among the gods themselves. (See

Il. 4.1 ff.) In some cases, however, Destiny itself, symbolized by the golden scales, contains a power, which may run counter even to the will of Zeus. According to the *Iliad* version, the gods cannot always be blamed for the Destiny of man. In the *Odyssey* Homer's standpoint is more outspoken. So Alkinoos addresses lamenting Odysseus as follows: "The gods did this, and spun the destruction of peoples, for the sake of the singing of men hereafter." (*Od.* 8.579-80) Except for the episode with Helios' threat, the disturbing questions of eschatology are never really dealt with in Homeric epic. But the destruction of living beings, of landscapes, and of cities provokes questions concerning the true nature of the gods. At times, the motives of the gods are indeed questioned.

War as a Pastime for the Gods

By way of their very nature the gods are considered to be beauty lovers, but strangely enough they also cause the destruction of beauty by afflicting strife and war upon humans. Humans are subject to all sorts of divine caprices stirring up the life of individuals and their destiny. Among such caprices is war. Thus the ten–year long warfare against Troy is due to games of competition between the goddesses. To the Olympians war is a game and a pastime. War stirs the emotional life of the gods, keeping them busy with each other and with their interest in humans, of whom some are favored and others subject to their hate. When not directly participating by their own presence, the gods take pleasure watching the gruesome games of killing from a distance. Athene and Apollo even appear at the war-theater disguised as vultures. (See *Il.* 7.58-59)

In the face of war and death it becomes manifest that the gods do in fact embody a value system that differs from that of human beings. Humans hold a taste for life itself and its beauty, but confronted with the stern order executed by the gods, they stand very fragile and vulnerable. Achilleus, at some point, refers to the lack of meaning in the warfare against Troy and says: "The gods themselves have no sorrows." (*Il.* 24.526) Then, the gods initiate and sustain war just for the sake of entertainment. While Achilleus is blaming Zeus for all the suffering, Homer tries to save the gods from blame. In other words: Homer's theodicy has many aspects to it. Though outstanding in wisdom Zeus, from time to time, makes his decisions by means of "golden scales." (*Il.* 8.69-70, 19.223 and 22.209-12) Thus suffering, destruction, and death are afflicted upon humans not only by Zeus, but also by Necessity. Necessity is a force to which even Zeus himself and other Olympians are exposed. Behind some of the most devastating decisions of Zeus operates some secret force, namely Destiny or Necessity. In some cases it turns out that Zeus is merely the executor of Destiny. In the end, Homer somehow claims that even Destiny holds a secret ordering principle. Its divine character is represented by the image of the golden scales, balancing good and evil, the beautiful and the ugly, and, finally, life and death. But Homer is ambiguous on this troubled issue as the destruction of beauty taking place at the war-theater is indeed overwhelming.

The Meadow of Skamandros as War-Theater

The war-theater is established on "the blossoming meadow of Skamandros." (*Il.* 2.467) Here, in this lovely landscape, described in a manner which resembles the description of *the Elysian Field*, the beautiful young heroes from both camps are going to lose their lives in a war, which has no real winners, and where the warriors on both sides bury their dead "with their hearts in sorrow." (*Il.* 7.428-431) The enemy is of course described as inferior to the Greeks, but only slightly so. Like the Greek heroes the enemy is courageous too and of noble lineage, being descendants from the gods.

As a consequence of the war game, initiated by the gods, Nature itself is damaged. By his mother Hephaistos is ordered to let lose his devastating fire, which burns down the grass and dries out the soil: "Then he turned his flame in its shining into the river. The elms burned, the willows and tamarisks, the clover burned and the rushes and the galingale, all those plants that grew in abundance by the lovely stream of the river." (*Il.* 21.349-52) Also the eels and the other fish are suffering. Instead of flowing the water is boiling. But after all, the river Skamandros, by the gods called Xanthos, belongs to the race of immortals. Therefore, Hera having reached her goal calls back the order: "It is not fitting to batter thus an immortal god for the sake of mortals." (*Il.* 21.379-80)

At least there is a limit to the sufferings of Skamandros and to the destruction of the landscape because of the special union between the Olympic gods and the Nature gods. But as to humans no sort of covenant protects them from suffering and losing their lives. Most of the Homeric heroes sooner or later are to lose their lives as the victims of warfare. At the war-theater the heroes gain fame and glory by paying the highest possible prize, namely with their lives. And though they are bold and courageous the heroes cry bitterly, facing the possibility of early death. Like Homer earlier elaborated in great detail the beauty of ordinary life in general, he now confronts us with a grim scenario of rage, a craze for blood, turmoil, and endless scenes of the killing and destruction of the sacred human body. "There the screaming and the shouts of triumph rose up together of men killing and men killed, and the ground ran blood." (*Il.* 4.450-51) The epitome of horror Homer describes by the image of purple rain: "And the son of Kronos drove down the evil turmoil upon them, and from aloft cast down dews dripping blood from the sky, since he was minded to hurl down a multitude of strong heads to the house of Hades." (*Il.* 11.52-55)

While the Underworld to a major degree was exposed in all its ugliness, the scenes of killing go beyond the very sense of ugliness. For each hero killed Homer has in advance described to us his beauty and excellence. Death comes to the heroes as violent destruction of the beautiful and admired body, but added to it is the description of the moment of death itself, which Homer imagines as being struck by ultimate darkness. As discussed earlier, the description of Erebos in the Underworld was lacking in detail. Likewise, Homer's description of the deathly darkness shirks from elaborating in further detail. The lack of description, or the poverty of imagination concerning the experience of death stands as the utmost horror in the Homeric universe, being crystallized to this very moment where darkness comes to the eye and the contact to the terrestrial world vanishes. The moment of transition is the real horror. And Erebos, the particular location in the Underworld where the souls of the dead are supposed to dwell, represents the utmost negative.

The Prize of Glory

As humans are victims to the caprices of the gods, they only play their own game to a minor degree. Therefore, to win glory becomes loaded with ambiguous feelings which, from time to time, force the heroes to air contradictory viewpoints. In moments of extraordinary reflection the heroes give way to their abhorrence of warfare and killing, realizing the grim facts. Thus Menelaos in the middle of a deadly fight, reflects on the Trojans who seem to be insatiable in warfare. (See *Il*. 13.639) And he becomes captured by grief in watching the fierce twin brothers being killed by Aeneas. (See *Il*. 5.561)

Of all the heroes Achilleus fights with a strength that is inhuman. His craze leaves the earth soaked with blood: "Before great–hearted Achilleus the single-foot horses trampled alike dead men and shields, and the axle under the chariot was all splashed with blood and the rails which encircled the chariot, struck by flying drops from the feet of the horses, from the running rim of the wheels. The son of Peleus was straining to win glory, his invincible hands spattered with bloody filth." (*Il*. 20.498-503) Looking like Ares, Achilleus has become seized by the spirit of war becoming even more horrifying than the god of war himself. But when the craze for blood in between fades, Achilleus questions the very reason for warfare. Tired of fighting, killing, and plundering he admits: "For not worth the value of my life are all the possessions they fable were won for Ilion." (*Il*. 9.400-402) Compared to life itself, all booty, they might gain, comes down to nothing. As to console himself, Achilleus imagines for a while a life in peace, longing for marriage and enjoying a good life. (*Il*. 9.393-400) Mourning the death of Patroklos and facing his own Destiny which is to lose his life soon after Hektor who he is now going to kill, Achilleus says: "I wish that strife would vanish away from among gods and mortals, and gall, which makes a man grow angry for all his great mind, that gall of anger that swarms like smoke inside of a man's heart and becomes a thing sweeter to him by far than the dripping of honey." (*Il.* 18.107-10)

In these episodes Homer gives voice to the depths of despair and grief, but he also suggests ways to overcome situations without hope and the strokes of grim Destiny. In the *Iliad*, Book 24, Achilleus is facing the fact that his Destiny, having fated him for an early death, is soon to be fulfilled. Achilleus suddenly finds himself in company with Priam, the enemy. In this strange situation they share deep despair. Together they mourn; Priam for the loss of his sons and, in particular, of the death of Hektor; Achilleus for the loss of Patroklos and his own Fate, that is, premature death, which will also prevent him from taking care of his old father. But after a while Achilleus returns to the routine of everyday life, saying: "Now you and I must remember our supper. For even Niobe, she of the lovely tresses, remembered to eat, whose twelve children were destroyed in her palace." (*Il.* 24.602-3) The recollection of the story of Niobe emphasizes the gesture of consolation and self-preservation against the capricious and jealous gods. Even in situations of the deepest sorrow and in face of death man should not turn away from life, but keep up his spirit and nourish life as far as possible.

Yet, in the *Iliad*, Book 19 one more hard aspect of war is revealed. Before the terrifying war game, in which the gods participate, Xanthos, one of Achilleus' horses, is for a short moment given voice as to air the mutual Fate of Patroklos and Achilleus. The horse bears in mind that Patroklos was indeed killed by a god and then Hektor was the one who won glory. Now, Achilleus, in a similar way, is going to kill Hektor by help of the goddess Athene. Though Achilleus already is familiar with his own Destiny, which is to be killed by an arrow from Apollo, Xanthos adds that also a human being is participating: "Yet still for you there is destiny to be killed in force by a god and a mortal." (*Il.* 19.416-17) Also the dying Hektor knows of Achilleus' Destiny. Like Apollo was behind Hektor when he killed Patroklos, the same god shall stand behind Paris, when he in the near future is going to kill Achilleus. (See *Il.* 22.359) In this fashion, humans are *nolens volens* subject to a strange pattern of balance and symmetry, unfolding within Destiny itself. In combat with Hektor, Achilleus says: "Pallas Athene will kill you soon with my spear." (*Il.* 22.270) By this laconic piece of information Homer indeed shows the tormented mood and consciousness of Achilleus. As noticed by Malcolm M. Wilcock, the significant victories in the *Iliad* are not really heroic contests.[6] The great warriors, Patroklos, Hektor, Paris, and Achilleus lose their lives due to divine

---

6   Malcolm M. Wilcock: *A Companion to the Iliad.* Based on the Translation by Richmond Lattimore. Chicago and London 1976, p. 245.

interventions. Hence, gods initiate the killing; man wins the glory, but paying with his own life.

At the end of the *Iliad* no final piece has been established. On the contrary, after endless suffering on the plains of *Skamandros*, Book 24 opens up to still another day of war, suffering, grievance, and grim death. The new day is to witness the lamenting and burying of Hektor. Still, on such a day of sorrow, dawn breaks in gleaming colors. With this overwhelming experience of beauty as a counterbalance to the endless suffering and killing Homer closes his story of the war against Ilion. Even war and death cannot turn Homer from focusing on sunrise. To Homer life itself remains a sacred mystery.

9. The Legacy: The Infinite Beauty of the World

In Plato's *Republic* Socrates refers to Homer as "the poet who educated Greece." (*Rep.* 606e) However, Homer also happens to be he who makes tradition regarding what are to become cornerstones in all later reflections on the beautiful. Homeric epic articulates the infinite beauty of world, and the number of beauties on which Homer dwells are *legion*. The fan of beauty arches from the splendor of sunrise to the fringes on Achilleus' helmet to dancers playing with a wine–red ball at the court of Alkinoos. Also Homer is able to imagine not only the beauty of the gods and their residences at Olympos, but he even applies some beauty to the Underworld and to some of the divine monsters.

While the scope of beautiful phenomena is infinite, Homer at the same time sets up a hierarchy between between the beautiful and the ugly. And, accordingly, he ranks living beauty above artificial beauty. But both forms of beauty are important for the good life. Finally, the beautiful wherever it may appear, is shining.

The Hierarchy: The Beautiful versus the Ugly

Through his poetic-mythological descriptions Homer shows the world to us in great variety and splendor. Homer's approach is one of wonder, and the expression: "Wonder takes me when I look at it" is a standing remark. So the structure of the Homeric universe embodies a unified worldview based on images of beauty. Order and beauty are found to vest in all sorts of phenomena, reaching from Olympos down to the Underworld. But Homer nevertheless does not restrain from pondering over the ugly. His knowledge of life is far more subtle than just painting the canvas with a rosy brush. In particular, his descriptions of the events at the war-theater are heartbreaking. Certainly, the destruction of order and beauty runs counter to the image of the ordered universe. Homer's solution to this problem is as follows: On the one hand, he secures the grand scheme against the idea of eschatology, while human beings, on the other hand, are not protected from destruction and death. Though the ugly is hardly a part of the grand structure, so war and destruction is indeed experienced as a powerful dimension of human of life.

Homer's ideas of the beautiful and the ugly unfold within a mythological universe. This means that there are lots of blind spots and caprices. Especially, in cases where Homer's ideas of the ugly become linked with the divine monsters, new aspects of the ugly appear. Or, in other words, the ugly becomes differentiated. In other cases the ugly is just perceived as the ugly, as is the case with Thersistes and Dolon. But when dealing with warfare and the destruction of beauty Homer's description of the ugly goes beyond his mythological descriptions. As he describes the ugly destruction of the beautiful heroes, a certain realism takes over. There are no really good explanations as to why all the suffering and destruction occurs. Then, it might be argued that the real ugliness in the Homeric universe is indeed to be found at the war-theater as representing the utmost dark aspects of the ugly destruction. War is a rift in Homer's rosy and high-spirited view of the world and a potential threat to his mythological cosmology, and the war descriptions are a severe threat, endangering his whole worldview. Only his ardent will to stay optimistic saves his grand mythological system. Homer does not fall out with his fundamental optimism. The will to endure and to experience again and again "the sweetness of life," the bright sunlight, and all the shining beauty on earth are what makes Homer maintain his spirit.

Even in the utmost darkness of things Homer does not really give in to a pessimistic worldview; buoyancy remaining his true companion. Like the gods despising the ugly, so ancient man seeks to escape the ugly, simply because it does not meet his desires and hopes for "the sweetness of life." Throughout Antiquity this attitude remains a distinctive feature of ancient aesthetics. In fact, the hierarchical ranking of the beautiful above the ugly becomes *conditio sine qua non* of all later aesthetics. In Homeric epic the boundaries between the ugly and evil are somewhat blurred, but in most cases there is a clear tendency to link the ugly with evil. Hence, the ugly becomes the conspicuous sign of something evil. And it is a common human experience that evil is infectious. Therefore, devoting oneself completely to focus on evil is a dangerous task as it consumes the soul and cripples the mind. In his descriptions of the war–theater Homer does not avoid the ugly and evil. But this aspect somehow strenghtens Homer's main view which runs throughout his epic. Homer keeps up his spirits to nourish this one message: Life is sweet.

The images of beauty are elaborated in a sanguine and hymnal manner. While Homer treats the ugly with some embarrassment, the phenomena beyond the ugly such as the sheer destruction of beauty, is treated with despair. By elaborating the description of the beautiful in a sanguine and hymnal manner and treating the ugly with embarrassment, the wish to hide the ugly becomes a long–standing tradition which will echo through the centuries. As we shall see, also Plato agrees to this approach.

Living Beauty versus Artificial Beauty

Setting a hierarchy between the beautiful and the ugly is a first important step in the development of an aesthetics. Another more subtle but important feature of Homeric epic is the hierarchy between living beauty and artificial beauty. Living beauty ranks always above artificial beauty. But it is crucial to emphasize that to Homer both levels of beauty are needed and cherished, and both of them are seen as wonders that add a festive and dignified stance to life. Also this feature of Homeric aesthetics becomes canonical. In later aesthetic tradition the hierarchy between living beauty and artificial beauty prevails until the beginning of the Enlightenment. With the Enlightenment this hierarchy is turned upside down. Now, artificial beauty becomes the centre of philosophical interest, while living beauty slowly becomes downgraded as a subject for philosophical discussion. Finally, under the influence of modern ideology also the beauty of art is abandoned.

The Epiphany of Beauty

To conclude, I want to call attention to yet one more important feature of Homeric epic which gives rise to a long-standing tradition. Homer introduces the idea that the beautiful lights up things, and hence has the power of shining. To Homer the diversity of beautiful phenomena is vast, and the numbers of beautiful phenomena wherever they may appear – in Nature, in the world of gods, goddesses, heroes, heroines, courtly manners, artificial objects etc. – are countless. But all beauties share in one common feature, namely that of carrying *a shining quality.* Beauty radiates a shine that attracts the eye and makes glad the human heart. Hence, Homeric epic can be read as the epiphany of beauty. The idea that beauty has a shining quality also becomes a cornerstone in all later reflection on beauty. As we shall see, both Plato, and later Cicero give their consent to this idea. And, in the case of Plato, his whole *oeuvre* can be seen under the perspective of shining beauty.

As my analysis has shown, the number of beautiful phenomena discussed by Homer is abundant. However, beauty is not only to be found as a directly addressed subject but it is also a strong feature of Homeric epic as such. Beauty is interwoven in the Homeric style of storytelling. In conclusion, I wish to recall a few of these grand images with which Homer lifts up the events of life to a level of unsurpassed beauty. Homeric epic is brimming with images of great beauty that very often also contain a profound knowledge of life. The epitome of sorrow and grief, which is shown in the heartbreaking story of Niobe turning into a weeping stone because of the death of all her children, is an unforgettable image. Other images, such as the story of Helios who threatens that he might leave the firmament and instead let his light shine in the Underworld, are terrifying and interesting too. Furthermore, the images of the whole world "laughing" of well-being because of the beauty and the scent from the white narcissus, or because of Hera's perfume, are endlessly charming. Another hauntingly beautiful image that we have analyzed is the description of the silvery air hanging over the war camps at night-time, where the heroes await yet one more fierce day of fighting and grim death. Here, beauty stands out as a contrast to the war-theater and grim death, adding a dimension of an immense sorrow to the scene.

Thus, Homeric epic contains almost everything. It contains a mythological aesthetics that includes not only the life of humans, but also of the gods and their interactions with humans, and it contains a *canon* of education. It is also highly imaginative and playful, and at the same time serious and very realistic. Homer is an eye-opener to the wonder and beauty of life itself shown in all its multifarious aspects including the bright presence of natural things. This is the legacy of Homeric epic.

PART II

THE BEAUTIFUL, THE GOOD, AND THE TRUE

Plato's Philosophy of Beauty

Introduction: Philosophy and Beauty

With Plato the philosophical question "What is Beauty itself" is being asked for the first time in a European context. Like the mythological approach also the philosophical approach pursues a number of questions related to the experience of beauty. And from a philosophical point of view it becomes ardent to ponder on questions such as: how is beauty related to the good and the true, in which ways is beauty an inherent feature of cosmos, why does man so passionately pursue beauty, and finally, in which sense should beauty guide us in our choice of life style, and way of life in general. Such questions were already present in Homeric epic and, to some extent, in the *Theogony* by Hesiod. Also, the natural philosophers at times reflect on beauty, but all these former approaches to the phenomenon of beauty dwell on the diversity of beauty. But with Plato the aim becomes to catch the essence of beauty. Even though Plato represents a turn in approach, that is, a shift from myth to philosophy, it does not follow that the mythical approach is therefore made obsolete. As a matter of fact, even Plato uses myths to bring home his most essential theories on beauty. The myths, invented by Plato for these specific purposes, have been dubbed *philosophical myths,* and they become the vehicles through which Plato brings forth a rich body of reflections on beauty.

1. The Question

When Socrates in Plato's *Greater Hippias* raises the simple question: What is beauty,[1] the mystery of beauty is for the first time introduced as a philosophical

---

[1]   Among philologists there are varying traditions concerning the translation of the Greek word *kalon.* In *Plato. The Collected Dialogues.* Ed. by Edith Hamilton and Huntington Cairns, Princeton University Press 1989, the quote from *Greater Hippias* reads: "what is beauty by itself." (286e) In

issue. This event marks the beginning of the European philosophical traditions on aesthetics.

Without hesitating young Hippias comes up with the obvious answer that the ultimate example of beauty is a beautiful young girl. As the discussion advances, the next beauty in line to be suggested is a beautiful horse. Thus living beauties rank above precious metals such as gold and the beauty of artificially made tools and utensils, and this approach clearly shows the anthropocentric roots of aesthetic sense. However, the debate between Socrates and Hippias comes to a close without the questions having been solved on what things are beautiful and what things are ugly. Also the essential question "What is beauty?" blows in the wind. Socrates comforts himself with the wisdom of an old proverb: "What's fine is hard." In fact, most philosophical inquiries on the issue of beauty come to a similar conclusion as that of Socrates, and the echo from this dialogue can be found either as introductory or concluding notes in many aesthetic treatises. Generation after generation has puzzled itself in pursuing an answer. A basic problem brought to light in *Greater Hippias* is the complexity of the phenomenon of beauty; on the one hand there is the experience of an infinite diversity of beauty, and, on the other hand, there is the need to reflect upon the very essence of beauty. In *Symposium* Plato addresses these issues, and, as we shall discuss next, the very myth of Beauty itself emerges as a result.

2. The Passion for Beauty

Symposium is a tale about a drinking party, held in Athens in 416 BC at the house of Agathon. Since the guests had been partying heavily the day before in order to celebrate the victory of Agathon who had won first prize at the Dionysus theater, they decide to drink only moderately on this occasion. Instead of getting too drunk, they agree to entertain themselves by delivering a series of speeches in honor of the god Eros, or Love. The idea of giving speeches in praise of Love is suggested by Eryximachus, but, as he says, the idea comes from Phaedrus. Phaedrus finds it a scandal that no one has ever composed a hymn to the ancient and powerful god Eros, while people take time to write books on the usefulness of salt. "How *could* people pay attention to such trifles and never, not even once, write a proper hymn

---

Plato. Complete Works. Ed. by John M. Cooper, Indianapolis/Cambridge 1997, the very same text is translated as follows: "what the fine is itself." In a small introductory note to *Greater Hippias* Cooper says: "The Greek word here translated as 'fine' is *kalon*, a widely applicable term of highly favorable evaluation, covering our 'beautiful' (in physical, aesthetic, and moral senses), 'noble,' 'admirable,' 'excellent,' and the like – it is the same term translated 'beautiful' in Diotima's speech about love and its object in *Symposium*." Hence, Cooper gives no explanation as to why the word 'fine' should be a better choice of translation than the word 'beauty'.

to Love? How could anyone ignore so great a god?" asks Phaedrus. (*Sym.* 177c)[2] The participants decide for the idea, and Phaedrus becomes the first to deliver his speech.

Already in the first speech the theme of Eros is connected with the theme of beauty. Phaedrus calls upon Hesiod and others to prove that Eros is first among gods, and it is from this god that man receives the greatest experience he will ever have. Hence, to fall in love, changes man's whole being from his behavior to his worldview; everything becomes orientated towards the beautiful. The gods are in favor of those who walk in the path of beauty – the effects of which extend even beyond the boundaries of death. Phaedrus gives examples of lovers who have given their own life in order to save their loved ones and thus ended up on the Isles of the Blest. (See *Sym.* 179e)

In the following speeches still more aspects of Eros and his influence on plant life, animals, mankind, and gods are introduced. We cannot in this context go through the details, but it is generally agreed that Eros is a god that brings happiness and good fortune. (See *Sym.* 188d, 189d) Eros inspires to pursue the beautiful, be it in terms of behavior, actions, deeds, and ways of living etc. As stated by Phaedrus in the first speech, man must always look to beauty in order to accomplish great things in life. (See *Sym.* 178d) In fact, the passion for beauty has an educating, cultivating aspect to it.

According to Phaedrus, Eros was held to be one of the most ancient among the whole race of gods. However, in the speech, delivered by Agathon, we are suddenly introduced to the opposite opinion. Until now the speeches have been focusing on the gifts bestowed by the love god. But the very nature of the god has not yet been touched upon. Therefore, Agathon wants to re-focus the discussion on the very nature of Eros and then take a look at the importance of this god to man and the other gods. Claiming Eros to be the youngest of the gods, Agathon suggests that a new order of peace and harmony became the result when Eros replaced the goddess Necessity and was made king of the gods. On the whole, the speeches launch a bold variety of ideas about Eros, connecting this god with beauty, happiness, and progress on many levels.

Eros, the Daemon

Until now all the speeches in praise of Eros have introduced various myths of Eros. But when, finally, Socrates takes the floor and delivers his speech on Eros, the whole discussion takes an unexpected turn. Claiming to be unable to compete with the

---

2   For references and quotations are used *Plato. Complete Works.* Ed. By John M. Cooper, 1997. Further, in spelling of names in Part II, I follow the practice used in Cooper's edition.

eloquence of Agathon, Socrates announces that, for his part, he can only deliver a simple speech. This time, says Socrates, we are going to hear "the truth" (*Sym.* 199b) about Love. As we shall see, this turns out to be a truly ironic remark. Socrates starts to paraphrase a tale he once was told by Diotima, a wise woman from Mantinea, and by using the word *once* he remains in the realm of myths. But as the story unfolds, it becomes evident that Socrates' account is indeed very special.

Diotima teaches Socrates that Eros is not a god but a daemon. By number the daemons are countless, their task being to bring messages back and forth between man and the gods. "Gods do not mix with men; they mingle and converse with us through spirits instead, whether we are awake or asleep." (*Sym.* 203) Socrates then asks Diotima about the origin of this daemon, and we are introduced to yet one more mythic account. Diotima claims that Eros was conceived in the garden of Zeus on the very day where the gods celebrated the birth of Aphrodite. His mother Penia is poor while his father Poros is very rich. According to the logic of ancient thought, this origin indicates that Eros is neither poor, nor rich. When he gains riches, they will disappear, and Eros will always be struggling with need. However, his character is not only destined by his parental origin, but also by the spirit of time and place. Conceived at the very moment in time where the gods celebrate the birth of Aphrodite, Eros is destined to become a being that partakes in the affairs of that goddess. Hence, Eros must follow and pursue the beautiful, and the essence of his being is the passion for beauty. This is the idea of *participation mystique*. Like a hunter Eros is always on the watch for beauty. Therefore, Eros is a restless daemon and vagabondish. He is "tough and shriveled and shoeless and homeless, always lying on the dirt without a bed, sleeping at people's doorsteps and in the roadsides under the sky." (203d) In other words: Eros' great passion is to search for beauty.

The difference in nature between the goddess and the daemon is presupposed and therefore hardly addressed in Diotima's speech. However, it is stated that Eros' task is indeed to serve Aphrodite. Eros is a servant for forces beyond his own being, indicating that there is a fundamental ontological difference between the goddess and the daemon. While Aphrodite is the personification of beauty, that is, the mythological representation of the beautiful principle itself, she does not search for beauty for the same reason as Eros does. Eros, on the other hand is on a mission, the conquest of which is dependent on his ability to differentiate between the beautiful and the ugly. Therefore, Eros must become a skilled master in distinction. The goddess, in contrast, represents a more elemental attitude, which seeks to match and mate where it is possible. As a goddess Aphrodite is not in need of anything; when she acts, she is playing. Hence, Aphrodite does not necessarily look for the beautiful, but she seduces to mating by means of her own beauty, and in this playful way she furthers the beautiful. The fact that Eros is not a god but a daemon and, in addition, the servant of Aphrodite is a sign that anticipates the educational stance innate in the affairs of Eros.

Reaching this point in Diotima's tale, Socrates suddenly asks the prosaic question: is Eros useful to humans? Or, in other words, why is passion for the beautiful useful? All things considered, why does Eros pursue beauty? Diotima's answer is simple yet profound. Eros is in love with beauty, because beauty is also the good; and if you have found the good you are happy. This answer is so obvious that it cannot be further elaborated. That everybody wants to be happy is a fact. To pursue happiness, or the quality that makes life a good life is a common concern of everybody.

In fact, already at the beginning of his speech Socrates emphasized that Eros seeks what he himself does not possess, namely, the beautiful; and further, since the good must always be beautiful, Eros is at the same time pursuing the good: "Then if Love needs beautiful things, and if all good things are beautiful, he will need good things too." (*Sym.* 201c) This statement anticipates a crucial point made by Diotima, namely the interchangeable nature of the beautiful and the good. We shall later discuss how Plato in the dialogue *Phaedrus* emphasizes the visual aspect of beautiful, which to some extent contradicts the fully interchangeable character of the beautiful and the good. Hence, the beautiful is a means to *eudaimonia*, but not in the sense that man has any authority over beauty. In fact, as we shall see, it is the opposite way round.

The Dynamics of Beauty

In Phaedrus' speech the view was already put forth that without beauty nothing could prosper, neither in society, nor in the life of the individual. Hence, beauty seems to have an invigorating and cultivating effect. Diotima takes this idea to yet unseen depths. Diotima says:

> All of us are pregnant, Socrates, both in body and in soul, and, as soon as we come to a certain age, we naturally desire to give birth. Now no one can possibly give birth in anything ugly; only in something beautiful. That's because when a man and a woman come together in order to give birth, this is a godly affair. Pregnancy, reproduction – this is an immortal thing for a mortal animal to do, and it cannot occur in anything that is out of harmony, but ugliness is out of harmony with all that is godly. Beauty however, is in harmony with the divine. Therefore the goddess who presides at childbirth – she's called Moria or Eilithuia – is really Beauty. That's why, whenever pregnant animals or persons draw near to beauty, they become gentle and joyfully disposed and give birth and reproduce; but near ugliness they are foulfaced and draw back in pain; they turn away and shrink back and do not reproduce, and

because they hold on to what they carry inside them the labor is painful. This is the source of the great excitement about beauty that comes to anyone who is pregnant and already teeming with life: beauty releases them from their great pain. (*Sym.* 206c-e)

In these lines a number of vital statements are made about the nature of beauty. In essence, beauty is a dynamic force that arouses life from its most basic forms to the complex, spiritual life of man. First and foremost, beauty is a life sustaining force, and as such beauty is in harmony with the divine. Therefore beauty furthers and encourages reproduction, not only in terms of childbirth, but beauty inspires to reproduction on countless levels. Beauty kindles and supports the spirit of life. However, Diotima's description of beauty as a life sustaining force also reveals the opposite of beauty, namely the ugly, which lacks in power to produce. While beauty has an uplifting effect, the ugly stifles and suppresses the energy. Faced with the ugly living beings fall into a state of depression. They turn away and do not reproduce. And without beauty life itself winds back; all buoyant and creative forces get caught in stagnation.

However, it is crucial to notice that the opposition between the beautiful and the ugly is not absolute. While the beautiful does relate to something real, namely to Beauty itself, the character of the ugly does not contain such a quality so as to refer to something real. Ugliness, according to Diotima, is not anything substantial, but something which is out of harmony with the divine. Hence, the beautiful and the ugly are opposed to each other, but the relationship is not a symmetrical one as the ugly is being denied any substantiality. Plato never develops an eternal form of ugliness. This point embodies a crucial stance in Plato's aesthetics, and we shall discuss this issue at length later.

Wherever the beautiful appears, it arouses the passion of living beings. Hence, the nature of beauty is dynamic, and it has an energizing and potential educating effect. Thus beauty carries with it a drive that can direct man's whole being. However, to take full advantage of the educational power of beauty, the passion for it should be guided. In fact, there is a certain procedure to follow that can take man to the highest possible wisdom that he can ever obtain. Diotima calls this state of mind "initiation." Apparently initiation does not happen naturally, but must be guided.

3. Passion, Beauty, and Education

The inner relationship between passion and the educational aspects of beauty is vividly described through the activities of Eros. As a consequence of his passion for beauty, Eros must learn to discriminate between the beautiful and the ugly. He must train the eye and the mind in order to estimate things to discover both their visual and intrinsic values, and he must compare and reflect upon things. In brief, Eros must become a skilled aesthete *and* a philosopher. But this process can go wrong, and therefore passion has to be guided and directed. In fact, passion could easily get caught up either in an idiosyncratic stance for someone, or something, or get lost in the vast sea of beauty. But if treated in the right manner, the passion for beauty can lead to initiation, which is regarded as the highest and final level of revelation. Ideally, initiation might be obtained through following a specific practice, which stepwise brings about a conscious approach to the different levels of beauty, advancing from the concrete to the abstract and from the particular to the general. The process, leading to initiation, takes the apprentice through three stages. The ultimate step, the fourth, is beyond the reach of pedagogical advice.

The very first step to Beauty itself starts with the sight of the beautiful body. It is a common human experience to fall in love with a beautiful person, which means that in principle, the road to initiation lies open to everybody. The initiation process, however, must not advance further before the apprentice has fully gone through this common experience, namely, to fall in love. The major significance of this imperative finds its legitimacy in the fact that exactly the experience of falling in love contains the matrix that coins all later experiences of beauty wherever they occur.

When the sight of beauty has been experienced on the level of beautiful bodies, the sense of beauty must expand. Instead of staying spellbound by the sight of the beautiful body, the apprentice should now take the next step towards initiation. Passion for the beautiful *Gestalt* must be succeeded by a passion for the beautiful soul. However, it is crucial to notice that the fascination of the body should not fade away, but just become more balanced. The slight debasement of the body should not be carried to the excess that one should praise a beautiful soul in an ugly body.[3] The approach is still to appreciate the beautiful body, but now also to learn to put emphasis on the beauty of the soul. It is beyond doubt that Plato still honors the Greek ideal, that is, a beautiful soul in a beautiful body. A third step describes how passion should rise to the beauty of order, arrangement, and laws. Eros must learn to see beauty in order structures, in the arrangement of things, in the ordering of households, in laws of society etc.

In order to be initiated the apprentice must pass through all stages. No steps in the process must be neglected. Yet, moving from one step to another does not mean that the previous steps are left behind; rather, each step is founded by the following step. The educating Eros must not get entangled, or bound, and blindly stay with

---

3   Of course, the very appearance of Socrates does question this claim to a certain degree. For discussion of the topic, see further under the section: *The Ugliness of Socrates.*

the things for which he cares. But he must uphold a certain freedom, which makes it possible to keep a broader vision in mind. Like the old, traditional accounts of the all-embracing Eros, the philosophical Eros also aims at love of the whole. The difference, however, is that the philosophical Eros encourages the consciousness of distinction.

4. The Myth of Beauty

At the threshold of the fourth and final step to initiation all pedagogical guidance comes to an end. The ultimate vision of Beauty itself is beyond human control. If it occurs, it happens. Diotima says: "All of a sudden he will catch sight of something wonderfully beautiful in its nature; that Socrates, is the reason for all his earlier labors." (*Sym.* 210e-211a) Hence, the experience of Beauty itself cannot be planned, but might be experienced as a revelation. Indeed, when Diotima teases Socrates by saying that he might not be able to reach the ultimate vision, she indirectly refers to this problem. Beauty itself is a true enigma and by consequence beyond description. Even though Diotima outlines some features of Beauty itself, her description remains in the realm of myth. Thus her account of Beauty itself sums up to a likely tale of beauty, that is, a myth of Beauty itself:

> First, it always is and neither comes to be nor passes away, neither waxes nor wanes. Second, it is not beautiful this way and ugly that way, nor beautiful at one time and ugly at another, nor beautiful in relation to one thing and ugly in relation to another; nor is it beautiful here but ugly there, as it would be if it were beautiful for some people and ugly for others. Nor will the beautiful appear to him in the guise of a face or hands or anything else that belongs to the body. It will not appear to him as one idea or one kind of knowledge. It is not anywhere in another thing, as in an animal, or in earth, or in heaven, or in anything else, but itself by itself with itself, it is always one in form; and all the other beautiful things share in that, in such a way than when those others come to be or pass away, this does not become the least bit smaller or greater nor suffer any change. (*Sym.* 211a-b)

Despite the fact that Diotima can only deliver a mythic tale about Beauty itself, she does indeed delineate a truly powerful and complicated description of what Beauty itself is, and what Beauty itself is not. She starts in the positive and concludes in the positive. The first and the last statement is about what Beauty itself is: "First, it always *is* and neither comes to be nor passes away, neither waxes nor wanes." She concludes by saying that Beauty itself is always "itself by itself with itself," and "it is always one in form." Hence, Beauty itself is unchangeable in every respect, and it is eternal. In brief: *Beauty is.* This is the ontological statement about beauty, and we shall have more to say about this in a moment.

Between the first and the last statement Diotima lists all the things that Beauty itself is not. The negative description of all that Beauty itself is not, highlights a number of shortcomings experienced in the physical world. In essence, the experience of beauty in the physical world seems to be very different from the experience of Beauty itself. Beauty in the world of phenomena manifests itself in countless ways, and the forms of beauty are *legion.* Beauty might even look different under different circumstances, and thus the beautiful experienced in the physical world is inflicted by time, place, individual taste, size, relation, etc. This is the burden of relativity. Diotima touches upon a number of ways in which relativity might show in the physical world. While Beauty itself is "not beautiful this way and ugly that way," but always just the same and in one form, the beautiful in the physical world might vary according to viewpoint. For example, some people prefer the color red to blue, and others might take the opposite view. Again, the example of color also applies to the following statement. While Beauty itself is not "beautiful at one time and ugly at another," but always the same, the beauty of colors in the physical world might become subject to change and fade away. Hence, the aspect of time does take its toll on the beautiful in the physical world, while Beauty itself is beyond the influence of time.

Further, Diotima mentions the problem that beauty in the physical world is not stable but might easily change according to what it is attached to. Beauty itself is beyond the conditional and is never "beautiful in relation to one thing and ugly in relation to another." Location and human taste also come into view as an example of relativity. While Beauty itself is never "beautiful here but ugly there, as it would be if it were beautiful for some people and ugly for others," the beautiful in the human world is valued according to human taste. Taste is bound to the individual and, hence, to the passing of time and location. Taste can be a strong, directing, and even an educating force, but since taste is bound to the particular, it lacks in power to lead beyond a certain goal. Taste might, so to speak, limit the experience of the vast sea of beauty. As yet one more problem Diotima mentions the human fascination of the body, or the *Gestalt.* Things once beautiful might be worn out or damaged, decompose, or deteriorate. A beautiful shape might collapse, and a beautiful face might change due to bad circumstances, sorrows, old age, and other tribulations. Therefore, Diotima warns against the belief that the beautiful indeed dwells in the *Gestalt:* "Nor will the beautiful appear to him in the guise of a face or hands or anything else that belongs to the body." She further warns against thinking that the beautiful in essence might vest in detail and specialization: "It will not appear to him as one idea or one kind of knowledge." If, namely it were so, then there would be no rise of new beautiful ideas. Also, it would be the end of science as an ongoing process of achieving new knowledge. Finally, Diotima concludes that Beauty itself is not fixed in time and place: "It is not anywhere in another thing, as in an animal, or in earth, or in heaven, or in anything else." Hence, Beauty itself cannot be arrested in, or singled out in any particular feature in the world of beautiful phenomena. It is not dwelling in Nature, in the *Gestalt,* in taste, in the detail, in the ideas etc. Beauty itself is beyond such constraints. Hence, the experience of beauty in the world of phenomena is mixed with feelings of sorrow due to the fact that beauty in the physical world will always fade, or change.

The real enigma of Beauty itself is addressed at the end of the section: It reads: "And all the other beautiful things share in that, in such a way than when those others come to be or pass away, this does not become the least bit smaller or greater nor suffer any change." What Diotima gives voice to here is not a philosophical definition, but a myth of Beauty itself. To Plato a myth is "a likely tale," (*Tim.* 29c-d) and it is in this sense we have to understand Diotima's account. Beauty itself is a divine principle, and how it interacts with the physical world is beyond the capacity of humans to understand. Only the initiated might catch a glimpse of understanding the myth of Beauty. As mentioned already, a modern word for the interaction between the divine and the world of phenomena would be *participation mystique.* No matter in which worldly forms Beauty itself may show, be it in the *Gestalt,* in soul, orders, structures, patterns, knowledge, ideas, geometry, numbers, etc., *it does not change.* Hence, Beauty itself represents the great mystery in which the physical world partakes. The physical world shares something with the meta-physical world. The difference, however, is that while the beautiful in the world of phenomena is subject to change and relativity, Beauty itself is divine, stable, eternal, and always one in form. As to Beauty itself, all relativity has vanished; and Beauty itself in its one form dwells in Eternity.

According to the very nature of initiation, Diotima can only give an impression of what the view of Beauty itself might be like. The description of the ultimate vision reads as follows: "If someone got to see the Beautiful itself, absolute, pure, unmixed, not polluted by human flesh or colors or any other great nonsense of mortality, but if he could see the divine Beauty itself in its one form," (*Sym.* 211e-212a) this would, according to Diotima, be initiation. However, to see the beautiful in its eternal form is an ideal and something that might only happen to those who approach the beautiful in the manner, described by Diotima, that is, a stepwise rise from the experience of natural beauty to the experience of absolute Beauty. The initiated contemplates the beautiful not with the natural eye, but with the mind's eye. Then, the initiated has changed his view from a provincial view to an Olympic view of beauty. In fact, he has learned to view the beautiful from the perspective of the gods. Being initiated means that the initiated, now saturated with beauty, contemplates reality from a divine perspective. The aesthetic way of seeing carries with it an inborn tendency to see also the truth of things. At the ultimate level where the initiate contemplates reality with the eye of the mind, the beautiful reveals itself as a principle at the root of being and as a feature of reality itself. Hence, to contemplate Beauty itself turns out to be a view of truth. To obtain true knowledge, or insight to the divine reality, is the aim of the whole process.

Beauty Itself

A human being can be brought to the final step where "he comes to know just what it is to be beautiful." (*Sym.* 211d) However, there is still a huge difference between *to know* about the beautiful and *to meditate* Beauty itself. The apprentice might be initiated, but he does not become deified. The initiated is still a human being. Then, passion can lead all the way up, but the energy, knowledge, and happiness from being "in touch with" Beauty itself, or from facing the divine, must be contained by the initiated in order to guide his life in the present, physical, concrete world. Initiation, then, is linked with the aim of educating the initiated himself, but it also has a wider scope, namely that of conveying insight and wisdom to the world. The power from contemplating Beauty itself flows back into the world. The question as to how the initiate can transform the view of something totally different into the physical world remains obscure, but the significance of initiation is beyond doubt. Thus, initiation is not meant to be an escape from the world but is rather an encounter, that reveals to the initiated a true conception of reality, namely the ontological truth. Ideally, initiation should result in a profound knowledge of the principle, that rules everything from man, soul, society, state, and cosmos, and this insight must then guide every action. By nature knowledge is good because it saves man from being lost, or from being engrossed by the world, and knowledge is beautiful because it shows the way to true *eudaimonia*. That Plato does not perceive initiation as an escape from the world, but rather as an attempt to comprehend a true feature of reality, is further emphasized by the narrative structure of *Symposium*. After the story about Diotima and initiation the drinking party resumes, and the participants get more and more drunk. At the end only Socrates is sober. He leaves the party at dawn together with a friend, takes a bath and continues his daily activities as usual.

It should not be ignored that the stepwise rise to initiation is an account of total perfection that might be accomplished only by the few. This, of course, embodies a problem. As we shall see, Plato later develops other answers in order to get to the bottom of this dilemma. In *Phaedrus* Plato launches a new myth to explain how the soul is indeed initiated before it ever reincarnates into an earthly existence. A prerequisite to reincarnate as a human being is that the soul has indeed been introduced to Beauty itself, although in varying degrees. While some souls have been fully initiated, others have only caught a few glimpses of the divine Beauty. Finally, in *Timaeus* Plato renounces the idea that humans should be able to grasp a complete knowledge of absolute Beauty. But for a number of reasons the importance of viewing and contemplating the beautiful phenomena remains a leading feature in Plato's philosophical project.

Diotima's description of the way to divine insight suggests a mystic level that cannot be transformed into philosophical terms. At the ultimate step, before the vision of Beauty itself, the philosophical project as well as the pedagogical project collapses. Beauty itself remains an enigma beyond philosophical definition, and because beauty in the physical world partakes in this mystery, there will always be an atmosphere, an aura, a shine, or something about the beautiful that escapes definition. In brief: Beauty by its very nature contains a dimension that cannot be caught by philosophical language. Through the centuries and up to the present, aesthetic theories about beauty have been struggling with this problem, and they still do. Also efforts to fully articulate the experience of beauty seem to be doomed and to fail. Since Beauty itself can only be described by means of an image or a myth, the philosophical concepts of beauty will always be *ad hoc* definitions. Concepts of beauty might capture significant features of the phenomenon, but some dimensions of beauty dwell in the obscure. They might be sensed, or felt, but escapes detailed description and definition. Beauty itself is a divine principle and, as such, beyond articulation.

5. Myth and Philosophy

As we have discussed above, the passion for beauty gives rise not only to philosophical reflection but also results in launching a myth of beauty. Thus myth, as well as philosophy, are born out of passion. But in Plato's universe the relationship between myth and philosophy is full of twists and turns. Plato's ambition is a philosophical one, according to which philosophy should basically replace mythology. This idea already contains a critical approach to myth itself as it strives to set free the interpretation of the world from being engrossed by the caprice of mythic tale. But as discussed above, the philosophical project collapses at the final stage of the initiation. Here myth takes over. The view of Beauty itself can be articulated only in terms of myth, that is, "a likely tale," and not in terms of concepts and definitions. Hence, the use of myth embodies a unique feature of Plato's philosophy. In the following we shall briefly discuss Plato's conception of the relationship between myth and philosophy.

Philosophical Myths

Plato's myths including the myth of beauty have been called philosophical myths, and to our knowledge none of these belongs to the traditional stock of myths. Rather, they are assumed to be of Plato's own making, intended to be, as it were, enlightening myths. However, it is crucial to call attention to the fact that Plato does not completely banish the old-fashioned, or traditional type of myths. From time to time we find references to myths of old times, but in these cases Plato often remains neutral and does not really engage himself in a discussion of the theme in question. An example would be the discussion in *Phaedrus* on Boreas, the North Wind, who according to myth kidnapped the daughter of the Athenian king, Erechtheus. When Phaedrus asks Socrates if he really believes in that story, Socrates says: "Actually, it would be out of place for me to reject it, as our intellectuals do." (*Phdr.* 229e) Such inquiries are without end, and Socrates says: "But I have no time for such things; and the reason, my friend, is this. I am still unable, as the Delphic inscription orders, to know myself; and it really seems to me ridiculous to look into other things before I have understood that. This is why I do not concern myself with them. I accept what is generally believed, and, as I was just saying, I look not into them but into my own self." (*Phdr.* 229e-230a)

Also, at the end of *Phaedrus* Socrates shows a rather conventional approach to the mythic gods by suggesting that he and Phaedrus should deliver a prayer to Pan and the local gods before leaving the beautiful spot in which they held their discussion. Plato does not argue against the existence of the Olympic gods, but he, so to speak, enlarges the whole picture to a degree that undermines the power of the Olympic gods. In *Timaeus* the Olympic gods belong to the race of lesser gods as they are brought to life by the Demiurge. Hence, Plato's idea of myth is complex and rather sophisticated. It is beyond the scope of this study to give a full overview of Plato's use of myths. In this context we shall focus mainly on the use of a few of the philosophical myths, and further, why myths play a fundamental role in Plato's philosophy.

On Why Philosophers Must Surrender To Myths

Plato's whole *oeuvre* contains a number of great philosophical myths such as, for example, the Myth of Beauty. Among Plato's great myths is his cosmology, elaborated in the dialogue *Timaeus*, which has been called a hymn to cosmos. *Timaeus* contains a clear answer as to why the philosopher must surrender to the use of mythic tale. According to Plato, human capacity to investigate the profound questions of being as such is limited, and as a result myth, that is, imagination, has to come to the fore at a certain point. Basically, the use of myth provides a platform to permit the progress of a discussion which otherwise would come to a standstill.⁴ For example, in the field of cosmology the question: how did the world come into being? must at a certain point move into the realm of mythology. Therefore, Plato claims that cosmology, in essence, can only be a "likely tale," (*Tim.* 29c-d) or a "likely account" (*Tim.* 30b), and this condition links both philosophy and science with myth. According to Plato, Beauty itself dwells at the root of existence, and in order to gain profound knowledge of beauty the philosopher must turn to myth. As we shall discuss later, Plato is persistent in this point of view. Hence, the basic argument for using myth is that it is beyond the capacity of man to fully penetrate to the core of existence and reality. Consequently, in Plato's cosmology the mythical figure, called the Demiurge, is the only one to show a profound insight to Beauty itself, while this deep understanding is not attainable to humans. Therefore, yielding to myth appears to be a necessity showing a way out of a difficult situation, and it represents a sort of method that can produce wisdom and information at the very boundary of human capacity. In dialogues, where Plato articulates his most profound thoughts, myth is always involved.

A very moving situation from *Phaedo* can illuminate how deeply Plato valued myth. While in prison and approaching his death, certain dreams return to haunt Socrates. These dreams plead that Socrates should "practice and cultivate the arts." (*Phd.* 60e) Now, to console himself, Socrates uses his last days to write a hymn to Apollo and to re-write in verse the fables of Aesop. As Gerhard Krüger has emphasized, this is indeed the collapse of Socrates' philosophical project.⁵ In the face of death philosophy is short of guidance, and Socrates turns to myth, that is, to imagination. Myth, indeed, is the language of soul. Not only is myth the language of soul, but also soul itself can only be understood by means of a myth. As we shall discuss below, the myth of soul is told in *Phaedrus*, and this myth also sheds light on the bond between soul and beauty.

In conclusion, Plato shows that mythos and logos must co-exist and co-work in the process of achieving profound knowledge about existence and reality. Hence, to separate *mythos* and *logos* as has been the fashion since the Enlightenment is in opposition to Plato's sophisticated conception of the relationship between myth and philosophy. Plato's use of myth is very serious and far beyond the naive, and it demonstrates a humble attitude. While Homeric myths tend to illuminate and dwell upon the diversity of beauty, Plato uses myth to throw light on existential, ontological, and cosmological questions.

---

4   In his analyses of *Timaeus,* Hans-Georg Gadamer has noticed that by means of the mythological discussion new theoretical and scientific elements are indeed highlighted, see Hans-Georg Gadamer: *Idee und Wirklichkeit in Platos Timaios.* Heidelberg 1974, p. 16.

5   Gerhard Krüger: *Einsicht und Leidenschaft. Das Wesen des platonischen Denkens.* Frankfurt am Main 1992, p. 301 ff.

6. The Myth of Beauty Continued: Beauty, and the Myth of Soul

The intricate blend of myth and philosophy is taken to new heights in *Phaedrus*. The dialogue introduces several themes causing some confusion as to what is, in fact, the main theme under discussion. As we shall see, the dialogue starts as a discussion of rhetoric, but then changes focus to discuss other great themes such as Eros, divine inspiration, the structure of the soul and the nature of Beauty, and after this roundabout it finally returns to the topic of rhetoric. It is impossible in the following examination to pay full justice to all these themes; we shall therefore restrict our focus mainly to analyzing the relationship between soul and beauty. Also, it is beyond our scope to unravel all aspects of the multi-layered use of myth in this dialogue.

Under the Plane Tree

The very setting of the stage in *Phaedrus* deserves some attention. Socrates meets Phaedrus who barefoot is on his way to take a walk in the countryside. Phaedrus is following medical advice that maintains it is more invigorating to walk in the countryside than in the streets. Socrates finds this argument not worthy of any serious concern, and later he even lapses into arrogance, making ironic and playful remarks on the issue. Nevertheless, he decides to join Phaedrus for a walk in the countryside but only in order to hear what Phaedrus can report about his latest conversation with Lysias on rhetoric. In this way Socrates is lured outside the city wall, and as Phaedrus remarks, Socrates behaves like a tourist who needs a guide to show him around. Socrates excuses himself by claiming that Nature, here trees and landscapes, does not really teach him anything; in contrast, studying human activity leads to knowledge. However, as the dialogue unfolds this argument is undermined. First, they follow a small brook, called Ilisus, and walk barefoot in the water. They reach a small place with a tall plane tree and a chaste-tree in blossom. At the foot of the plane tree, a small stream runs with clear fresh water. Suddenly Socrates is overwhelmed by an unfamiliar feeling and says: "Feel the freshness of the air; how pretty and pleasant it is; how it echoes with the summery, sweet song of the cicadas' chorus! The most exquisite thing of all, of course, is the grassy slope." (*Phdr.* 230c-d) Even though Socrates, immediately after this exclamation of joy, repeats that landscapes and trees have nothing to teach him, the environment is so impressive that Socrates is truly captivated by the natural beauty of the countryside. At the beginning Socrates mocked Phaedrus' enthusiasm for Nature with witty irony; now the situation is turned upside down, and as the event unfolds, Socrates himself is made the target of witty irony.

How Socrates slowly gives in to this rural atmosphere, in which divine powers appear to be present, can be followed throughout the dialogue. First Socrates becomes inspired to speak the truth about Eros, inspiration, soul, beauty, and rhetoric, and, finally, the walk in the countryside ends with a prayer to Pan and other local gods of the environment near the lovely plane tree. Thus the formal frame of *Phaedrus* that takes the discussion outside the city walls into the countryside, that is, into Nature, prepares the ground for the mythic tales with which Socrates supports his argumentations. In fact, truth does not flow from studying human activity, but, rather, it is grasped under the influence of divine powers. And, as it seems, being in touch with these powers is easier, when man moves into their sacred dominions, namely Nature. As already announced at the beginning of the dialogue, Nature, among other things, represents healing aspects according to the advice about taking walks in the countryside. Then, location and geography are not without issue; properly chosen these things might lead to contact with the divine powers behind Nature. It is interesting to see how Plato paves the way for the proper mood in which man should exercise philosophy. In the face of Nature man is more predisposed to being aware of his own shortcomings. And this is exactly the frame of mind needed to further proper philosophy. Then, philosophy is a bold enterprise, but it must also strike a humble attitude to the themes in question, since man's capacity for absolute knowledge is limited.

When finally seated under the plane tree Phaedrus now reads aloud Lysias' speech which Socrates finds confusing and disorganized. Though the speech displays a lot of beautiful words, it does not impress Socrates. As a result, Socrates is being forced to deliver a proper speech on the same issue, namely on Eros. Reluctantly, Socrates does so, but he covers his head while delivering the speech. But afterwards Socrates feels ashamed, because both he and Lysias have spoken badly about Eros and his gifts to mankind. Then, having spoken falsely about a divine matter only proved that it is possible to give a well-organized speech, which, nevertheless, is wrong as far as its content is concerned. Suddenly, the conversation has revealed a dire problem. Hence, the essence of rhetoric does not hibernate in formal structures. Instead, Socrates holds that a true rhetorician should rather try to understand the object of rhetoric, and that is the soul. Soul is the real object of rhetoric, and, as Socrates says, it "is clear that someone who teaches another to make speeches as an art will demonstrate precisely the essential nature of that to which speeches are to be applied. And that, surely, is the soul." (*Phdr.* 270e) Therefore, to be a true rhetorician one must understand the nature of soul. Once again, now with his head uncovered, Socrates delivers a speech on Eros, that is, the *Palinode.* The great themes in this speech are Eros, divine inspiration, the nature of soul, the nature of Beauty itself and, finally, the interconnection between all these themes.

The Palinode, or the Myth of Soul

In the *Palinode* Socrates launches a mythic image of the soul in which soul is seen as a charioteer with a team of two horses. This image makes Socrates introduce the difference between the souls of gods and the soul of man. While the gods have horses of good breeding, human souls must operate a team of horses where one is obedient and the other evil. Hence, human souls are at a disadvantage compared to the gods; this is a situation which later epochs have dubbed *the human condition.* Nevertheless, the need to understand the nature of soul in general evokes again the reflection on Beauty. In *Symposium* the beautiful was highlighted from the perspective of passion. In *Phaedrus* Plato reconsiders the issue of beauty, but from a different angle, namely that of soul. Hence, new features of beauty are born out of a conversation on the nature of soul. However, the change in perspective does not create any major contradictions. In fact, in *Symposium* soul is described as a host for passion, and therefore, the discussion in *Phaedrus* just adds more features to the profound view on Beauty itself.

Soul is claimed to be self-moving and immortal. About its structure Socrates says: "To describe what the soul actually is would require a very long account, altogether a task for a god in every way; but to say what it is like is humanly possible and takes less time." (*Phdr.* 246a) Then, in order to give an idea of what soul is like Socrates develops an elaborate and far-reaching myth of the soul which even suggests some cosmological features: "Do you think, then, that it is possible to reach a serious understanding of the nature of the soul without understanding the nature of the world as a whole?" (*Phdr.* 270c) However, Plato's cosmology is only fully developed in *Timaeus.*

Although soul is said to be immortal and self-moving, it is not always in the same condition or shape. To illuminate this state of affairs the myth of soul is brought into play. Whether the soul is in good or in bad shape shows in the condition of its wings. Hence, soul in its pre-earthly existence is assumed to be winged. As long as the wings are in perfect shape the soul travels the entire universe and enjoys the sight of Beauty itself. Only when its wings are damaged or shed, the soul must in-carnate into an earthly existence. Socrates gives a vivid image of the conditions that make the wings either grow or shrink: "By their nature wings have the power to lift up heavy things and raise them aloft where the gods all dwell, and so, more than anything that pertains to the body, they are akin to the divine, which has beauty, wisdom, goodness, and everything of that sort. These nourish the soul's wings, which grow best in their presence; but foulness and ugliness make the wings shrink and disappear." (*Phdr.* 246d-e) As in *Symposium,* the main contradiction is between the beautiful and the ugly. While the sight of the beautiful furthers growth, the sight of ugliness disheartens the soul. What is stated here is a recycling of Diotima's wisdom. However, the account of the soul's experience of Beauty goes far beyond Diotima's teaching of initiation. In *Phaedrus* it is claimed that the soul, in fact, is initiated before it ever incarnates into an earthly existence.

To give a vivid picture of the soul's experiences before it incarnates, Socrates brings into play an image from the Homeric cosmology, namely that of the Olympic gods and their banquets where they gather together to feast and celebrate. Then, in the likeness of this image Socrates describes how all souls travel the universe, but in a specific order. As ruler, Zeus is in front of the trains of gods and spirits. There are twelve such trains, and each soul or spirit is by destiny associated to one of these twelve trains. Each soul will resemble the god or goddess in whose train or chorus, "he danced, and emulates that god in every way he can." (*Phdr.* 252d) The train of gods and spirits travels all over the universe, and during these travels the soul is shown "many wonderful places." However, when the train of gods and spirits goes to the banquets, the climb upwards is said to be so steep that many souls cannot follow because of each individual soul's problems with the horse team. But a few souls make their way up together with the gods, now standing at the rim or the border of the universe, from where they gaze upon Beauty itself outside the present universe: "The place beyond heaven – none of our earthly poets has ever sung or ever will sing its praises enough! Still, this is the way it is – risky as it may be, you see. I must attempt to speak the truth, especially since the truth is my subject. What is in this place is without color and without shape and without solidity, a being that really is what it is, the subject of all true knowledge, visible only to intelligence, the soul's steersman." (*Phdr.* 247c-d) This is, according to Socrates, the banquet of the gods, and the gaze of Beauty itself outside or beyond the universe is the image upon which they feast. In brief: they feast upon Reality. They feast on what really is: "Now a god's mind is nourished by intelligence and pure knowledge, as is the mind of any soul that is concerned to take in what is appropriate to it, and so it is delighted at last to be seeing what is real and watching what is true, feeding on all this and feeling wonderful, until the circular motion brings it around to where it started." (*Phdr.* 247d)

It is interesting to notice that Socrates entertains the Homeric image of a banquet to the very end of this particular section in *Phaedrus* (from 246e-248) by telling that the charioteer after the journey feeds the horses with ambrosia and nectar; indeed, this is the sort of food that Homer imagined was consumed by the gods. Thus, on the one hand Plato gives some credit to tradition but, on the other hand, he also transcends Homeric mythology as well as other mythological accounts of the gods' banquet as it is told by Hesiod and Pindar. To illuminate the issue in question here we must make a small detour and take a brief look at various elements of the myth of the gods' banquet.

In *The Iliad* Homer depicts a grand image of the gods' banquets. But he also shows that food, wine, merry company, discussions, quarrels, laughter, and the beautiful setting with Apollo playing his lyre are not sufficient. For a true banquet the singing of the Muses is needed. (See *Il.* 1.601-04)[6] To confer names on objects and deeds is to reveal the true and divine nature of the world, and therefore Homer describes the singing of the Muses as a highlight and a completion of the festive atmosphere. However, the Muses do not only perform at festive and happy events; they are also present at the funeral pyre of Achilles in order to give voice to sorrow. (See *Od.* 24.60-64) Hence, the world must be identified and articulated in all its aspects.

Hesiod further elaborates the feature of completion. According to him, the Muses are ordained to sing about how everything came into being, that is, about the race of the gods, the race of giants, and the race of men. The Muses are themselves goddesses, born at the foothills "not far from the topmost peak of snowy Olympus." (*Theogony,* lines 62-63)[7] They, therefore, show a certain predilection for natural surroundings where they have "their gleaming dancing-places and their fair mansions; and the Graces and Desire dwell beside them, in feasting." (*Theogony,* lines 62-65) The Muses keep company with the Graces and with Desire, which means, that inspiration from the Muses will materialize as something enhanced and that longing and passion might be part of it. Hesiod further tells us that when they sing and dance, their feet touching the ground, the earth responds with an echo: "The dark earth rang round them as they sang." (*Theogony,* lines 69-70) By the act of name-giving and touching the ground the Muses bring real knowledge to the world, and the act is met with response.

The aspects of identification, articulation, and praise are fully worked out in Pindar's now lost Zeus hymn.[8] Having created the world, Zeus calls upon the other gods to ask if something is missing. Overwhelmed by the beauty of the world, they, however, find themselves in need of a voice to glorify the splendor. Therefore, Zeus together with Mnemosyne gives birth to the Muses, their task being that of praising the beauty of the world. But to praise things one must also interpret them. By interpreting the world and by singing at the gods' banquets, at their festivals, and singing and dancing in Nature, the Muses contribute to both the solemn and the festive atmosphere of life. The singing of the Muses is an act of eternal praise without which the experience of the beautiful order, that is, *kosmos* in the original sense of the word, would fall back into oblivion. Therefore, their service is a con-

---

6   References are to *The Iliad of Homer*. Translated with an Introduction by Richmond Lattimore. Chicago and London 1961, and *The Odyssey*. Translated with an introduction by Richmond Lattimore. New York 1991.

7   Quotations are from Hesiod: *Theogony and Works and Days*. A New Translation by M. L. West, Oxford 1988.

8   See Eike Barmeyer: *Die Musen. Ein Beitrag zur Inspirationstheorie.* München 1968, p. 124 ff.

tinuous remembrance of the true nature of the world. In this way they embody the essence of their parental origin. Mnemosyne is the goddess who is a repository of all knowledge of how things began and what has happened in the worlds of gods and man. Hence, from their mother, whose memory includes everything, they know of the past, the present, and the future. From their father Zeus, who is the epitome of order, and who guarantees that the cosmic order will prevail, they possess the skill of conferring order on things. Thus the singing of the Muses points to crucial dimensions of language. Words are never only neutral, or mere technical tools; they are loaded. Words refer to a much wider context, which, in the end, links all phenomena to a cosmic whole. Hence, the image of the gods' banquet is linked with the theme of getting in tune with the deeper principles of reality. This is the mythological heritage that Plato brings into play in his own philosophical myth about the soul's encounter with Beauty itself, or with a true feature of Reality.

After this minor detour we return to our analysis of *Phaedrus*. Plato's aim is to show the obscure basis for order that dwells at the root of existence. Most souls in the trains of gods and spirits are not able to follow the gods all the way up, and, by consequence, they get varying and insufficient views of Reality itself. The individual soul, then, will incarnate according to the level of insight, gained in its pre-earthly existence. This condition is called "the Law of Destiny," and it contains the matrix for a number of different lifestyles. Those who followed in the train of Zeus and grasped an almost complete view of Beauty will become philosophers. Then in a declining line follows a list of different lifestyles, that is, the lifestyle of: 2) a king, or a warlike commander, 3) a statesman, financier, or manager of a household, 4) a trainer of sports, or a doctor, 5) a prophet, or a priest, 6) a poet, or an artist, 7) a handy man, or a farmer, 8) a sophist, and a demagogue, and, 9) a tyrant. Souls who have not grasped the slightest feature of truth will not incarnate as humans, but in other types of living beings. It remains obscure why Socrates lists exactly nine ways of life; in fact, it is said that the trains of gods and spirits are twelve in number.

In conclusion, a pre-condition for the human soul is that she has already been in-troduced to the beautiful. Therefore, when the soul in its earthly existence discovers traces of the beautiful, she will be reminded of her former existence. A vision of the beautiful awakens memory and thus guides the soul back to a true perception of reality. In this context Socrates introduces an important feature on the special nature of beauty: "Now beauty, as I said, was radiant among the other objects; and now that we have come down here we grasp it sparkling through the clearest of our senses. Vision, of course, is the sharpest of our bodily senses, although it does not see wisdom. It would awaken a terribly powerful love if an image of wisdom came through our sight as clearly as beauty does, and the same goes for the other objects of inspired love. But now beauty alone has this privilege, to be most clearly visible and most loved." (*Phdr.* 250d-e) Then, the most characteristic feature of beauty is that of being visual – either to the eye, or to the inner eye. If beauty does not appear in order, form, or structure, it might appear as light, brilliance, shine, and splendor. The vision of beauty enters through the eyes, and the eyes are said to be "the natural route to the soul." (*Phdr.* 255c-d) This means that Plato's conception of beauty also embraces the aphrodisiac nature of beauty, that is, warmth pouring out and in of the eyes that are dwelling on beauty.

7. Beauty and Rhetoric

Socrates introduces yet one more myth in *Phaedrus,* which concludes what has previously been said about rhetoric. When Phaedrus and Socrates sat down under the plane tree, Socrates referred to the "sweet song of the cicadas." Later, he returns to this subject much to the surprise of Phaedrus who happens to be ignorant of the myth of the cicadas. Socrates says: "Everyone who loves the Muses should have heard of this. The story goes that the cicadas were human beings who lived before the birth of the Muses. When the Muses were born and song was created for the first time, some of the people of that time were so overwhelmed with the pleasure of singing that they forgot to eat or drink; so they died without even realizing it. It is from them that the race of the cicadas came into being." (*Phdr.* 259b-c) Hence, devoted to singing, the cicadas participate in praising the truth of the world, and they are bestowed with the task of reporting back to the Muses on those who have been living a philosophical life in honor of the Muses. Among the Muses, Calliope and Urania are the oldest, Calliope being the Muse of the stories of gods and men, while the Muse of the whole universe and for "all discourse, human and divine" is Urania. Urania is she who "sings with the sweetest voice," (*Phdr.* 259d) and if someone has participated in singing the praise of reality as far as he is able to grasp the truth, the cicadas carry the message further to Urania.

However, listening to the singing of the cicadas is a somewhat dangerous pastime as it can easily make man doze and thus make him sink back into a state of oblivion. Thus, natural surroundings can easily lure man back into a state of regression. The solution, of course, is that man should keep clear-headed and continue conversation, no matter the outer circumstances. Hence, mental or philosophical laziness is not acceptable. Even in the heat of noon the discussion ought to go on. Then, on the one hand, the true rhetorician is guided by the soul's inner voice, that is, the daemonic voice to which Socrates refers and which encourages him to speak the truth. On the other hand, according to the myth of the cicadas, the rhetorician is also being kept under close watch by divine powers. When Socrates argues that the rhetorician should be able "to speak and act in a way that pleases the gods as much as possible," (*Phdr.* 273e) it indicates that the search for truth can only be achieved on this road. In brief, rhetoric consists of speeches to the soul about truth. This is the ideal on which Socrates' question: "When is a speech well written and delivered, and when is it not?" (*Phdr.* 259e) can be put to the test. As we shall see later, this theme becomes the cornerstone in Cicero's whole *oeuvre*.

8. The Beauty of Cosmos

In *Symposium* it was argued by Diotima that Beauty itself is a divine principle at the root of being. Thus Beauty itself as a profound feature of reality is endowed with an ontological status, and its manifestations are countless. Diotima speaks of "the great sea of beauty." (*Sym.* 210d) In *Timaeus* these ideas are to become the cornerstones in Plato's cosmology. In other words, Plato's cosmology is a consecration of the principle of beauty and its countless forms. It is not possible in this context to deliver an extensive analysis of *Timaeus*.[9] However, we shall discuss a few highlights in order to show how the principle of beauty runs like a *leitmotif* through Plato's cosmology.

From the very beginning of Plato's cosmology, we are introduced to the special relationship between the beautiful and the good. Only when beauty is linked with the good, it may be said to be real. Therefore, the mythical figure, called the Demiurge, becomes a focus of interest since he is the one, who brings forth the cosmos and puts it into order. It is crucial to stress that the Demiurge does not bring forth the cosmos out of nothing, but this operation is based on a number of certain pre-conditions.

Plato's Demiurge belongs to the distinguished clan of daemons and love gods, and goddesses, of whom Eros and Aphrodite are prominent examples. Like his forerunners he shows an inclination towards buoyancy and cheerfulness, and he reveals a taste for light, for brilliance, and for order and beauty. But the love of beauty is a feature that we find in almost every mythological creation story. And in that sense Plato follows a traditional track. Already in *Symposium* Plato gives a somewhat witty but still serious reference to these mythological accounts. Socrates and Agathon agree namely that the gods designed the world because of their love of wonderful things. As Socrates emphasizes, "there is no love of ugly ones [things]." (*Sym.* 201a, see also 197b-c) By inventing the myth of the Demiurge, Plato brings this tradition to a spectacular culmination. However, in comparison to love gods of former times, the Demiurge represents a more refined and sophisticated aesthetic sense. The Demiurge embodies a love for order in the original sense of the word *cosmos,* namely cosmos meaning beautiful order. Also, being in favor of perfec-

---

9   For an extended analysis of *Timaeus*, see chapter 8: "Plato's Cosmology. Consecration of the Idea of Beauty" in Inga R. Gammel: *The Passion for Order. Myth and Beauty in the Writings of Plato, Heisenberg, Pauli, Jung, John D. Barrow, and Others*. Shaker Verlag. Aachen 2015.

tion, he surpasses his predecessors. But it is not only in aesthetic matters that the Demiurge is superior to former love gods. Plato clearly states that the Demiurge is a divine being, embodying a higher degree of existence than, for example, the Olympic gods.

The Demiurge is described by a number of names. He is called an organizer, a craftsman, and a father. He is the one who creates or, to be specific, organizes the universe. By his divine agency the universe and the World Soul are brought to manifestation. Before the arrival of the Demiurge the universe and the World Soul were non-existent, but after his actions have been accomplished, the universe is said to be complete and perfect. Even the issue of mortality, which to humans is a disturbing fact, is said to be necessary in order that the universe could obtain perfection. The Demiurge is a divine being, but not omnipotent. There are forces stronger than him, for example Law, Fate, and Necessity, although he manages to persuade Necessity to a certain degree. As a divine being he might be immortal, and he might be uncreated. I say *might*, because Plato is not specific in these matters. But more to the point, the Demiurge is presented as an individualized and personalized being. And it is, of course, by means of such features that we learn about his mental and emotional character. The Demiurge is described as follows:

> Now why did he who framed this whole universe of becoming frame it? Let us state the reason why: He was good, and one who is good can never become jealous of anything. And so, being free of jealousy, he wanted everything to become as much like himself as was possible. In fact, men of wisdom will tell you (and you couldn't do better than to accept their claim) that this, more than anything else, was the most preeminent reason for the origin of the world's coming to be. (*Tim.* 29e-30)

A number of things are stated here. First, the Demiurge is good and not jealous. A jealous person is supposed to be stingy, keeping everything to himself. But the Demiurge wants to contribute with what he has to give, namely something that echoes his own being. As he himself seems to be a living example of exquisite order, he wants to bestow order upon things. Funnily enough, Plato claims that the Demiurge creates the world because he is good, but in fact *shows* that the Demiurge creates because he is a lover of beautiful order. Hans-Georg Gadamer has argued that the essential motivation for creating the Universe is really never revealed.[10] But while the Demiurge's ultimate purpose dwells in *clairobscur*, he nevertheless reveals a lot by his passionate way of acting.

---

10   Hans-Georg Gadamer: *Idee und Wirklichkeit in Platos Timaios*, Heidelberg 1974, p. 11.

By transferring his vision the Demiurge generates a whole range of life forms from the Universe, the gods, the human race, the animals, and down to the single seed. In this way the Demiurge shows himself as a dynamic, intelligent being. But it is crucial to stress that being a superior mind is only one part of his talent. Equally important is his passion. Indeed, it is passion that guides his activity in one direction and not in another. As noticed by Hans Georg Gadamer, the beauty of the world is totally in the hands of the Demiurge.[11] If the Demiurge had been a bad judge with bad taste, he might have looked in the wrong direction, or looked upon the paradigm of matter, also eternal, but originally in a state of disorder which would, of course, have led to an unstable creation. But the Demiurge's excellence *and* reliable aesthetic taste turns his awareness towards the perfect and the good. In brief, he is moved by the sight of the beautiful and feels a natural attraction to it. This orientation, to some extent, reduces the aspect of free will. As Gerhard Krüger has argued, the lover when he really loves, does not have any choice.[12] Although self-moving, the Demiurge seems to be dependent on the beautiful paradigm in order to draw inspiration for his creative impulse. Reason as such does not invent the beautiful, but beauty is discovered because of its calling attention to itself by form, light, brilliance, and endurance. Therefore, the object, or the eternal forms, or the ideas, have the character of a revelation to the Demiurge. And the result is simply this: he falls in love.

Then, in conclusion, the beauty of the Universe has a double origin. First, it originates within the paradigms in which the Demiurge seeks guidance when devising his plan. And, second, it also originates in the very nature of the Demiurge, who embodies goodness with love of the beautiful.

Cosmos as Beautiful Order

In the creation of cosmos, different types of matter as well as a number of different principles of order are used. The sun is made of fire, and fire is held to be the most refined material. In fact, all visible gods [e.g. the nature gods] are made "mostly out of fire, to be the brightest and fairest to the eye. He made them well-rounded, to resemble the universe, and placed them in the wisdom of the dominant circle [i.e., of the Same], to follow the course of the universe." (*Tim.* 40) We notice that we are immediately exposed to aesthetic features. Thus refined matter, here fire, has a shining quality to it. Further, the planets and the stars, made from this divine material, by their very forms participate in a most noble figure, namely the circle. Finally, a strict type of order determines the whole process and the movements of

---

11   Gadamer 1974, ibid., p. 9.
12   Gerhard Krüger: *Einsicht und Leidenschaft. Das Wesen des platonischen Denkens.* Frankfurt am Main 1992, p. 9.

the planets. I cannot go into detail here, but we are introduced to concepts such as proportion, symmetry, rotation, equipoise, and harmony. But to our surprise the Demiurge also exercises another type of order when distributing the rest of the visible gods, namely the stars: "He spread the gods throughout the whole heaven to be a true adornment [*kosmos*] for it, an intricately wrought whole." (*Tim.* 40) The distribution of the stars in the night sky represents a spontaneous order. Hence, to form a true cosmos different types of order are used, including a spontaneous, decorative order. This is a surprising feature of Platonic thought, but in fact, it is said here, that randomness may also contribute to enhance things. However, it is crucial to stress that the enhancing of the night sky, and thus the use of randomness is only exercised *after* the creation of a comprehensively ordered structure.

The Demiurge is a happy god, enjoying the process as well as the result. It is said directly that he is both pleased and delighted. (See *Tim.* 37c-d) The special trick of making the sky look like a spangled banner and the careful strapping of the bonds around the World Soul are all signs that the Demiurge is indeed enjoying his activity. Hence, joy might simply be understood as part of his secret motivation. His joyous and buoyant activity might even suggest a festive stance, namely a Demiurge who for a moment celebrates his own mode of existence. In fact, this attitude links back to the unsolved problem in *Timaeus*, that is, whether the Demiurge is immortal, or not. The Demiurge might only be endowed with a sort of semi-immortality. And if so, it becomes meaningful to celebrate a certain moment in time, as does the Demiurge.

The Beauty of Living Beings

On top of Plato's hierarchical list of beauties we find the living cosmos. Estimated from this perspective other forms of beauty must by necessity count as lesser beauties. Hence, the Platonic idea of the emergence of species turns out not to be a tale of evolution, but of devolution, describing a descending curve in regard to beauty and consciousness. The hierarchical order of living beings reveals a variety of forms from cosmos to the gods, of whom some are visible, others invisible, and it also includes men, women, birds, animals, plant life, and, finally, the aquatic race. Even the aquatic beings in their muddy darkness, that is, in the deep sea, participate in soul and, therefore they are not totally excluded from the world of beauty. Also, the single seed participates in soul, and therefore belongs to the world of beauty. But the beauty of the animal kingdom and plant life remains somewhat unsung. The reason for this only appears indirectly. From the perspective of reincarnation any level beyond man represents a detour of the soul and, consequently, a decline in terms of beauty, which may be viewed as a key to the somewhat sudden ending of Timaeus' speech, treating the generation of the third and fourth race rather derogatively.

In ancient aesthetics the beauty of living beings ranks above the beauty of any man-made artificial artefact, and Plato's cosmology wholeheartedly brings this feature in the forefront. In Plato's dialogues the issue of human beauty is touched upon several times. Symmetry between inner and outer beauty remains the much admired ideal which has profound roots in ancient Greek culture. It is the notion of *kalos kakagathos*. Thus the "great sea of beauty" appears to contain a diversity of forms beyond measure, but in Plato's description focus is on the beauty of living beings, and, in particular, on the beauty of the human soul and the human body. Also, in *Timaeus* it is demonstrated that the forms when used in the great enterprise of creating the ordered universe only become truly beautiful when animated. Indeed, they were beautiful before, but now they become even more so.

In *Symposium* there is a ranking in terms of beauty going upwards from the body, to soul, order, and, finally, to the forms. The argument of hierarchy is very crucial in Diotima's speech as it leads to the Mystery of Beauty itself. It also shows why aesthetic theory can hardly be developed without using some sort of hierarchical thinking. Aesthetic theory cannot be without orientation and direction. But equally important is to keep in mind that the beautiful bounds out on the whole world. Beauty embraces everything. Beauty dwells in the Universe itself and in all other living beings, in thoughts, in laws, in actions and deeds, in things and in artefacts. In brief, beauty is to be found not in a particular dominion or area of life, but, in principle, beauty might manifest itself through an abundance of forms and phenomena. This is one of the real great achievements in Plato's theory on beauty. In comparison, modern aesthetics has made a point out of reducing the discipline of aesthetics to the area of art.

9. The Ugly as a Border Concept

In the *Odyssey,* Book 1,32 the question of evil is articulated for the first time in Western thought. Here, Zeus offers a defence speech against mortals who accuse the gods of being the source of evil. Zeus argues that evil is a self-inflicted phenomenon caused by the mortals themselves.[13] Thus the gods are without fault, but the actual question: "what is the origin of evil?" is not being asked. While ancient myth is confronted directly with giving form to the problems of the ugly and evil, philosophy has a tendency to fight the ugly and evil powers by exposing their lack of essence.

Also Plato is eager to show that evil does not derive from the Demiurge. That said,

---

13   The verses referred to in *The Odyssey,* Book 1, 32-34 read: "Oh for shame, how the mortals put the blame upon us gods, for they say evils come from us, but it is they, rather, who by their own recklessness win sorrow beyond what is given." Quoted from *The Odyssey of Homer.* Translated with an Introduction by Richmond Lattimore. New York 1991.

Plato does indeed air a number of different answers as to why the phenomenon of evil exists. According to the discussion in *Theaetetus,* evil will never die away as there must of necessity be something opposed to the good.[14] In the *Republic* evil appears to be a defect in creation itself. (See IV, 444d-45a-e) And, finally, Plato returns to the issue of evil in the *Laws* (See X, 896e-99a) with a vague hint of the existence of an Evil World Soul.[15] In *Timaeus,* however, Plato develops a detailed cosmology, in which pre-cosmic matter belongs to one of the cosmic preconditions from which the Universe originated, and he is eager to emphasize that matter as such cannot be associated with evil. Thus, also Plato evades a substantial reflection on the ugly. Hence, the ugly is identified mainly as disorder, and disorder is claimed to have no essence.

The claim that the Demiurge fashioned just one copy of the Universe is a further, strong argument against the possibility of destruction, caused, for example, by unexpected evil forces. As there is only this one Universe, created by the Demiurge, there would be no hiding place for such forces. Finally, the claim that there is only one Universe, is further supported by the claim that no matter was left unused; therefore, one more world could not have come into existence. (See *Tim.* 33a) Along the same line, it is also stressed that the Demiurge is very cautious to use up the blend from which he created the Universal Soul, thus excluding the possible emergence of another kind of soul, that is, an evil World Soul. Also, the very shape of the Universe, being spherical, eliminates "up" and "down" as true categories, that is, the very form of the Universe contradicts the idea that there might be regions of the Universe where evil might reign. Evil as such simply has no place to hide. Therefore, to maintain that the world is evil is not only considered a sheer blasphemy, but also false. The very existence of evil as an eternal form would be an assault, or violation of the beauty, indwelling generation itself. (See *Tim.* 29a) We do indeed hear of unpleasant and remote regions to which the aquatic race, the fishes, and oysters find themselves exiled, but these regions are not hiding places for evil.

According to ancient Greek thought, it is in general regarded as sheer blasphemy to discuss evil, and there is a strong tendency in ancient Greek mythology and philosophy not to make the ugly and evil the center of attention but to focus on the beautiful and the good instead. Plato is no exception in this respect. In *Timaeus* he

---

14   In the discussion on evil, Socrates says: "But it is not possible, Theodorus, that evil should be destroyed – for there must always be something opposed to the good; nor is it possible that it should have its seat in heaven. But it must inevitably haunt human life, and prowl about this earth." (*Tht.* 176)

15   The notion of an Evil World Soul in the *Laws* and, hence, a dualistic cosmology, is the subject of heated debate. For a thorough discussion, see T. M. Robinson: *Plato's Psychology.* Toronto, Buffalo, London (1970) 1995, pp. 145-157.

even articulates this approach very clearly: "After all, good things have more of a claim to be the subject of our speech than bad things. Now all that is good is beautiful, and what is beautiful is not ill-proportioned." (*Tim.* 87c) Therefore, it is highly interesting that the theme of eschatology is touched upon in *Timaeus*, although in an evasive fashion. The point, however, is that the theme is addressed at all. Before the Demiurge leaves the cosmic stage, we get the following information: "When he had finished assigning all these tasks, he proceeded to abide at rest in his own customary nature." (*Tim.* 42e) This is of course a riddle, or a true mystery, and really nothing substantial is said about what a divine being is doing when not in action. But he gives a promise. The Demiurge addresses his creations, the semi-mortal gods by saying:

> O gods, works divine whose maker and father I am, whatever has come to be by my hands cannot be undone but by my consent. Now while it is true that anything that is bound is liable to being undone, still, only one who is evil would consent to the undoing of what has been well fitted together and is in fine condition. (*Tim.* 41a-b)

This is the Promise made by the Demiurge, and the best he can come up with. At least, he himself will not destroy what he truly loves. The Demiurge could in fact draw back his creation, but will not do so. However, to give a promise is to link oneself, or to create bonds with the subjects to whom you give this promise. Then, in this way the Demiurge is indeed linked with the ordered universe and vice versa.

But the question remains: on which grounds, on which conditions does the Demiurge give this promise? We keep in mind the worrying fact that the Demiurge is not an omnipotent being. Therefore, it becomes somewhat eerie, uncanny, and unsafe that the Destiny of the Universe dwells in the mind of the Demiurge. This uncertainty is not neglected, but it is overcome, or calmed by the Great Promise. But the eerie hypothesis, of course, remains that the Demiurge for unknown reasons might become subject to powers that he himself cannot master. If his mind, for unknown reasons, fails, or becomes subject to weakness of some kind, the Universe will accordingly descend into disorder and perish together with its originator. In this sense, the Destiny of the Universe is uniquely linked with the Destiny of the Demiurge. The eternal forms, on the other hand, still shining in eternity, would be unmoved and untouched, but in need of some kind of force, or activity which would be able to meditate upon them and to witness them.

Plato employs a sort of asymmetry in his philosophy. He describes the idea of the beautiful and good, but never admits any idea of the ugly and evil. The hierarchical order of the beautiful and the ugly, then, is an order in which the beautiful is the cardinal concept while the ugly is a pseudo-concept that does not describe anything substantial, but only a temporary situation of disorder. As was articulated in *Symposium* by Diotima, ugliness is something which is out of harmony with itself and also with the godly.

The Ugliness of Socrates

While Plato is rather straightforward when dealing with the general discussion of the beautiful and the ugly, things become more complicated and even paradoxical when the issue of beauty becomes linked with individual appearance. The ideal is articulated in the *Republic* as follows: "Therefore, if someone's soul has a fine and beautiful character and his body matches it in beauty and is thus in harmony with it, so that both share in the same pattern, wouldn't that be the most beautiful sight for anyone who has eyes to see? It certainly would. And isn't what is most beautiful also most loveable?"(*Rep.* 402c-d) Indeed, this argument for human beauty, which is in line with the ancient Greek ideal of *kalos kagathos,* comes from the mouth of Socrates who himself is far beyond this ideal of perfection. Again, we see how Plato in a playful manner is pushing the limits of former tradition, and the case of Socrates' physical appearance is just one among many examples of Plato's many paradoxes.

Socrates' bizarre appearance was legendary, and through the accounts of his contemporaries we have a fairly good idea of what he looked like, and how he behaved. It is said that Socrates had a snub nose, swollen lips, roving eyes, and a swaggering gait; he is also accused of being ascetic to a shocking degree, walking barefoot even in winter and wearing only a thin cloak. In *Symposium* Socrates' lack of beauty even becomes a topic of discussion, when Alkibiades gives his speech. In describing exactly what a person looks like it is a common feature to turn to comparison, but Alkibiades has trouble in finding anything or anybody that matches the appearance of Socrates. In fact, Socrates cannot be compared to anything human, and thus, in need of a suitable comparison Alkibiades uses the image of Silenus, the elderly head of the satyrs. Although it may look like a joke, the choice of this image is a very serious one. As Alkibiades says, "it [the comparison] aims at the truth." (*Sym.* 215b) Socrates is also compared to the satyr, Marsyas, who was able to mesmerize people with his music. According to tradition silens and satyrs were semi-divine beings dwelling in Nature. In form they look like mutations between man and the animal world. Thus a silen, or a satyr, is imagined to have a head and a body like a human being, but with horns, pointed ears, a flat nose, broad lips, claws, and a tale. In behavior they are mischievous, roguish, and animal like and always interested in seduction and procreation. Thus, close to Nature they represent in outer appearance and behavior a challenge to the taste and ideas of civilized man.

Yet in spite of his bizarre appearance and also his habit of teasing people Socrates is, nevertheless, endowed with an irresistible charm. While Marsyas uses musical instruments to captivate the attention of people, Socrates uses words only. And he does so to the extent that men, women, and children are spellbound and want to listen to him. But his rhetoric is one of simple words, and he has the habit of using the same examples "making the same tired old points in the same tired old words." (*Sym.* 221e) However, if one seriously considers these simple words, they open up to true knowledge. According to Alkibiades, Socrates' speeches are worthy of a god, and they contain everything that man has to ponder upon.

Even though Socrates in both appearance and habit deviates from the Greek ideal of *kalos kagathos,* he is incorruptible in character. This is the point. Bodily beauty, money, or social rank cannot make Socrates deviate from his own moral strength. Alkibiades also stresses that in times of hardship as, for example, in the military camps, Socrates is above all the one who is able to cope with hunger, and in times of peace the one who is able to enjoy life in full measure. In conclusion, Alkibiades presents a picture of Socrates that, in fact resembles the ideal Socrates himself is advocating. In *Phaedrus* Socrates suggests that he and Phaedrus should offer a prayer to the local gods before they leave the beautiful place. The prayer reads: "O dear Pan and all other gods of this place, grant that I may be beautiful inside. Let all my external possessions be in friendly harmony with what is within. May I consider the wise man rich. As for gold, let me have as much as a moderate man could bear and carry with him."(*Phdr.* 279b-c)

Hence, in rank soul is superior to body, and therefore inner beauty, that is, the very nature of the soul ranks above visual, bodily beauty. To have an ugly soul is worse than suffering from an ugly appearance. In fact, to have an ugly soul is the worst thing that can befall a human being. If the soul degenerates and becomes corrupt and ugly, it is like a violent act against the higher, divine orders. Thus, in Plato's philosophy, inner beauty deserves more praise than outer beauty. This is one of the points that Plato gets across with his emphasis on Socrates' appearance and character. It is, of course, a common human experience that the outer appearance of living beings does not always match their inner nature and character, but in the case of Socrates we are tempted to look for even further meaning than the one already presented. The image of the ugly-looking Socrates from whose lips we learn about the mystery of beauty is one of Plato's many witty and deeply fascinating paradoxes that goes beyond the sheer function of irony and playfulness. And, indeed, hidden in the complex image of Socrates dwells yet one more important theme. By his very appearance Socrates links back to Nature, a condition which, as a matter of fact, indirectly argues that Socrates somehow has access to the instinctive wisdom in Nature itself. Like Marsyas mastered the musical, so Socrates likewise instinctively knows how to use words. In brief, both of them know about rhythm and harmonies and thereby have access to the divine, that is, they know how to get in harmony with the divine order of the Universe. But contrary to Marsays, who suffers a grim fate, Socrates is endowed with inner wisdom, and therefore he becomes such a unique figure in Plato's *oeuvre*.

In Greek mythology as well as in Plato's philosophy it seems that beings with access to the divine harmonies are beings that one way or other are lingering on the periphery of mankind, such as semi-divine beings, or, in the case of Socrates, a human being of an extraordinary quality. In conclusion, the discussion of the ugliness of Socrates not only reveals a clear point about the ranking of inner beauty over outer beauty. It also launches a strong reminder that even when man has risen to a sophisticated level of wisdom and knowledge, the inner spirit, or wisdom, or rhythm and harmony dwelling in Nature, must never be forgotten. Hence, the harmony and rhythm present in Nature is one of the keys that links man with the divine.

While myth in general is hostile toward visual ugliness, Plato's approach is softened by the philosophical claim that inner beauty, that is, the beauty of soul, ranks above visual beauty. But even so the concept of inner beauty is linked to the visual; inner beauty also partakes in the visual in the way that it is said to *appear* to the inner eye.

10. Paideia and Beauty

The interest in *paideia,* that is, education, is a major theme in ancient Greek culture, present already in the epic poetry of Homer and Hesiod. With Plato the subject of education is closely linked to the theory of Beauty, and also to Plato's cosmology, which altogether adds a major significance to this issue. Julius Stenzel once claimed that Plato's whole *oeuvre* might indeed be viewed from the perspective of *paideia*.[16] This claim is not beyond the point which can be seen by the far-reaching consequences of *paideia*. In the first speech in *Symposium,* Phaedrus says "nothing fine or great can be accomplished, in public or in private" (*Sym.* 178d) if man does not look to beauty. In effect, beauty contains an educating, cultivating aspect. Education is not only a matter of living a good life, but education, or lack thereof, will even affect one's life after death. If, namely, the soul in its earthly existence has not received proper education, it might be too confused to make a wise choice for a future incarnation. (See *Rep.* X, 620a-d) What you do in life echoes into Eternity. Also, Plato claims that no man becomes bad voluntarily, but he might turn to evil conduct because of lack of order and education. (See *Tim.* 86e) Hence, proper education, guided by order and beauty, is a remedy against evil. In the *Republic* the issue

---

16 Julius Stenzel: *Platon, der Erzieher*. Felix Meiner Verlag. Leipzig 1928. See also Werner Jaeger: "Die platonische Philosophie als Paideia" in Konrad Gaiser (Hrsg.): *Das Platonbild*. Zehn Beiträge zum Platonverstandnis. Hildesheim 1969, pp. 109-24.

of *paideia* is already a great theme, focused on how to educate the class of watchers. But in Plato's last work, the *Laws,* the ideas of education are of a more general sort and argued with the gentle authority of old age and wisdom. In the following we shall concentrate mainly on the latter in order to illuminate how Plato imagined the dimension of beauty to be transformed into rules and standards to live by. The *Laws* not only concerns the the written laws on how to run a state, but also the laws that govern everyday life, and by which men should relate to other human beings, to his own soul, and finally to the divine dimension of existence. As the *Laws* is a voluminous work with numerous examples, the context here only allows for a very brief outline to illustrate how Plato links beauty and education.

The Lawgiver

The very first line in the *Laws* opens with the speaker, called the Athenian, putting the following question to his companions: "Tell me, gentlemen, to whom do you give the credit for establishing your codes of law? Is it a god, or a man?" (*Laws* I, 624) The answer to this question is elegantly woven into the very setting of the stage which deserves some attention. The *Laws* unfolds as a conversation between three old men while walking from Cnossos to the shrine of Zeus. As his name suggests, the Athenian comes from Athens, and he is on a visit to Crete, where he keeps company with Clinias who is a Cretan, and Megillus, whose native country is Sparta. Thus the three gentlemen come from different backgrounds representing three different constitutions, a situation which provides grounds for a far-reaching discussion. The Athenian suggests, they should launch a draft of the very best laws that man is able to attain. The breathtaking beauty of the route to the cave of Zeus is revealed to us through the dialogue between the Athenian and Clinias: The former says: "I've heard it said that from Cnossos to Zeus' cave and shrine is quite a long way, and the tall trees along the route provide shady resting-places which will be more than welcome in this stiflingly hot weather." (*Laws* I, 625b) Clinias' reply emphasizes the beauty of the area: "And as you go on, sir, you find tremendously tall and graceful cypress trees in the sacred groves; there are also meadows in which we can pause and rest." (*Laws* I, 625c) In this fashion Plato again shows a playful, yet serious attitude to tradition. Hence, the beauty of the geographical setting leads to the shrine of Zeus. According to legend, the god Zeus was born in a cave on Crete. Paying a visit to the shrine of Zeus signifies a symbolic act in which the three gentlemen show their reverence to the very principle of which Zeus is the epitome, namely order. And further, as the three gentlemen slowly approach the shrine of Zeus, they finally agree on the answer to the question put forth at the beginning of the *Laws,* namely that law-making is indeed man-made, but only the laws inspired and guided by a god are good laws. He, or those, who lay down the laws must humbly ask for inspiration and guidance from the gods.

Hence, laws are indirectly given to man, but in order to materialize these and to make them function, those who are concerned with constitutional problems must give voice to and articulate these laws. In fact, if humans were fully aware of the divine order, no state would need laws at all. As this is a far cry from reality, laws must be prescribed in order to guide life. As laws and rules of conduct must always be defined in such a way that they pay tribute to beauty, the lawgiver himself must be able to differentiate between the beautiful and the ugly, and between the good and the bad. (See *Laws* V, 728a-b) As we shall touch upon below, to strike the golden mean, and, to avoid ascetism are too crucial elements. Then, it becomes an art in itself to lay down the *Laws*. In fact, to lay down the *Laws* in order to form and run a state is considered the most elevated task man can carry out, and compared to, for example, that of writing a tragedy. Hence, in themselves the laws are found to be the most beautiful tragedy. (See *Laws* VII, 817b)

Laws as Magic Songs

Originally, the Greek word *nomoi* derives from the musical sphere (See *Laws* III, 700b and VII, 800a), and Plato puts new emphasis on this fact in surprising ways. As mentioned earlier, laws are seen as a blend of something divine and accumulated human experience, but this blend must always comply with the harmonious and the beautiful. This is the reason why Plato maintains that the written laws must be allowed to take the prize as the most beautiful of texts in the state. Laws are in a way just one genre among the musical genres, and they must strike a balance, or the golden mean. Also, laws must avoid the ugly in every respect such as, for example, ascetism, the disproportionate, and extreme austerity. Plato imagines that the songs of old have over time become *unwritten laws*. Thus the unwritten laws, by which we to some extent live in everyday life, are a sort of bond that links the present with the past as well as with the future. Together with experience these unwritten laws are meant to fuse into the written laws too.

While the laws on how to run the state and how to guide the social and cultural life should be put down in written words, the greater part of how man should be educated cannot be made subject to laws and regulations in the same manner. If the lawgiver would implement laws on, for example, how many hours the individual were allowed to sleep, his choice of hairstyle, his manner of walking etc., the lawgiver would only make himself the subject of ridicule. Thus there is a limit to what can be regulated by laws as such. But Plato does not really see this as a problem. To get hold of people, young and old, Plato resorts to a very sophisticated and magic trick, namely that of playfulness and gentle persuasion.

To captivate the souls and minds of people Plato introduces a specific, pedagogical trick of employing a sort of charm songs to induce the proper approach in children and people in general. (See *Laws* II, 664a-b) Such charm songs may take many different forms. Charm songs may literally be songs such as those used in the various performances by the different choruses. But, in a discussion for example, the magic might be found in "a form of words to charm" people "into agreement." (*Laws* X, 903b) And because such ways of persuasion are performed in a cheerful, yet serious fashion they are called "charms" or even "spells." Thereupon, by praising the values, or making the guidelines known for proper living and an appropriate attitude towards life itself, the "charm songs" are supposed to take on a number of different forms. The Athenian says: "About this – that every man and child, freeman and slave, male and female – in fact, the whole state – is in duty bound never to stop repeating to each other the charms we have described. Somehow or other we must see that these charms constantly change their form; at all costs they must be continually varied, so that the performers always long to sing the songs, and find perpetual pleasure in them." (*Laws* II, 665c)

Besides the written laws it is an imperative for the state to make known its fundamental values by means of a number of pedagogical tricks. Then, the voice of the law, or rather the spirit of law, should be made known through songs, in stories, in fables, and by means of doctrines and discourse. Hence, to guide and educate animals, children and adults in a subtle way Plato resorts to a sort of playfulness. How to develop man's whole being should ideally result in encouraging the development of a gentle mind.

Sing and Dance

Plato's fundamental ideas are argued on the basis of experience supported by stunning myths. As *paideia* is one of Plato's fundamental ideas, we are also in this case introduced to a great myth in support of his pedagogical advice. When Plato advocates that man should play, and sing and dance, it might sound as promoting a somewhat carefree life-style, but as we shall see, his counsel is in line with the serious cosmological outlook of the *Laws*.

As everyday life is the main focus of discussion in the *Laws,* this factor has indeed some effect on the style in which the metaphysical background is presented. In vivid words a picture, or rather a myth, is launched in which it is said that man is the property of the gods. Man is made as a toy to please the gods, and therefore he is destined to sing and dance and play. This claim, however, is only an assumption, and Plato leaves open the issue of wheather there should be other and more serious reasons for the existence of man. But in spite of man being compared to a puppet, he still has a free will. He can freely choose if he wants to follow the inner golden cord, that is, "the gold in us," (*Laws* I, 645) or, if he wants to deviate in other directions. But because man is assumed to be the property of the gods, it is indeed his duty to play. How Plato understands this decree is a far-reaching theme. Only by playing, singing, and dancing does man honor the gods and his own divine origin. Hence, the gods and life itself must be celebrated, and according to this command man should stay cheerful and optimistic. To fall into depression over the tribulations of life is disgraceful, and it does not help anything either. Plato further adds a certain detail to the mythic image, namely that the gods in particular have assigned Apollo and the Muses as advisers in achieving a proper sense for rhythm and harmony and thus educating man in good taste. (See *Laws* II, 654) Hence, the sense for rhythm and harmony is a gift from the gods, and *paideia* that embraces man's whole being is, in principle, musical.

However, these lofty, mythical explanations on why man should play, sing, and dance, are surprisingly linked with sober human experience. According to Plato, sound and movements have a healing effect on the worried and anxious, mentally as well as physically. As an example Plato dwells on the image of the mother, rocking the weeping child, while she is humming or singing a lullaby. Movements can heal both fear, frenzy, and disorder which for various reasons might have beset the soul. Hence, movement and the sound of voices are of major importance. From the very beginning the infant should be treated according to these prescriptions, that is, the baby should not be spoiled but, on the other hand, it should not be treated with too harsh rules either. The effect might turn out to be a child with no capacity to love, or a child who behaves like a slave.

The Golden Mean

Besides playfulness and gentle persuasion, Plato emphasizes the importance of striking always the golden mean or, in other words, always to avoid extremes. This approach should be exercised from the very beginning in the raising a newborn child. (See *Laws* VII, 792c-793b) Plato has a keen eye for how education can easily go astray. Therefore, precaution must be taken that the achievement of personal authority is pursued in the right manner.

The principle of the middle course applies not only to raising the newborn, but to young and old as well. Plato sees education as a never-ending process that also runs into old age. (See *Laws* I, 643a) When discussing the issue of drunkenness, the three old gentlemen once again consider the principle of the middle course. On whether one should indulge in pleasures or abstain from them, Megillus calls attention to the Spartan law, according to which drinking wine is totally forbidden. Even at the festival of Dionysus wine is not allowed. Having experienced the whole city of Tarent drunk at a Dionysus festival, Megillus finds this law suitable. As a

Spartan, he defends the laws of his native country. But the Athenian says: "Pleasure and pain, you see, flow like two springs released by nature. If a man draws the right amount from the right one at the right time, he lives a happy life; but if he draws unintelligently at the wrong time, his life will be rather different. State and individual and every living being are on the same footing here." (*Laws* I, 636e) As a matter of fact, the idea of balance, or the choice of the middle course, represents the Utopia of Platonic thought about education.

Finally, to Plato education is not education in this or that profession. *Paideia* is not about learning a specific skill, but *paideia* is about education in a very broad sense of the word. For example, to be a skilled musician in a technical sense does not imply that a person has obtained a just attitude towards the wisdom of *paideia*. According to Plato, education is "just about the most important activity of all." (*Laws* VII, 803d) Education is to learn about the nature of life and of how to live in accordance with the great order structures down to minute detail. Also, Plato's *paideia* includes everybody, male and female, young and old etc., and the major part of educational advice is best when demonstrated by example. From the very beginning education must be taken care of to make sure that the newborn does not become subject to corruption and adopt unsound habits. The first three years of the child's life are formative years, and here those in charge should see to it that the child develops a gentle character. We cannot dwell here on the various stages that are suggested in the process of *paideia,* but the goal enunciated by the Athenian is that man should aspire to conduct his life so as it bears a resemblance to the life of a god. Thus, to be godlike is the great example set before man. In the *Laws* it is argued, "it is God who is preeminently the 'measure of all things,' much more so than any 'man,' as they say." (*Laws* IV, 716c) The Athenian is indirectly arguing against Protagoras who claimed: "Man is the measure of all things: of the things which are, that they are, and of the things which are not, that they are not." (See *Tht.* 152) Not man is the measure, but the gods, and as a result man should strive to be godlike.

As mentioned already in *Phaedrus,* it was held that man resembles the god in whose train he once journeyed before incarnating into an earthly existence. Plato holds on to this myth of reincarnation in the *Laws*. Mankind originates from the gods, and therefore the individual soul must pay tribute to and acknowledge the special character and gift of skills originating from the god in whose trail she once traveled. (See *Laws* XI, 920d-e) In consequence, this means that the individual is by Fate endowed with a certain temperament and a strong drive and interest towards themes embodied by the guardian god, or goddess. Hence, education is basically meant to pull forth and shape the essence of the character. Then, in this way the individual becomes what he, or she, indeed is.

Eudaimonia

Education is – *per se* – an idealistic project, the goal of which is to develop a gentle character that man can live a happy and decent life. Man should be godlike as far as that it possible for a human being, and it is his duty to sing and dance to please the gods and also to sing the magic songs to honor his own soul. While *eudaimonia* is the goal of proper education, *paideia* also has the effect of being a mean against the ugly and against evil. As Plato never allows evil to participate in the eternal forms, evil is something that arises from the irrationality of the soul, in brief, from cases where the process of *paideia* has suffered havoc.

But musical education is dependent on a certain condition, namely the fact that proper education can only be carrid out during peace-time. The Athenian says:

> But in cold fact neither the immediate result nor the eventual consequences of warfare ever turn out to be 'real' leisure or an education that really deserves the name – and education is in our view just about the most important activity of all. So each of us should spend the greater part of his life at peace, and that will be the best use of this time. What, then, will be the right way to live? A man should spend this whole life at 'play' – sacrificing, singing, dancing – so that he can win the favor of the gods and protect himself from his enemies and conquer them in battle. He'll achieve both these aims if he sings and dances in the way we've outlined; his path, so to speak, has been marked out for him and he must go on his way confident that the poet's words are true. (*Laws* VII, 803d-e)

With the reference to the words of the poet is referred to a passage from the *Odyssey* in which Homer emphasizes that each person, besides educational advice, also must rely on the subtle advice from his or her inner guardian spirit.

It is easy to find a number of capricious and bizarre ideas in Plato's theory of *paideia*. Thus Gregory Vlastos is somewhat piqued to find that Plato in the *Laws* suggests that the person who rejects the divine cosmic laws, should be put into jail for five years. And if not convinced by the reality of these laws during his time in prison, the disbeliever should suffer the death penalty. However, death penalty should only be sanctioned in very special cases. The banishment of the poets from Plato's state is another heated issue. Counting among the exotic examples we also find the advice that slaves, or foreigners should be hired to perform the ugly parts of a performance, together with advice concerning the special treatment of unlawful animals etc. To a modern reader such examples are mere caprice. But as for a general view, Plato's ideas of *paideia* contain some truly significant insights into the realm of educating man, vital even to the present.

11. The Legacy: Beauty as the Bond between Man and the Divine

The love of the beautiful and the rejection of the ugly is a basic feature of Greek thinking that materialized in the epics of Homer, in the theories of the natural philosophers, and, also in Plato's philosophy. But, in the case of Plato, aesthetic tradition is not only carried forward, but it is brought up to an unprecedented, sophisticated level.

To Elaborate on Tradition

While Homeric aesthetics bounds out, indulging in listing a great variety of aesthetic phenomena and dwelling upon details such as origin, form, material, color, location, etc., Plato's ambition is rather to grasp the essential questions concerning the phenomenon of beauty. Therefore, Plato's aesthetics is not the place to look for descriptions of the endless variety of beauty. Instead, Plato introduces some deep and memorable insights into the nature of the beautiful.

Although Plato is rather critical of Homer, he, nevertheless, uses with stunning results a great many of Homer's thoughts and images as stepping stones. While Homer is guided by a natural inclination to concern himself with the beautiful, Plato brings about substantial philosophical arguments as to why focus must be on beauty and not on the ugly. And although the ugly is indeed experienced as an aspect of the world, it does not, according to Plato, deserve our attention. Therefore, from a philosophical point of view the ugly must linger always on the periphery. However, the main point in all this is the fact that Plato agrees with Homer on the fundamental hierarchy between the beautiful and the ugly. This point of general agreement between Homer and Plato should not be overlooked, because the effects from this agreement on all later aesthetic thinking are overwhelming. As Plato, consecrates, so to speak, the idea of the beautiful with his cosmology, which happens also to be a consecration of his aesthetics, the idea of beauty takes on the leading role in all later reflections on beauty and the ugly. And from this originates what is later addressed as classical aesthetics in which the beautiful becomes the cardinal category, while the ugly serves as a border category.

The Metaphysics of Beauty

In Homeric epic, beauty is mostly in the hands of the gods; this means that beauty can increase or vanish according to the whimsical moods of the gods. In comparison, Plato secures the very idea of beauty against such a confusion by developing a metaphysics of beauty. While beauty in the natural world is subject to time and must fade away, Plato safeguards Beauty itself against any such decline or decay.

In Homeric epic the connections between the beautiful, the good, and the true are loosely woven. But with Plato this triad becomes the point of focus. The three dimensions are closely linked, and Plato addresses each of them in turn. The unique status of beauty compared to the good and the true is emphasized in *Phaedrus*. Only beauty is endowed with the very quality of being radiant, or shining. Further, in Plato's cosmology, that is, *Timaeus*, Beauty itself belongs among the eternal ideas, or forms, which dwell in the metaphysical realm. Even here, beauty is somehow shining, being able to captivate the awareness of Demiurge.

To Plato, beauty belongs to the eternal ideas, or forms, lingering on the periphery of our universe, or maybe even outside our universe, and beauty becomes the building block in his grand cosmology. But even so, beauty is saved from any harm should this cosmos come to an end. Not even the question of eschatology can rock Plato's argument. If the beautiful cosmos should for unknown reasons go asunder, a hypothesis that Plato anyway rejects as sheer blasphemy, Beauty itself would still be shining in eternity. Thus, Plato's metaphysics adds an enormous depth to the most lasting conception held by Antiquity, namely that beauty ranks above the ugly and that beauty has a tremendous life-giving power. And it further underscores the profound experience made through the ages, namely that beauty seems to always radiate a shining light.

Beauty as the Shining Bond between Man and the Divine

Plato's main argument that beauty is basically an intrinsic feature of reality leads to the development of a cosmology in which beauty is the leading principle. Beauty as such is an intrinsic force of reality, rooted in the metaphysical realm. Beauty is a part of life itself, and therefore beauty participates in ontic dignity. It is brought into play by divine agency that, by means of beauty, bestows order upon cosmos and the soul. Thus both cosmos as such and the soul in her cosmic and earthly existence are closely linked with beauty. Therefore, the encounter with even the slightest traces of beauty will always remind the human soul of this eternal beauty. Hence, beauty becomes the shining bond which has the power to link man with the divine and to bring him in harmony with the divine. In this manner the phenomenon of beauty has a deep impact on man, on culture, and on society, and beauty has the ability to guide man in his education and way of living.

Plato's idea of the beautiful is brought about in a specific, historical and cultural context. But this fact does not belittle the achievements of Plato. Even today, Plato's concepts are vital to us. As mentioned already, Plato is the very first to delineate what could be called a classical aesthetics, and it stands out as one of his great achievements. It is not beyond the point to stress that the aesthetic vocabulary emerging from his philosophy is indeed consecrated by being linked to his cosmology, a fact that adds great depth and lasting value to his aesthetic ideas. Plato's metaphysics on beauty has had a long-lasting effect on European thought. That beauty, among other things, shows by a shining quality, is, of course, a general statement, but it is, nevertheless, a description used also today. In common language we use the phrase: to set a shining example etc. Throughout the classical tradition up to the present, we still feel that beauty is manifested by a shining quality.

Already the mythological approach to beauty linked with idealism. With Plato it becomes totally evident that aesthetics in essence contains quite a portion of idealism. To Plato beauty is very real, and it holds the key to *pure* being. But in comparison to the metaphysical realm, the traces of beauty in the physical world represent both a bond and a challenge to man. In his search for answers man must look to beauty in order to find guidance for his way of life. Hence, with beauty comes too the idea of improvement, education, and enlightenment.

The concept of beauty might be exiled from contemporary philosophy, but as human beings we are still faced with similar existential questions and experiences as was Plato in his day. Therefore, we even today find ourselves engaged in the great conundrum of beauty. Whether we are aware of it or not beauty, in some way or another, still dwells at the root of our concerns in everyday life. And, also, when we embrace the future with hopes for a good life, the idea of beauty is never far away.

PART III

DECORUM

Cicero's Ideas of Beauty in Everyday Life

Introduction: Beauty in Everyday Life

With Cicero the Greek reflections on beauty are brought into play on a new battle-ground, namely that of Roman rhetoric. Cicero never wrote any treatises on aesthetics as such, but in line with the tenor of Platonic philosophy, the reflections on beauty in Cicero's case are also generously spread over his entire *oeuvre*. Hence, the discussion of aesthetics is to be found in his books on rhetoric, in the philosophical books, in the letters, and in his speeches. Cicero, time and again, informs the reader about his ideas of the beautiful and the good and how these dimensions in unison should be put to test in practice. In his own fashion, Cicero becomes the successor of Greek culture in which beauty is a concept of great importance on all levels of human conduct and activity.

The fact that Cicero's ideas of aesthetics are an integrated part of his whole *oeuvre* calls for a systematic research which, however, cannot be satisfied in this context. As mentioned in the general introduction, my presentation of the aesthetics of Antiquity is carried out under certain constraint, namely that of the eclectic method of selecting the most important issues for discussion and letting go of the rest. This restriction, or point of focus, includes also the following discussion of Cicero's ideas of aesthetics.

1. Cicero, a Man of the World

Among the illustrious personalities from Antiquity, Cicero is almost certainly the person about whom we have the most detailed records in terms of life, destiny, and activities. Besides Cicero's own information and comments, generously scattered throughout his writings and his letters, a rich material of ancient sources adds to the intriguing and complicated portrait of this genius, whose influence on European culture to this day has not ceased to exist. From Cicero, mottos, phrases, sayings, and a rich vocabulary originate, all of which have become a natural part of our everyday life, even to the extent that we do not realize the origin of these terms let alone their full implications. Terms such as *individuum, curriculum vitae, decorum, otium,* and *humanitas* are just a few examples. In many ways his ideas have been assimilated to the degree that they have become almost natural ideas. Of phrases still in use, one of the most well-known is the following: "errare humanum est." Hence, his legacy to European culture is beyond measure.

In this context we shall not deal with the biography of Cicero as such. But since Cicero's ideas are intimately linked to his temperament and his everyday life experience as a rhetorician, lawyer, politician, statesman, and writer on philosophical issues, we shall allow to dwell briefly on his appearance, character, and background. Ancient sources agree that Cicero had been favored with a pleasant apperance and good health. Even in old age he retained his good looks. In his *Suasoriae,* Seneca the Elder quotes one of Cicero's opponents, Asinius Pollio, as saying: "Nature and fortune smiled alike on him; for good looks and good health remained with him to old age." (*Suas.* VI, 24) Also Plutarch, in his comparison of Demosthenes and Cicero, refers to Cicero's good looks by saying that he had a smiling face. Plutarch further nurses the idea that it is "possible to get a glimpse of the character" from the style of Cicero's rhetoric. Hence, according to Plutarch, Cicero was "naturally prone to laughter and fond of jesting" (Plutarch, Bd. VII: *Lives. Demosthenes and Cicero* I, 4-6) even to the extent that he often got carried away, a habit that Plutarch does not appreciate. Finally, Plutarch accuses Cicero for singing his own praises and overestimating the function of rhetoric, when claiming that words, or speech should replace the sword. Hence, being of Greek descent, Plutarch had a keen eye for Cicero's Roman arrogance and zest for glory and superiority. It is definitely true that Cicero aspired to fame and glory, but, as we shall see, not for the sole reason of glory itself.

Being a Man of Letters

In his description of Cicero, Plutarch puts emphasis on the fact that Cicero's rise to fame was founded on his broad and erudite education. Even in the speeches, written for the Forum and the courts, says Plutarch, Cicero clearly desires to display "a considerable acquaintance with letters." (Plutarch, Bd. VII: *Lives. Demosthenes and Cicero,* I, 1-4) Also modern scholars have paid attention to the remarkable fact that Cicero's rise to fame in public life first as a lawyer, then as a statesman, and finally as consul and life member of the Senate, was due to his great knowledge in various arts. Cicero had studied not only the discipline of rhetoric but also philosophy, religion, history, law, and physics. Hence, in his rhetoric he was able to use all his knowledge, and that made Cicero superior to his competitors. The most famous orator among his contemporaries was Hortensius, and it was with him, Cicero wanted to compete.

Although it is beyond question that Cicero's skills in various disciplines and his knowledge of philosophy, in particular, play an important role in his rise to fame, there are other crucial elements in his upbringing than just education. In a number of ways his personal experiences of the terrors of civil war contain a key to both how he came to see the world and to the values that he cherished. Cicero was about eighteen years old when the civil war between Marius and Sulla broke out. Thus Cicero witnessed the collapse of the old order, and all the values that he had been taught to love and honor were suddenly disregarded. Also, during this time Cicero experienced the sudden and violent deaths of teachers and mentors. In the face of civil war and the horrors of proscriptions, life and destiny could turn from bad to worse in the blink of an eye. Normal civil rights were suspended, and the courts were closed. When finally the courts opened again, Cicero appeared at the Forum with his defence of Sextus Roscius of Ameria. Sextus Roscius had been accused of patricide by those who themselves had killed his father, and deprived him of his heritage. This speech immediately catapulted Cicero into fame among his contemporaries, but it has also won admiration from later generations. Still today, this speech is considered outstanding because of its seriousness, wisdom, and elegance. Cicero was about twenty-five years old when he concluded his defence for Roscius in the following manner:

> Banish this cruelty from the State, gentlemen; do not allow it to stalk abroad any longer in this republic; for it not only involves this evil, that it has removed so many citizens by a most atrocious death, but it has also stifled all feeling of pity in the hearts of men generally most merciful, by familiarizing them with all kinds of evils. For when, every hour, we see or hear of an act of cruelty, even those of us who are by nature most merciful lose from our hearts, in this constant presence of trouble, all feeling of humanity. (*Pro Sexto Roscio Amerino*, 154)[1]

These are remarkable words put forth by a young person. Living at a time of civil wars and proscriptions Cicero had already witnessed many actions of terror and atrocities. This personal background adds a worldly, wise, and experienced character to Cicero's ideas and views. And it also shows that his idealism and optimism were never achieved on cheap grounds.

---

[1]   Quotations from and references to Cicero's *oeuvre* are from The Loeb Classical Library Edition. In spelling of names I follow the practice of the Loeb translations.

Vocation and Grand Ambitions

It is beyond question that from an early stage Cicero aims at a political career. To be a politician and to take part in the affairs of the state was his main ambition. Late in his career, Cicero recalls how even as a young boy he had already nourished the burning ambition of becoming a politician and serving the state. (See *De re publica* I, 10) Only after Cicero happens to become cut off from the political scene, does he turn to what might be called his second ambition, namely to educate the Roman people.

As a young man Cicero had fallen in love with the Greek masters of rhetoric and philosophy, and he found that this rich storehouse of wisdom and knowledge should find its way into the Roman culture to the benefit of the state and its population. Indirectly, Cicero began to realize this plan already through his speeches at the civil court and through his political activity and career as consul and member of the Senate. At two periods in his life, he experienced being cut off from political activity due to serious political turbulence and upheavals, and under these circumstances he turned to the task of making available in Latin as much Greek knowledge and culture as possible. Hence, besides his main goal, that is, his political ambitions, Cicero wanted to educate the Roman people. The contour of this second *curriculum vitae* and the commitment to it is most touchingly articulated at the end of Cicero's life. In a discussion with Varro, Cicero reveals that for a long time he had nursed a secret plan to educate the Roman people in philosophical matters. (See *Academica* I, 11) In brief, Cicero wants to popularize the Greek sources in Latin. (See *Academica* I, 19) In one of his last philosophical works, *De divinatione*, Cicero again gives voice to his grievance and sorrow at being excluded from the political scene, and he repeats that, in this situation, the best he can do in order to serve the state is "to conduct my fellow-citizens in the ways of the noblest learning." (*De divinatione* II, 1) Then, he goes on to list a conspicuous number of works already completed; he further reaffirms that he intends to proceed in this way: "For what greater or better service can I render to the commonwealth than to instruct and train the youth." *(De divinatione* II, 4) Even though Cicero considers his engagement in philosophy as a substitute for his political activity (see *De divinatione* II, 7), he hopes that he can still make a political and cultural difference for the better and thus gain an influence on the state.

2. The Mission

Though the mission to bring knowledge, education, and refinement to the Roman people only arises as a secondary task in periods where Cicero is cut off from his political life, he nevertheless considers this task a political act. Hence, when Cicero turns his attention and energy to translating a number of Greek sources to make the Greek culture accessible in Latin, he has very clear ideas as to why he should take on this task and, further, how he should carry it out.

If one wants to take part in public life, being acquinted with philosophy is indispensable. And for the rhetorician the study of philosophy is an absolute necessity, because "the foundation of philosophy rests on the distinction between good and evil." (*De divinatione* II, 2) But to Cicero the Roman culture lacks in philosophical knowledge, and, still worse, the Romans are somehow dependent on Greek philosophy. Cicero writes: "Furthermore, it would redound to the fame and glory of the Roman people to be made independent of Greek writers in the study of philosophy, and this result I shall certainly bring about if my present plans are accomplished." (*De divinatione* II, 5-6) Hence, Cicero's mission contains a double agenda: To educate the Roman people in philosophical matters is only one part of the agenda, the other is to make the Roman people independent from the embracement of Greek culture.

Cicero's Approach to Philosophy

Cicero passionately stresses the necessity of studying philosophy, an interest that was to stay with him all his life. (See *De officiis* II, 4 and *De natura* I, 6) However, Cicero did not see himself as a philosopher, but more as a person who introduces a philosphical content to the Roman people. Furthermore, Cicero's approach to philosophy is characterized by a certain reserve. While advocating the need for philosophy, Cicero also warns against getting lost in endless speculation. To Cicero, philosophy is a nesessary tool that qualifies one's activities and prevents one from taking a false or naïve approach to reality.

As a man of the world Cicero knows that Plato's philosophy cannot be brought into play directly at the Forum. The class of philosophers lacks in edge and candidness. Even Plato would lack in power had he appeared at the Forum. At the Forum and at the courts special skills are needed. In these settings the destiny of the individual may at times change for the better, or for the worse, depending on which words are used. This experience, that a lawsuit may be won, or lost, merely because of a single word or the choice of style, is of cardinal importance to Cicero. That makes him consider the difference between being a philosopher or a rhetorician. Just as philosophers would not be able to stand the test if met with the demands of the turmoil and dust at the Forum, it must be admitted also, says Cicero, that Demosthenes' style would do no good in the halls of philosophers. (See *Brutus*, 121) In this respect, Cicero acknowledges that philosophy and rhetoric are disciplines in their own right. While the style, or the tenor, in a philosophical debate is more like a conversation, rhetoric is an art that is directed towards a goal. Even though rhetoric may improve and enhance the conversation between philosophers, the *raison d'être* of rhetoric is indeed orientated towards a desired goal, and persuasion is the tool.

In *De oratore* the reservation towards philosophy and Plato is voiced by one of the discussants who warns the orator not to get lost in obscure philosophical speculation without end. (See *De oratore* I, 224) The orator must be a man of the world, he must be in touch with the pulse of everyday life with all its conflicting agendas, he must know about people's needs, feelings, fears, and hopes. A rhetorician must not stand estranged from the very society in which he finds the justification for his talents and skills. Rhetoric can stand well without much philosophy. But, for Cicero it is in general a necessary condition that the orator achieves knowledge in philosophy. However, genuine philosophical questions, as such, should not be brought into rhetoric directly. As mentioned earlier, to lose oneself in the mess of endless philosophical speculation should be avoided. Rather, insight into universal problems should add color and depth to the speech. Normally, a case contains a general level as well as a special time- and person-related level. The orator must aquire the skills to be able to link any specific problem, or case, to a more general level, because only on this level will he find answers that might highlight the case in question. The benefit, thereupon, is that solutions, which are accepted on the general level might in turn become acceptable also with regard to the special case. But the orator must be sure that the general discussion of things should be in line with the special case. (See *Orator,* 46, 125, 126) In brief, Cicero does not approve of armchair philosophy. On the contary, he, emphasizes, time and again, that speculative knowledge should always, one way or the other, be made useful to society. This is one of Cicero's key ideas. In his own words: "for mere speculation is self-centered, while speech extends its benefits to those with whom we are united by the bonds of society." (*De officiis* I, 156) This critical approach to philosophy adds a certain vitality and drive to Cicero's engagement.

The Rural Greeks and the Urban Romans

There are three heroes in Cicero's life, namely the admirable philosopher and writer Plato, the great rhetorician Demosthenes, and, then, Cicero himself as the one who brings inspiration further from these two Greek giants in order to educate the Roman people. In Cicero's view the benefit of this task is beyond measure. If this enterprise is brought to a successful completion, it would bring forth the yet unseen, but dormant powers and abilities of the Roman people. In fact, in Cicero's view the Roman culture and Latin language are already superior to Greek culture. Cicero founds this estimation on the argument that the Romans possess traits that are lacking in the Greek character, namely those of determination and courageousness. And, as for the Latin language, it is just as rich in vocabulary as the Greek language. Further, Latin is spoken with a certain charm and accent, both of which are "peculiar to the Roman race and to our city." (*De oratore* III, 44) But in some sense the Romans need to be educated, especially in terms of philosophy and rhetoric. It would shape their dormant skills so that they would become independent of Greek culture. In this way, the Romans would finally surpass their teachers.

Although Cicero deeply admires Plato for his philosophy and brilliant style, he is also capable of looking at this great philosopher with some detachment and reservation. In *Brutus*, Cicero says: "Where will you find a writer of greater richness than Plato? Jupiter would speak with his tongue, they say, if he spoke Greek." (*Brutus*, 120-121) But needless to say, Jupiter speaks Latin! Cicero is constantly on guard to save, strengthen, and braze Roman identity while researching the heart of Greek culture.

No matter how learned and sophisticated the Greeks might be in philosophical debates, Cicero considers the Greek habit whereby rhetoricians can give a speech on any topic at any time as childish. (See *De oratore* III, 129) He also disapproves of the Greek habit of being carried away by discussion, a practice that Cicero finds equally naïve. Finally, according to Cicero, the Greeks lack in taste! The *aemulatio Graecorum* was an old theme in Roman thought, and Cicero indeed made his contribution to keeping the quest for superiority alive.

Tradition

Indirectly, Cicero anticipates his future fame by letting Crassus state that, in principle, it is possible to transfer "the outstanding wisdom" of the Greeks to the Romans. But, says Crassus: "It needs persons of advanced learning," and adds: "If they do ever arise, they will deserve to rank above even the Greeks." (*De oratore* III, 95) In fact, Cicero himself was the man who took on the enterprise of educating the Romans in Greek philosophy and rhetoric. In this sense Cicero becomes one of the very first intellectuals in European culture to transfer an entire philosophical tradition from one culture to another.

This task is undertaken with the attitude of being superior compared to the culture from which traditions are being transferred. We have already touched upon the issue of how Cicero struggles to enhance Roman identity and make it independent. Such examples are *legion* in Cicero's writings, and they reveal a key to the understanding of Cicero's contribution to the field of aesthetics. They, namely, allow us to realize that genuine tradition is not a matter of simple imitation, but as the very word *traditio* proclaims, it means to bring something further. Hence, as we shall see, the important achievements that Cicero brings forth with an air, or an attitude of self-assurance are unique and surpass the Greek sources. In spite of the fact that Cicero deeply admires Greek philosophy and, Plato in particular, he had from the beginning a very clear idea of the deeper meaning behind the task of translation. In *De finibus,* Cicero proudly states that he does not intend taking on the role of the translator. He says: "But, while preserving the doctrines of our chosen authorities, add thereto our own criticism and our own arrangement." (*De finibus* I, 6) In conclusion, Cicero sees himself neither as a mere translator, nor as a philosopher, but as a critical writer and mediator. Furthermore, Cicero also holds a sound and clear idea of his own unique style. In *De legibus,* Cicero's brother, Quintus, makes the remark that Cicero might try to copy Plato, not insofar as content of the conversation, but in respect to style. To this suggestion Cicero says: "It is very easy to translate another man's ideas, and I might do that, if I did not fully wish to be myself. For what difficulty is there in presenting the same thoughts rendered in practically the same phrases?" (*De leg.* II, 17 ff.) As Cicero sees it, being a writer on philosophical isues does not prevent him from exercising a critical stance in what he is bringing further.

Cicero's method in dealing with the Greek sources is one of eclecticism. As Quintilian later phrased the leading principle of eclectisicm, it means to select the best from every source. According to the general approach of his time there was nothing dubious in such a method. And, as a matter of fact, it seems that this method fitted well with that which Cicero wanted to achieve.

3. Eloquence

According to Greek mythology the dominion of sweet persuasion is ascribed to Peitho.[2] But Peitho is a tricky goddess that can be called upon for good, or bad. As such Peitho does not necessarily intervene with content. She guides the aspects of form. Cicero is very clear about this problem from early on, and in *De inventione* he addresses the *pros and cons* of eloquence: "I have often seriously debated with myself whether men and communities have received more good or evil from oratory and a consuming devotion to eloquence," and he proceeds: "For my own part, after long thought, I have been led by reason itself to hold this opinion first and foremost, that wisdom without eloquence does little for the good of states, but that eloquence without wisdom is generally highly disadvantageous and is never helpful." (*De inventione* I, 1) Also later in his career Cicero reflects on this problem and arrives at the same conclusion. This specific question is only one example among a multitude of themes that shows continuity in the thoughts of Cicero from his younger days until the very end.

---

2   According to Hesiod, Peitho is a goddess of Titanic origin, see *Theogony,* lines 331-365. In Greek art and poetry Peitho is perceived as one of the companions in the retinue of the goddess of love and beauty, Aphrodite.

After the death of his friend and rival, Hortensius, Cicero feels that he together with Brutus are destined to take care of "orphaned eloquence" (*Brutus,* 330) and, in particular, the Roman eloquence, which has been under way for many generations. In order to show how the art of eloquence is a significant dimension of human life as such, Cicero calls attention to an episode from Homer's poetry. In the *Iliad,* Phoenix is sent along with Achilles in order to teach him proper eloquence and to be a man of action too. (See the *Iliad* IX, 443) The conspicuous point in this story is the fact that Phoenix, the old master of horses, serves as a teacher in matters of eloquence as well as in matters of actions. To Cicero this fact is of major importance, and, as we shall see, it becomes an issue of great consequence to Cicero's fundamental approach to rhetoric. Hence, life and eloquence are intertwined. In everyday life language is crucial in order to communicate ideas to one's fellow citizens. Therefore, eloquence is needed whether in the private or public space, in the arts, in court, and in politics. Eloquence, then, is a fundamental part of being human and living in a society. Even in solitude eloquence counts as thoughts and ideas depend on words.

Eloquence is involved wherever people want to communicate their ideas. Hence, ideas must be clothed in words in order to gain power and become materialized. As it is not possible to separate the soul from the body without causing the death of the body, so it is not wise either to separate words from their meanings. This is the reason why no real style can ever arise where no firm ideas are present. As Crassus puts it, the ultimate argument for eloquence is this: "It is impossible to achieve an ornate style without first producing ideas and putting them into shape, and at the same time that no idea can possess distinction without lucidity of style." (*De oratore* III, 24) Time and again, Cicero gives voice to this holistic view.

Then, proper eloquence is first and foremost linked with knowledge, wisdom, and life experience. And Cicero's idea of what it takes to become an orator is indeed all-embracing as it shows in the following remark, made by Crassus: "Whereas eloquence is so potent a force that it embraces the origin and operation and developments of all things, all the virtues and duties, all the natural principles governing the morals and minds and life of mankind, and also determines their customs and laws and rights, and controls the government of the state, and expresses everything that concerns whatever topic in a graceful and flowing style." (*De oratore* III, 76) Hence, to perform a good speech takes all that the orater can possibly embrace. But even so, eloquence is hardly an art. Eloquence is more like *the art of life,* which means that the goal of this art is one to which a person can only aspire. As such *the art of life* is a never-ending process of making things better. Therefore, the art of eloquence cannot be reduced to theory and rule, or pinned down as a scientific study. But that does not mean that the reflections on strategy and methods are all in vain. On the contrary. At the Forum and at the courts, for example, it pays off to have reflected upon how to meet the challenges and not just go along without preparation and strategic planning. And, further, even though it is beyond the point to set up strict rules for eloquence, any speech will always be measured against the ideal standards for its delivery. Then, if one claims to be an orator, it follows that the delivery should ideally be done with distinction, order, and beauty. Hence, the orator can never escape being measured always against an unwritten standard which demands a certain degree of order and beauty in every speech. The aspect of beauty is a natural part of eloquence, and may take as many forms as there are speakers.

Cicero sharpens his ideas of eloquence to the point that if eloquence had had the upper hand, the sword would by necessity yield to the toga. Hence, the toga-dressed rhetorician should ideally be master of circumstances and guide people for the better, just by means of his very words. Thus, eloquence, at the end of the day, would ideally illuminate the case in question to the benefit of everybody. This is Cicero's utopian idea.

Rhetoric

Rhetoric is the crowning point of eloquence. Although rhetoric is late born among the arts, it is, nevertheless, according to Cicero, the most important. Nothing compares to the eloquence of the perfect orator in terms of aesthetic splendor and satisfaction. Rhetoric is the art in which every word is chosen with skill, every argument placed in the proper order, and every section of the speech composed in an appropriate style etc. It is even argued that a speech may surpass music, poetry, and play. The beauty of rhetoric is described as follows: "Is there aught more wonderful than the lighting-up of a topic by verbal brilliance, or aught richer than a discourse furnished forth with material of every sort?" (*De oratore* II, 34) Although Cicero admits that virtues are equal in rank, the virtue of being eloquent takes the prize as being the most beautiful and distinguished. The splendor of the words are intertwined with the actual situation in which they are used. Hence, to Cicero beauty is intertwined with usefulness. We shall return to this issue later.

The Rhetorician

Yet, the goal of rhetoric is in fact more than just persuasion although this is the main concern. The ideal orator has more tasks to fulfill. Cicero says: "The supreme orator, then, is the one whose speech instructs, delights and moves the mind of his audience. The orator is in duty bound to instruct, giving pleasure is a free gift to the audience, to move them is indispensable." *(De optimo* I, 3) Then, if one aspires to be a rhetorician by profession, it is necessary to learn the means by which to obtain the goal of one's desires. The task of being a rhetorician must be undertaken with enthusiasm and almost with "the passion of love." Like most things in life have to be undertaken with enthusiasm in order to prosper, it is equally held that without passion, or love, "no man will ever attain anything in life that is out of the common, least of all this success which you covet." (*De oratore* I, 134) First of all, the orator must obtain wisdom and knowledge on a variety of levels. He must know about the divine, about nature, and about the human heart. He must be familiar with the tribulations of human life, and he must know about the complications of human feelings. Further, the orator must be familiar with the laws and society in general. Equally vital is a knowledge of history and the past as the orator will need this store of examples and guiding images: "To be ignorant of what occured before you were born is to remain always a child. For what is the worth of human life, unless it is woven into the life of our ancestors by the records of history. Moreover, the mention of antiquity and the citation of examples give the speech authority and credibility as well as affording the highest pleasure to the audience." (*Orator,* 120) Finally, knowledge of philosophy is essential. Without a philosophical background it becomes too difficult to differentiate between the beautiful and the ugly, the good and the bad, the true and the untrue. Last but not least, the orator must not stand as a stranger in front of his fellow citizens.

On the other hand, it is not requested that the orator should know everything. Cicero does not approve of specialization, but every orator must, in a moderate sense, have access to a store-house of knowledge from where he can always find support and upon which he can sharpen his arguments. In fact, such knowledge is essential. The rhetorician will always, one way or the other, end up dealing with right and wrong, good or bad, the beautiful, or the ugly. Brought down to this basic statement, it becomes obvious how Cicero is influenced by Plato's famous triad: the beautiful, the good, and the true, but Cicero brings these linked terms into practical use.

Finally, the rhetorician must be in good shape, well groomed, and he must be in possession of a pleasant appearance in terms of gesture, bearing, and presence, together with a resonant and pleasing voice. Crassus admits that in a Roman context the physical appearance of the rhetorician plays a greater role than it does to a Greek audience. (See *De oratore* I, 131-132) However, Cicero knows by experience that those who by nature are less naturally gifted still have a chance if they are skillful enough to turn their disadvantages into something positive. Cicero refers to a rhetorician who was a rough and ungroomed type who used an unpleasantly rough language (see *Brutus* 117), but who, nevertheless, proved himself to be of a reliable and steadfast character and thus won the applause of the audience. Cicero gives other examples too in order to show rhetoricians that have overcome considerable difficulties. Among these examples is the story of the most famous and cherished of all rhetoricians who, according to Cicero, was Demosthenes. At first, Demosthenes could not even pronounce the first letter in the discipline in which he later outshon everybody else. (See *De divinatione* II, 96) But, in the main, the key to success is, as always, to excel in good taste and above all, to be a master of *decorum*, that is, to always make the proper choices in a given situation.

However, all things considered, the most important issue is the actual delivery of the speech. To emphasize this argument Cicero again calls attention to Demosthenes. When asked what was the first, the second, and the third in oratory, Demosthenes' famous answer was: Action, action, action. (See *Brutus,* 142) Even a modest degree of eloquence may at times appear to be successful. (See *De oratore* I, 116-117) The orator must learn the skill of delivering his speech with stamina, with wisdom, and with charm and wit. No fixed rules can be launched to achieve a unique style, only advice and guidelines. Therefore, the orator will have to rely on his own sense of the situation and what sort of style, phrases, and wit might be used. Above all, he must know what sort of style and wit he, as an individual, can make use of. In particular, the issue of wit immediately shows how the individual is intimately linked with his presentation. In essence, wit, one could say, holds the key to the personal uniqueness of style.

Nobody, would deny, says Cicero, that the elegance of the actor Roscius is a boon. This applies to his voice, its tone and modulation, his facial expression, and his posture and movements. (See *De oratore*, I, 251) Still, the orator is not an actor like Roscius. Cicero warns the orator not to be too much absorbed in training because too much focus on training may easily lead astray. The precondition for learning the skills how to become an excellent orator is that the orator can perform truly from the basis of his individuality. Although it is a natural and common faculty to be able to speak, not everybody can therefore aspire to become an orator. Nature and destiny in unison are decisive agents too. Nature as such must be respected, and it means that the individuality of a person is the basis on which the rhetorical skills are built up.

4. Details of Beauty

The beauty of a speech depends on a number of things. The content must be arranged according to order, style, and wording. In addition, things like quality of voice, facial expression, posture, gestures, bodily features, and movements must be carefully considered. It is not possible in this context to consider all the minor tools that are involved in achieving excellence of style such as how to use metaphors, rhetorical figures, rhythm, etc. Therefore, in the following we shall only discuss the major features of the concept of style.

Style

At the root of Cicero's conceptualization of style we find the crucial notion that form and content cannot be separated without creating disaster as a result. In everyday communication we all make use of a number of styles, even within one and the same conversation. Likewise, in a rhetorical speech a number of styles may be needed. A case at the courts, or a political speech, might be lost or won because of style. Among orators past and present Cicero always emphasizes the greatness of Demosthenes. Because Demosthenes was the supreme master of all styles, Demosthenes was seen as a champion in rhetoric. Therefore, to obtain perfection, or eloquence, the orator must ideally be able to master all styles. As in everyday life, a case at the court might require various levels of style to get an argument through.

In practice, there are as many different styles as there are orators. This is because style, basically, is something that is an innate part of the individual personality. (See *De oratore* III, 32 ff.) As we shall see later, this point is best demonstrated in what Cicero has to say about the use of humor, wit, and charm. On the other hand, it does indeed make sense to systematize the main levels of style as guiding principles for official and political speeches and for speeches at the courts. Ideally, there are three levels of style, namely the plain style, the middle style, and the grand style. The main goal of eloquence is persuasion, and Cicero differentiates the methods of persuasion into three steps: "To prove is the first necessity, to please is charm, to sway is victory; for it is the one thing of all that avails most in winning verdicts." (*Orator* 70) As for the first part of a speech, Cicero advises the use of a plain, simple, and pointed style to introduce and explain the facts of a case; for the entertaining part of a speech another style is needed, namely a style that can bring about wit and humor, that is, the middle style. Finally, a third style is advised to arouse the emotions, that is, the grand style, the effects of which are impressiveness, dignity, and weight. In order to achieve this triple task, the orator must be so skilled as to choose among the different levels of styles.

One of the secrets about style is never to forget for whom, and for which purpose, it is chosen. The all-important rule of style is always to customize, or mould the style according to who the addressee is, and to choose the right levels of style for each case is a skill that is not easy to achieve. Thus, to present a minor case in the grand style would be ridiculous. The orator must always be prepared to estimate the nature of a situation and of things and cases as this is the basis of his further decisions. In each case he must select and adjust the levels of style that can carry home his arguments. In brief, he must know about *decorum*. With *decorum* Cicero refers to the decision on which style should be used for the case in question, and this decision-making ability takes knowledge, excellent judgements, and taste.

Hence, Cicero's aesthetics is able to embrace different talents as, for example, people having a talent for precision and profundity, or people having sonorous voices, great force, weight, or smoothness. The road that leads to being a successful orator may take its departure in a number of very different skills. Any orator can be "eminent in his own particular style." (*De oratore* III, 28) In that sense, style is closely linked to each single person and, therefore, style is something that cannot really be taught. For that reason, the grace of style dwells in the mystery of character and personality.

In spite of the detailed advice for the use of different styles, it cannot be determined which of these styles is the most beautiful. But this lack of philosophical definition does not in any way obstruct the aesthetic valuation of a speech. Hence, the best of styles is always the style that brings about the wanted results and thus leads to a successful completion. This fact leads into the very core of Cicero's approach to the aesthetical dimension. To Cicero the aesthetic elements are almost never considered beautiful as such, but they are found to be beautiful as they interact with and further a purpose. Beauty is mainly linked with function. Hence, the beauty of a speech is always measured on the level of eloquence; on the other hand, the concept of beauty to Cicero, is one of great breadth. In nature beauty always appears in relation to something embraced by necessity. In other words, beauty is not a free-floating phenomenon, but beauty is bound. This is a crucial statement which Cicero applies to life in general and to the arts. Beauty and function are linked.

Proper Wording

To make the various styles work an orator must develop a sense for words. One of the charms of style lies hidden in the actual words. Julius Caesar who was much admired for his use of Latin (See *Brutus* 252) and praised for his exquisite choice of words, wrote a book on Latin grammer, in which he emphasized the necessity of using the proper words. The orator must know how to dress the words. First of all, he must shun a trivial vocabulary and instead choose every single expression with diligence, making every word glow and shine so that the ideas and arguments may become illuminated. The orator must find conspicuous images to support the course of thoughts and arguments in order to make vivid his whole argumentation. Only, when things are presented to us through appeal to the eye, it can touch our feelings. Then, mastering a rich vocabulary is something that must be prepared already from childhood. As a result social background and family background such as the language ability of the mother, the nurse, and the teachers are crucial elements in achieving a beautiful language. Finally, the sense for words is further improved by reading history and poetry.

The perfect design of the sentence, that is, the whole choice of style, of wording, their combination, the rhythm etc., compares to the order of the universe: "But in oratory as in most matters nature has contrived with incredible skill that the things possessing most utility also have the greatest amount of dignity, and indeed frequently of beauty also." (*De oratore* III, 178)

On Charm, Wit, and Humor

As already touched upon, style basically springs from the very nature of the individual. Therefore, there are limitations as to what sort of rhetorical tools might be used, and not every person can use, say, for example, the same joke. Hence, every orator must bow down to nature and pay respect to his own individuality and temperament. But it is, of course, a rather delicate act to be clear about what sort of wit and humor links with one's personality. To choose witty remarks that go either beyond, or above one's own character will immediately be noticed by the audience. As a consequence, the use of wit and humor in a speech is an area that depends on the orator's understanding of his own personality. Ideally, he must be fully aware of his own character and temperament. The reason that it may have a negative effect to embark on witty remarks that somehow go either beyond, or above a person's own nature, is that they may clash with what is natural for this or that person. Crossing this invisible line may create some grim effects.

The bad thing, however, is that wit and humor cannot be taught, nor systematized. Books on these themes usually end up as being rather ridiculous. Therefore, once again *decorum,* that is, the wise decision-making in relation to a special case, or situation, is of major importance when using wit and humor in a speech. For example, it is embarrassing when people who have a natural talent for wit are capsized by their own talent and air witty and pointed remarks that do not suit the occasion.

As stated earlier, to Cicero a speech ought to be like a bonfire of knowledge and delivered with much energy. Also every performance, says Cicero, should be delivered with "a certain humour, flashes of wit, the culture befitting a gentleman, and readiness and terseness alike in repelling and delivering the attack, the whole being combined with a delicate charm and urbanity." (*De oratore* I, 17-18) These are high standards, and Cicero knows that to claim charm, humor and wit to be part of a delivery is a delicate claim because these thing can hardly be learned. Man is not a *tabula rasa* at birth. Nature has already put her stamp on both body and soul. Thus, the seed of education is already inborn in man, but, says Cicero, as to the most important, Nature has left open for man himself to bring this education to a conclusion. (See *De finibus* V, 59 ff.) Hence, man is in many ways conditioned by Nature, but he also possesses free will and responsibility. As for his actual personality and character, man must work to improve himself, but there will always be a natural limit to what he can actually achieve. As a consequence, not everybody can be an orator.

To Cicero, the elegant witticism goes together with *urbanitas*. Among other things an urban behavior meant being able to speak sound Latin, behave in a dignified manner, and capable of blending this urban behavior with a certain charm. (See *De oratore* III, 29) Hence, eloquence and charm are key elements in *urbanitas*. To return a remark in an elegant and witty style shows not only style and *savoir-vivre*, but also superiority with a certain stoic ring to it. It follows by consequence that humor and wit should never be vulgar, but somehow good-natured, making use of fine irony. Thus "the manner of jesting itself ought not to be extravagant or immoderate, but refined and witty." (*De officiis* I, 103) Even in jesting "the light of the pure character" should shine forth. But the use of amusements must be guarded. Otherwise, witticism can easily carry man away from proper and decent behavior. Altogether, Cicero sees the use of humor and wit as a way of adding color and life to things.

Time, and again, Cicero stresses that a speech should ideally be like a bonfire. Therefore, to make a speech takes all that the rhetorician can come up with. Wise considerations must be made as to the choices of styles, much delicacy must be exercized in the choosing of words, proverbs, and sayings, and, finally, the very deliverance must be performed with energy, liveliness, and charm. In a playful description of the perfect speech with its order, style, and proper wording, it is compared to the colored stones of a mosaic with the main image at the center. (See *De oratore* III, 171)

5. Decorum as the Great Concept for *the Art of Rhetoric* and *the Art of Life*

The concepts used in *the art of rhetoric* spring from the experience of life itself. This is the main tenor in Cicero's approach to rhetoric. Hence, *the art of rhetoric* and *the art of life* are closely related. We have already touched upon how Cicero links eloquence and life by referring to the old horseman, Phoenix, who was sent along with Achilles to educate him "in order to make him 'an orator and a man of action too'." (*De oratore* III, 57) Therefore, the principles taught in rhetoric are such that they should be of service also when it comes to the question of how man should act and behave in everyday life. Rhetoric, then, becomes the prism that allows Cicero not only to develop a rhetorical vocabulary but also to comment on a variety of general aesthetic and educational issues. In brief, *the art of rhetoric* sets a shining standard for good conduct, embracing art as well as life itself. This approach makes Cicero's contribution to aesthetics truly unique. One term, in particular, signifies the character of Cicero's all-embracing aesthetics, and that is the term *decorum* which we have already come across a number of times.

Basically, *decorum* describes the special balance achieved when Nature renders living beings to be perfectly suited to their purpose. Likewise, man must treat things so they become suited to their purpose. As Cicero says: "In an oration, as in life, nothing is harder than to determine what is appropriate. The Greeks call it prépon, let us call it *decorum* or "propriety." Much brilliant work has been done in laying down rules about this; the subject is in fact worth mastering. From ignorance of this mistakes are made not only in life but very frequently in writing, both in poetry and in prose." (*Orator*, 70) Then, *decorum* is about estimating people, behaviors, situations, and events in order to decide what to do; *decorum* is about exercising sound judgement in all kinds of situations, and, *decorum* is about showing good taste in all things related to human life, to Nature, and even to the divine. From the following quotation we see how *decorum* is understood as an inclusive concept embracing both the aesthetical and the ethical dimension: "For, as physical beauty with harmonious symmetry of the limbs engages the attention and delights the eye, for the very reason that all the parts combine in harmony and grace, so this propriety [decorum], which shines out in our conduct, engages the approbation of our fellow-men by the order, consistency, and self-control it imposes upon every word and deed." (*De officiis* I, 98)

First and foremost, to Cicero *decorum* and, hence, beauty, originates in Nature herself shown in the harmonious body. Therefore, man should always look to Nature as the model for good conduct. *Decorum* embraces both the inner and the outer approach to the world and to life itself. When it materializes, it shows in our deeds and actions as visible, or audible beauty. Then, *decorum* as an aesthetical-ethical concept holds the key to all the qualities that Cicero values. If the concept of *decorum* is furthered and encouraged, it leads into a world of pleasant manners and gratifying and entertaining conversations. In other words, *Decorum* is the tool that leads to mastering an urban and cosmopolitan lifestyle.

Although *decorum* is a fundamental concept in Cicero's aesthetics, it is not possible to lay down the rules for *decorum* into a system, or a theory. The essence of *decorum* lies hidden in the very situation and is bound to this particular context. Therefore, in each situation sound estimation of what would be the right thing to do is necessary. As *decorum* can never be translated into square rules, *decorum* must be taught from life itself, and, last but not least, from good counsel. This is the reason why Cicero presents his idea of *decorum* by means of numerous examples that, in each single case, illuminate what sort of *decorum* would be proper. Cicero draws on cases from both rhetoric as well as from everyday life.

As for the orator, he is constantly exposed to the problem of *decorum*. In each situation he must make a very qualified estimation of the whole situation in order to decide the style of his speech. Mastering *decorum* is, according to Cicero, equal to the act of showing good taste. But even for Roscius, the great artist, the rules for good taste are difficult to state. Crassus says that he has often heard Roscius saying "that the chief thing in art is to observe good taste, though how to do this is the one thing that cannot be taught by art." (*De oratore* I, 132-133)

The Beauty of Decorum

Decorum, says Cicero, is "a sort of polish to life," (*De officiis* I, 93) and it embraces everything from physical appearance, posture, movements, dress, speech, conduct, actions, self-control, and inner life. Cicero has a razor sharp eye for what is revealed by all the small gestures we all use in our communication with our fellow citizens: "We observe others and from a glance of the eyes, from a contracting or relaxing of the brows, from an air of sadness, from an outburst of joy, from a laugh, from speech, from silence, from a raising or lowering of the voice, and the like, we shall easily judge which of our actions is proper, and which is out of accord with duty and Nature." (*De officiis,* I, 146) Therefore, good manners and decent conduct must always be taken into account. Cicero considers it indecent to run and to sing in the streets. Such things bring our looks into disarray. But more crucial than such whimsical advice are Cicero's guidelines for our mental condition. He namely warns against falling into the pit of depression, which he thinks is indecent, and he does not approve of acting overtly aggressive, or emotional. Immoderate conduct, in whichever field it might appear, is always a violation – either of one's own dignity, of the good opinion of others, or of the community. In fact, there are no aspects of rhetoric, of art, of politics, and of life as such in which *decorum* is superfluous, or unnecessary. In Cicero's words: it is bad if a harp player is out of tune, but it is worse if something in our life is out of tune. Cicero compares the orderliness of conduct to the balance and harmony that are the characteristics of a finished speech.

Finally, *decorum* also links with Cicero's ideas of how to maintain individuality, dignity, and *humanitas.* In fact, Nature itself teaches us what *decorum* is about, and Nature also teaches us how we aught to behave. For example, one should not without reason offend other people's feelings. Cicero concludes that we in our day-to-day dealings should show a certain "reverence toward all men – not only toward the men who are the best, but toward others as well." (*De officiis* I, 99)

Lack of Decorum: Ugliness and Evil

A number of examples of nasty habits violating the unwritten laws of good conduct are listed in Cicero's letters and, in particular, in the *Philippics*. In Cicero's opinion Marcus Antonius has turned into an enemy of the state, and in 14 speeches Cicero launches a portrait of Marcus Antonius in order to show not only his appalling lifestyle, but also his brutality and his viciousness. Antonius is described as a brute who, time and again, fails to respect the *decorum* suitable for a gentleman and a person of official rank. Already long before Marcus Antonius turns into Cicero's fierce enemy, Cicero ridicules his lack of manners in a letter to Atticus. Cicero writes that Marcus Antonius sleeps until nine o'clock, he refuses to receive the envoys and suggests that they return later because he wants to take a bath and take care of himself. (See *Letters to Atticus,* 205 (X. 13) § 1, May 7, 49)[3] To Cicero, such behavior for a man of offical rank is a dire scandal, showing that Marcus Antonius is ignorant even of the most common rules of conduct. Also, by overtraining his body Marcus Antonius has become vulgar to look at. He looks like a gladiator, says Cicero. But physical excess, such as the overtraining of the body, is a lesser wrong among all that Cicero has to say about his enemy. During the performance of state affairs he is not dressed properly, he is always drunk and smelly. He sets all good manners aside by reading aloud in public a private letter from Cicero. At a wedding party Marcus Antonius gets so drunk that the following day he vomits while conducting state affairs. As Cicero puts it: "But at an assembly of the Roman people, while in the conduct of public business, a master of the horse, for whom it would be disgraceful to belch, vomitted and filled his own lap and the whole tribunal with fragments of food reeking of wine." (*Philippic* II, 63) The tone in Marcus Antonius' edicts is vulgar and arrogant, but worse still: the edicts reveal his ignorance. He is unreliable and, therefore, not a person with whom you can negotiate. The list of crude habits that violate all customs for decent behavior, is comprehensive. Marcus Antonius illegally uses state money to pay a rhetorician. As Cicero phrases it, Marcus Antonius takes lessons in how to become a fool. (See *Philippic* II, 43)

Marcus Antonius is a hothead, he is arrogant, and foolish. But among the more grim and vicious examples is his total lack of respect for people and property. Cicero asks the question if the warfare carried out by Marcus Antonius and his men amounts to anything but one prolonged act of "depopulation, devastation, massacre, and rapine." And, Cicero continues: "Hannibal was not guilty of these: he kept much for his own use; but these men, who only lived for the hour, have not given a thought, I do not say to their fortunes and the goods of citizens, but even to their own advantage." (*Philippic* V, 25) Cicero lists other disgraceful examples in order to show how Marcus Antonius excels in laying things waste. After Caesar's death Marcus Antonius illegally moves belongings from Caesar's household to his own. Further, Marcus Antonius also illegally takes over a number of villas and farm

---

3   For *Cicero's Letters to Atticus* and *Cicero's Letters to Friends* are used D.R. Shackleton Bailey's translations, The Loeb Classical Library Edition, Massachusetts/London 1999.

houses, among which are the estates of Pompeius and Varro. As to how Marcus Antonius treated the belongings of Pompeius, Cicero says: "It is incredible, and almost portentous how in so few days – I do not say months – he squandered so much property. There was an immense store of wine, a very great weight of the finest silver, a costly wardrobe, much elegant and magnificent furniture in many places, the belongings of a man not indeed lavish, but fully supplied. Of these in a few days nothing remained." (*Philippic* II, 66-67) As for the estate of Varro, this was overnight turned into a veritable inferno in which all sorts of unspeakable acts were carried out. Cicero writes: "The whole place rang with the voices of drunken men; the pavements swam with wine; the walls were wet." (*Philippic* II, 105) Marcus Antonius' greed for property, gold and siver is boundless.

The examples of Marcus Antonius' cruelty are many. Cicero writes: "No sport seems to him more joyful than bloodshed, than massacre, than the butchery of citizens before his eyes." (*Philippic* IV, 11-12) Among the extreme atrocities mentioned by Cicero is the occasion where the legions protest against some absurd plans made by Marcus Antonius. Immediately after this event Marcus Antonius invites a large number of trustworthy and loyal centurions to his private dwelling, whereupon they are executed in front of himself and his wife. (See *Philippic* V, 12) According to Cicero, more than 300 hundred centurions and Roman citizens were murdered on this occasion just because Marcus Antonius could not control his temper. (See *Philippic* III, 10)

6. The Origin of Beauty

Cicero's ideas of beauty encompass a vast range of natural phenomena and artistic skills. In this way his aesthetics bounds out on the world, including even a fragmentarily articulated cosmological outlook. We have already come across how Cicero, time and again, refers to the order of Nature and the order of cosmos. Cicero translated Plato's cosmology *Timaeus,* which also advocates the view that the ordered universe sets a shining example for us in respect to order, beauty, and intelligence. And from Aristotle, Cicero was familiar with the argument that beauty should be understood in relation to its function. It is not possible in this context to discuss at length the Platonic, Aristotelic, and Stoic influence on Cicero's cosmology, but it is crucial to stress that even though Cicero is not interested in elaborating a detailed and comprehensive cosmology, his cosmological outlook is, nevertheless, fundamental to his ideas of beauty.

The fundamental argument in Cicero's cosmology, which is based on the Ptolemaic assumption that the sun travels around the earth in an orderly pattern, is one of usefulness, beauty, and harmony. As to the order of the universe, it is stated: "This system is so powerful that a slight modification of it would make impossible for it to hold together." The order of the universe is further held to be "so beautiful that no lovelier vision is even imaginable." (*De oratore* III, 179) The principle of unity between form and content applies to all living creatures. Cicero writes: "You will discover that the body has no part added to its structure that is superfluous, and that its whole shape has the perfection of a work of art and not of accident." (*De oratore* III, 179) Therefore, order, beauty, and usefulness are linked. The trees, for example, are suited to render the idea of utility and beauty as a unique whole: "In these the trunk, the branches and lastly the leaves are all without exception designed so as to keep and to preserve their own nature, yet nowhere is there any part that is not beautiful." (*De oratore* III, 179-180) Cicero provides the reader with numerous examples of how utility and beauty are linked. In a discussion on rhythm and how to please the ear Cicero suddenly takes us from the detail to the whole, or from the level of sense perception to cosmology. Through the reflections of Crassus in *De oratore,* Cicero launches a sketchy frame of a cosmology that provides backing for the argument of the unity of utility and beauty. Thus it is held that "nature has contrived with incredible skill that the things possessing most utility also have the greatest amount of dignity, and indeed frequently of beauty also." (*De oratore* III, 178) Hence, to Cicero the origin of beauty is basically founded in Nature.

Like the harmony between utility and beauty is displayed by Nature in living beings, such as humans, animals, and trees, this very order ought to be applied in *the art of rhetoric* and *the art of life* as well. To bring home this argument Cicero lets Crassus launch yet one more conspicuous example to show that also in the man-made world utility and beauty are linked. If, says Crassus, the Capitol were built in Heaven, where it never rains,[4] it would need no pediment. Hence, without a pediment the building would lack sadly in dignity and beauty. Other examples mentioned by Cicero are the construction of a ship with all the different parts, building of temples with pillars to support the structure etc., all of them examples of how utility and beauty go together. In sum, beauty is not a free-floating phenomenon, but beauty is linked with utility. Hence, beauty is an aspect, innate in Nature itself. Therefore, according to Cicero, the universe and Nature itself display to us the standards of beauty, and from the universal order and from Nature derive all the basic aesthetic rules that matter. Then, if we want to understand the secrets of beauty, we have to pay attention to Nature.

---

4   According to Homer the weather conditions on Olympos were always nice with no wind, rain, or snow. (See the *Odyssey* VI, 44)

Natural Aesthetics

Then, to Cicero, Nature itself is the wise teacher in terms of aesthetic and ethical issues. Cicero says "the first road on which it conducts us leads to harmony with Nature and the faithful observance of her laws. If we follow Nature as our guide, we shall never go asray, but we shall be pursuing that which is in its nature clear-sighted and penetrating." (*De officiis* I, 100) As mentioned already, Cicero's main concept *decorum* originates in Nature. Hence, the aesthetical-ethical principles spring from reality itself, but, of course, it is the duty of man to mold, refine, and apply these principles in *the art of rhetoric* and in *the art of life*. And, since natural forms and man-made artefacts show a great number of diversities, beauty has many faces. In surprising detail Cicero nails down how *decorum* even applies to our understanding of our own individuality and personal freedom. Nature not only sets the basic agenda for man's activities, but from Nature we also obtain subtle, but strong pointers, or guidelines when it comes to making the proper choice of lifestyle and vocation. Hence, following Nature shows us how to educate our sensibility in aesthetic matters. In spite of the fact that Cicero is usually the spokesman for tradition, he does indeed advocate personal freedom in choice of lifestyle and vocation so that the individual can follow his natural disposition and excercise his personal talents. The natural tendency, or the natural gifts must be respected. As Cicero says: "For it is of no avail to fight against one's nature or to aim at what is impossible of attainment." (*De officiis* I, 110) Therefore, it becomes crucial that the individual knows what are his own special talents, and holds on to these as long as they are not vicious. Hence, Nature's gifts rank above other obligations such as the family background and social groups. To follow in the footsteps of forefathers, that is, to follow tradition, does not mean, says Cicero, that one should therefore repeat the failures of the past. (See *De officiis* I, 121) Indeed, Cicero's idealism is tinged with a certain realistic approach.

Decisive powers are at work when the individual chooses a way of life and a vocation At times other powers such as Fortune may run counter to a person's choice of lifestyle. If, says Cicero, a person's natural disposition cannot be brought to prosper, it becomes like a fight between man and divine powers. As a remedy to meet such an unhappy situation Cicero stresses yet one more aspect of *decorum,* namely the psychological trait of persistence and not giving up: "There is nothing so essentially proper as to maintain consistency in the performance of every act and in the conception of every plan." (*De officiis* I, 125) Then, endurance, withstanding idleness, despair, and other ailments are ways of behavior that are also embraced by *decorum.*

Decorum applies to every aspect of life, and *decorum* originates in Nature. A final example of this is Cicero's advice on the flow of words and its rhythm. The tasteless habit of the Greeks who indulge themselves in an unbroken flow of words must be avoided, because as to the question of rhythm in a speech, the ear is entitled to be the judge and arbiter: "For our ears are only gratified by a style of delivery which is not merely endurable but also easy for the human lungs. Consequently, the longest group of words is that which can be reeled off in one breath, this is the standard given by nature." (*De oratore* III, 181-182) Hence, the human ear is by nature musical. The Roman audience at the Forum was familiar with listening to speeches and had therefore become very skilled and trained in estimating the eloquence of the orator. Matters dealt with at the courts were important to the individual, and this fact in itself sharpened the ear and the awareness of speech in general. This circumstance should be kept in mind when Cicero says that the ear is naturally predisposed to differentiating between the beautiful and the ugly. In ancient aesthetics the eye is normally considered superior to other senses, and in *De oratore* also Cicero gives his consent to this order of things. (See *De oratore* II, 357 ff.)

First and foremost, Cicero's aesthetics is founded in Nature, and his *credo* is this: follow Nature. Another main tenor in Cicero's aesthetics is his focus on education. In conclusion, Cicero's aesthetic principles aim at molding, or transforming the teachings of Nature into everyday life. In this way aesthetics becomes a means to improve and enhance life in general.

On the Ugly

Cicero has much more to say about the beautiful than about the ugly. Thus Cicero follows a common tendency in ancient philosophy to concentrate the discussion on the beautiful and to dwell less on the ugly. The point, however, is that the ugly is acknowledged as a real phenomenon but one which can to a great extent be overcome by education and good counsel. Moral ugliness is worse than physical ugliness (See *De officiis* III, 105-106), and also in this respect Cicero follows in the footsteps of Socrates and Plato. When the unwritten laws of *decorum* are violated, ugliness and evil are the results. Cicero speaks about a "demoralized soul." To violate the social instinct, that is, to violate the human feeling of co-existence produces ugliness: "For there are some acts either so repulsive or so wicked, that a wise man would not commit them, even to save his country. Posidonius has made a large collection of them; but some of them are so schocking, so indecent, that it is immoral even to mention them." (*De officiis* I, 159) Hence, such very grim examples of the ugly are best condemned to be stored away. In fact, Cicero is here delivering some building blocks to later enterprises on how to avoid extended discussions of the ugly. About some two hundred years later, Plotinus brings the discussion of the ugly and evil to a remarkable juncture with the following glorious remarks:

> Evil is not alone: by virtue of the nature of the Good, the power of Good, it
> is not Evil only; it appears, necessarily, bound around with bonds of Beauty,

like some captive bound in fetters of gold, and beneath these it is hidden so that, while it must exist, it may not be seen by the gods, and that men need not always have evil before their eyes, but that when it comes before them they may still be not destitute of Images of the Good and Beautiful for their Remembrance. (*The Enneads* I, 8)

With Plotinus the ancient world is coming to a close, but we still find the attitude of Hades being very embarrassed that the world should be exposed to the ugliness of parts of his kingdom. According to Homer, Hades tried to hide the ugly from the sight of gods and men. Plotinus, in his ardent fight against the Gnostics, argues the same idea that the ugly should be hidden to the world.

However, Cicero is a man of the world, and through his lifetime he himself experienced at close hand appalling atrocities. Instead of delving into a profound analysis of the ugly and evil, Cicero turns his focus to discuss more mundane, or day-to-day problems of evil. For example the question of whether one should always keep a promise. The answer is *no*. If, for instance, the circumstances under which a promise was given have changed dramatically, and further, that keeping the promise will result in harming the person to whom it was given, it is wiser not to keep the promise. Cicero illustrates this problem with a few conspicuous examples from mythology. For example, the Sun god has made a promise to his son, Phaëton, that he can have any wish come true. Then, the son asks be the driver of the his father's horse-drawn chariot, that is, the vehicle in which the Sun god performs his daily tour upon the firmament and down again. But the son cannot master the horses, and the result is pretty grim. Phaëton by his unwise ride happens to bring the burning Sun god close to endangering the whole earth. Zeus must come to the rescue, and Phaëton is hit by Zeus' thunderbolt and burns to death. Another example is Agamemnon, who had promised to the goddess Diana to sacrifice to her the most beautiful being born in his kingdom the year ahead. This happens to be Agamemnon's own daughter, Iphigeneia. Agamemnon keeps his promise to the goddess, and Iphigeneia is sacrificed. (*De officiis* III, 94-95) Cicero does not approve of such cruelties, although they are not intended. The mythological examples highlighted by Cicero demonstrate *in nuce* how evil is the outcome when common sense is suspended. As always, Cicero's inclination is to defend something, and his skills as a defence lawyer shine through. As a remedy against situations as those mentioned, Cicero calls for the use of common sense, or, in other words of *decorum*. Cicero's main concern is always to improve every human enterprise, and in this way his aesthetics becomes focused on how to apply the aesthetic principles to everyday matters.

7. Tusculum: The Art of Civilized Living

Cicero did not only articulate utopian ideas of how he imagined a free person ought to behave in public and in private life in order to achieve a good life, that is, *vita beata*, but he also tried to mold his own life and lifestyle according to these high standards. Such an enterprise is of course vulnerable to failure and shortcomings, and it is easy to find harsh criticism of Cicero and of his activities in the writings of Cicero's contemporaries. Here, however, we shall take a look at how Cicero paints a picture of the etiquette of civilized living. From Cicero's writings on rhetoric and philosophy we have already come across many of his ideals in the art of civilized living, the settings of which are very often town houses and country estates. Also through his letters we gain access to interesting details on the aesthetics of everyday life that he himself was familiar with from his youth and adult life.

As a lawyer the issue of real estate plays an important role in Cicero's vocabulary, and he often refers to his own town-house and country estates of which we get brief glimpses, especially through the prologues to his treatises. Cicero stresses that a man of rank must carefully consider his surroundings, that is, everything from location to interior decoration. Because a man of rank will receive many clients and guests, the house must be spacious and customized to this purpose. Cicero warns nevertheless against being too luxurious: "A man's dignity may be enhanced by the house he lives in, but not wholly secured by it; the owner should bring honour to his house, not the house to its owner." (*De officiis* I, 139) Ideally, there should be an inner relationship between the owner and his house. A house should never be an empty showpiece, but it should truly represent the rank of the owner, no more, no less. Cicero ridicules people who copy the villas and the luxurious lifestyle of Lucius Lucullus, the former general and one of Cicero's good friends. People who just copy the rich and famous, says Cicero, are not able to stand the test when it comes to the virtues that Lucullus represented.

As Cicero slowly rose to power the need for a representative habitat became mandatory. Then, about 67 BC Cicero becomes the owner of a villa at Tusculum, a former owner having been Sulla. After his year as consul Cicero also buys a town-house on the Palatine hills where he could receive his clients. However, Cicero seems to prefer staying at his country estates. Although Cicero was not rich compared to the Roman aristocracy in general, he became the owner of at least nine villas, most of which were in the vicinity of Rome, making it possible to reach Rome in about two or three days. Staying in the countryside was of course a retreat from all the hassle at the Forum and from city life, but it did not mean being cut off from what was taking place on the political scene. The infrastructure provided for good roads which allowed couriers to speedily bring letters back and forth to the centre of power in Rome, and therefore most villas were built not too far from the main roads. For example, in *De legibus* Cicero sings praise of his estate at Arpinum, as this area is a healthy location and convenient too, being not too far from the capital city. (See *De legibus* II, 3)

However, among his estates the villa at Tusculum becomes his favorite place. Cicero writes to Atticus: "It is the one place where I rest from all troubles and toils." (*Letters to Atticus*, 1 (I.5), § 7, November 68) In his next letter to Atticus, Cicero emphasizes his fondness of Tusculum: "I am delighted with my plan at Tusculum, so much so I feel content with myself when, and only when, I get there!" (*Letters to Atticus*, 2 (I.6) § 2, shortly after November 23, 68) Cicero even chose the name *Tusculum* for one of his most famous philosophical treatises, that is, *Tusculanae disputationes*. Hence, Tusculum becomes almost a metaphor for what Cicero saw as a civilized lifestyle. As we shall see in the following, life at the country estates becomes associated with the values that Cicero cherished most and in which he believed.

The Beauty of the Environment

From Plato, Cicero was familiar with a certain style of setting the stage for a dialogue. Most famous in that respect are Plato's settings of the stage in *Symposium*, *Phaedrus, Timaeus,* and the *Laws*. In *De legibus* Cicero refers to both *Phaedrus* and the *Laws,* both of which are conspicuous for their setting of the stage. In Plato's *Phaedrus* the conversation starts during a walk along the river bank. Finally, Socrates and Phaedrus find a place to rest, sitting on the grass in the shade of a plane tree in a very beautiful landscape. Also in the *Laws* Plato sets the stage by depicting the special beauty of the landscape. Three old gentlemen decide to walk quite a distance to reach the shrine of Zeus, while discussing which laws would be proper for the utopian state. This famous walk takes place on a warm summer's day in surroundings that are breathtaking with the beauty of cypresses and soft meadows.

In *De legibus* Cicero himself sets the stage of location, namely Arpinum, where he was born and raised and where he owns the country estate of his forefathers. On a walk in the beautiful vicinity of Arpinum, Cicero is escorted by his brother Quintus, and his much beloved friend, Atticus. Hence, the inspiration is due to Plato, but what is presented in *De legibus* is truly adapted to Roman history and culture, including the landscape and the attitude to it. By setting the stage to take place in Arpinum, his own place of birth and the location of his forefathers, Cicero clearly emphasizes the tenor of *De legibus*. Despite Cicero's admiration of Plato being boundless (see *De legibus* III, 1), he, nevertheless, ends up writing something quite different. As always, Cicero molds the inspiration from Plato – whom he considers the greatest of philosphers ever (see *Tusculanae I*, 22) – into his own unique style, and with emphasis on being Roman and not Greek.

To Cicero, the aim of the various stage settings for the treatises is to show how the beauty of the environment adds a certain historical, cultural, and urban dignity to the conversations, whether they take place in a town-house or are carried out at one of his country estates. In *Brutus* we hear that the discussions take place at Cicero's town-house on the Palatine hills. The discussants sit on the lawn beneath a statue of Plato. (See *Brutus*, 24) But as mentioned earlier, Cicero was particularly fond of Tusculum, a love manifested by the fact that several of his treatises use Tusculum for stage setting. Thus, discussions often take place in his own villa, or at the neighboring villas of friends at Tusculum.

In a letter to Atticus, Cicero refers to his country estates as "those pearls of Italy, my little houses in the country." (*Letters to Atticus*, 414 (XVI.6) § 2, July 25, 44) And at his estates Cicero allows himself the freedom of a certain playfulness. Hence, at the villa at Tusculum he arranged for two sections of recreational areas, one of which was named after Plato's *Academy*, and the other, named *Lyceum*, with reference to Aristotle. Thus, meetings on philosophical issues took place at the *Academy*, while lectures on rhetoric took place in the area called *Lyceum*. (See *Tusculanae* II, 9 and III, 7) At Arpinum Cicero plans to build a shrine to Amalthea, the nymph that according to Greek mythology nursed the divine child, namely Zeus. Cicero confers with Atticus on how to erect such an Amaltheum with running water, the symbol of the creative power in Nature. Atticus already owns such a shrine, and Cicero asks: "I should be grateful for a description of your Shrine of Amalthea, its furnishings and layout, and would you send me any poems or narratives you have about her? I have a fancy to make one on my own place at Arpinum." (*Letters to Atticus*, 16 (I.16) § 18, beginning of July 61) Cicero plans to decorate the walls around the Amaltheum with fragments of texts from the myths telling the story of the nymph. The use of inscriptions on the walls in private houses seems to have been popular. One of the more conspicuous ideas that gripped Cicero from time to time was a plan to have golden walls made with inscriptions and records of his own deeds. Atticus already had decorated the walls in his villa with inscriptions that glorified the statesmanship of Cicero. Like Romans in general, Cicero also was concerned with his future reputation. In a letter to a friend who was supposed to write about Cicero's political achievements, Cicero writes: "I have a burning desire, of a strength you will hardly credit, but ought not, I think, to blame, that my name should gain lustre and celebrity through your works." (*Letters to Friends*, 22 (V.12) § 1-9, ca. April 12, 55)

In general, there is much focus on the interior of the various sections of the villa, and careful consideration was given to ensure that the function of rooms was in alignment with their decoration. For example, Cicero refuses to have a statue of Mars, the god of war, in his house. Also, he rejects the idea of having any statues of satyres in his library. In fact, the idea of how rooms should be decorated in accordance with their use, is later elaborated in detail by Vitruvius. (See *The Ten Books*, VII 5.2)

Dress, Polite Manners, and Hospitality

The etiquette of life at the country estates in Republican time is ideally and vividly described by Cicero in *De oratore*. At the villa of Lucius Crassus, also at Tusculum, a gathering of friends meets for three days to discuss at length issues such as the orator, eloquence, and the state. On the first day the discussion continues until late in the afternoon. A civil war seems to be unavoidable, and the atmosphere in which the discussions take place becomes more and more gloomy. Finally, the host takes over; after having bathed and taken his place at the dinner table, Crassus shows all his charm and wit to elevate the atmosphere with the result that "it seemed as though a day in the Senate-house was closing with supper at Tusculum." (*De oratore* I, 27) Such stamina, or disciplined character like that of Crassus, Cicero describes with the term *humanitas*.

It is suggested that a suitable setting for the next day's discussion might resemble that in Plato's dialogue *Phaedrus*. In this dialogue Socrates and Phaedrus are having their discussion, lying on the grass beneath a plane tree near a small creek. However, the host does not find such a setting appropriate; instead he provides cushions to be placced on the benches around a plane tree. (See *De oratore* I, 28-29) Hence, the natural setting is made urban with benches and cushions. Thus a Roman gentleman, dressed in toga, must put emphasis on urban behavior and, above all, keeping up a certain dignity.

The whole atmosphere, even if some of the political discussions are somber and the philosophical discussions tough, is pervaded by a certain *esprit*. Though conversing about serious issues, the discussants treat each other with great courtesy; they never become bad-tempered or rude – all behaving in a civilized manner. The discussants deliver their remarks "with a smile," or, they take the floor "smiling," or, they might even deliver an elegant witty remark. Again, in *Tusculanae Disputationes*, Cicero describes the fashion of meeting with a group of close friends to discuss important issues at length. At his own villa at Tusculum, Cicero gathers with friends and students for a five day long discussion on philosophical issues, such as how to lead a good and happy life. Cicero ends the discussion on the first day by saying that "the richest fruit of the whole field of philosophy" is "all that tends to alleviate distresses, terrors, lusts." (*Tusculanae* I, 119) In Cicero's dialogues both the exchange of viewpoints and teachings of the younger generation are carried out in an atmosphere of urban, gentle and pleasant behavior. Seniors are treated with respect, and there is time for rest, pleasant dinners, and walks etc., while the young are embraced with interest and hope.

Although a great number of the topics discussed at the villas involved Greek rhetoric and philosophy, the *decorum* of life at a Roman villa differs from what was common to Greek philosophers. From the dialogues we realize that Cicero put much emphasis on showing that learned conversations ideally should take place under pleasant conditions, ranging from personal grooming, well-being, polite manners, to the interior of the residence and, last but not least: the whole atmosphere for the discussion must be civilized. The elegance of socializing that Cicero paints has been characterized by Paul MacKendrick with the Italian word *sprezzatura*.[5]

Cicero also reflects on the issues of good reputation, kindness, and hospitality; to be kind and always offering pleasant companionship to one's fellow men is considered a moral imperative. Furthermore, it is sheer irresponsibility not to care about reputation and hospitality. If one is a lawyer or rhetorician, one must receive clients every day, but besides that, every man of reputation should be able to open his home to his equals. Living in isolation is negative, not only for the individual but for society as well. Hence, social contact is regarded as a remedy against isolation and loneliness, but to socialize also appears to be a powerful tool in the game of politics. In *De officiis* Cicero writes: "It is most proper that the homes of distinguished men should be open to distinguished guests." (*De officiis* II, 64) When on long journeys the villas of friends functioned as a sort of base camp for the traveler. On his way to Vibo, Cicero stays overnight at a villa at Velia belonging to Talna, one of Cicero's good friends. Talna is not present, but his household staff does everything to make the stay confortable for Cicero. A reception is organized in which Cicero can receive clients and guests. Cicero writes: "My reception, particularly as he was away, could not have been more handsome." And on a stay at another friend's villa at Vibo, Cicero writes: "Here of course it is like being in my own home." (For both quotes see *Letters to Atticus* 414,(XVI.6) § 1, July 25, 44).

Cicero, likewise, received guests at his villas. A most conspicuous example of such an event is briefly referred to in a letter dated December 19, 45 BC to Atticus. Cicero is at one of his villas at the Bay of Naples when Caesar is on a visit at a nearby villa. Suddenly Cicero receives a message that Caesar with his armed escort of 2,000 men wants to pay a visit to Cicero the following day. To meet this challenge Cicero immediately takes action and works out a strategy that caters for the logistics and the food. A camp is set up in the open field in front of the villa, so as to prevent any damage to the villa, and the entrence to the villa is guarded in order to control access. According to Cicero, the whole event turned out to be a success in spite of the fact that his household staff had to provide food not only for Caesar but also for his huge escort. Cicero writes: "It was really a fine well-

---

5   See Paul MacKendrick: *The Philosophical Books of Cicero*. London 1989, p. 41.

appointed meal, and not only that but 'cooked and garnished well, good talking too – in fact a pleasant meal.' " Caesar's men are being served according to rank in three neighboring dining-rooms: "The humbler freedmen and slaves had all they wanted – the smarter ones I entertained in style," says Cicero, and adds: "In a word I showed I knew how to live." But he also makes the following comment: "But my guest was not the kind of person to whom one says: 'Do come again when you are next in the neighbourhood. Once is enough.' " (All four quotes are from *Letters to Atticus*, 353 (XIII.52) § 1-2, December 19, 45)

This episode is of course conspicuous because the guest is Caesar in person and because of the number of people involved, but it is also revealing as to the political game of net-working. In the very same letter to Atticus, Cicero writes: "We talked of nothing serious, but a good deal on literary matters." (See § 2) Nevertheless, the event is ruled by a hidden, political agenda. The relationship between Caesar and Cicero was a complicated one. Caesar needed Cicero, and vice versa. Thus, their partnership may be characterized as a sort of mutual dependency. In conclusion, Cicero shows that to be actively engaged in the welfare of the state, one almost needed villas in order to socialize. Thus the exchange of news and information, and the discussions of philosophical and political issues carried out at the villas were of major importance in order to take part in the life of the state and in its culture and politics.

Libraries

Books, of course, play a major role in Cicero's life. Therefore, it comes as no surprise that collecting books was a cherished pastime for Cicero and his friends. The establishment of a private library was an act that earned the owner much admiration, an example of which is Lucullus, Cicero's long-term friend and his neighbor at Tusculum. One could say, Lucullus, suffered the same unpleasant fate as Cicero, having been cut off from the political scene. However, contrary to Cicero, Lucullus turned his energy into living a rather luxurious life for which he became legendary. Nevertheless, he did not totally forsake paticipating in public life and performing some service to society. According to Plutarch, Lucullus established a huge library on his estate. This library was open to the public, and in particular Greek scholars were allowed to use the study rooms. As it seems, Lucullus' library might have counted as the very first public library in Rome. Also, Lucullus took pleasure in guiding scholars around in his library, making himself useful by helping them to find the books they desired to read. Then, circulation of books was a part of life at the villas. If one needed a particular book, the owner of the nearby villa might lend out a copy. In *De finibus* III, 7, Cicero makes use of a charming anecdote to set the stage for his meeting with M. Cato, whom he meets at the library of Lucullus, now owned by Lucullus' son. Thus the stage for Book III and Book IV of *De finibus* is

Lucullus' library. Furthermore, it is suggested that the stage for Cicero's now lost treatise called *Consolation; Hortensius,* which is only restored in fragments, might indeed also have been at Lucullus' library.[6]

Humanitas

Cicero's ideas of the good life is not a matter of isolation and seclusion, and accordingly life on the country estates is never a matter of retreat. Time and again Cicero emphasizes that *humanitas* cannot be realized in solitude. *Humanitas* is about interchange and communication. In essence, the high standard of *humanitas* is about being with people and being responsible not only in respect of one's own being, but in respect of the common condition of society and culture. Thus rhetoric, and in particular eloquence, are genuine aspects of *humanitas*. Whether in public life, or in the sciences, man needs the skill to communicate in order to introduce others to his ideas, knowledge, and requests. But Cicero is very persistent in stressing that *humanitas* does not require any skills to be taken to their extremes. Though concerning refinement of taste, Cicero does not advocate an ideal of refinement carried to the point of caprice. The very learned person not knowing how to communicate his knowledge in an apt, or appropriate style does not earn any applause from Cicero. Neither does the person who might be the master of form but whose speech has no content. As Cicero saw it, conversations in everyday life should add to hightening the level of information and knowledge, and should also add to the festive aspect of life. Conversation should be lively and elevated with wit and never heavy and dogmatic. This was the ideal that Cicero saw as a great advancement of society. Then, *humanitas* is about a certain attitude to life which sets a shining standard not only of pleasant courtesy and how to interact though decent conversation, but of decent human behavior in all aspects. With Cicero the word *humanitas* becomes coined, or loaded with rich meaning, which includes the dimensions of the Greek words *philanthropia* and *paideia*. Thus *humanitas* in all its depth and fine distinctions covers a huge specter of civilized and urban behavior: from being kind and polite, showing pleasant manners, to knowing how to behave with eloquence, humor, wit, and tolerance. The goal, indeed, is civilized living.

8. Dignity

To Cicero the necessary condition to realize *vita beata* is, first and foremost, to be educated in philosophy. To know about the world and about oneself are two

---

6   See Paul MacKendrick 1989, p. 109.

constituents that are fundamental to a happy life. (See *De finibus* V, 58) A third requirement is education in eloquence so that the individual can communicate his knowledge and ideas to his fellow citizens and to society. In support of this approach there are yet two other fundamental values that run through Cicero's *oeuvre*, namely that of personal freedom and dignity. In the following we shall see how personal freedom and dignity are of major importance to Cicero.

According to Cicero, the ideal *curriculum vitae* is first of all to serve the state and rise to power, then in old age to offer service as a legal adviser. (See *De oratore* I, 199, and *De legibus* I, 10) To Cicero, the only excuse for not contributing to society either with philosophical, literary, or political contributions would be bad health. Even in the face of personal and social tragedy, being forced into retirement, it is vital to remain active. In *De officiis* II Cicero tells that in spite of all his sorrows, he did not give in to pessimism, but always kept his spirit. To yield to idleness or despair, or to give up hope, is to cause harm to one's dignity. Hence, keeping up one's personal freedom and self-respect is a necessity. In fact, it is a moral obligation not to lose oneself, or to sink beyond the level of personal abilities. As touched upon at the beginning, Cicero saw himself to the very end of his life as a man of action and not one of contemplation. Having obtained life experience and knowledge, it is crucial, says Cicero, that this expertise somehow flows back into society to the benefit of one's fellow citizens.

Vita Activa and Vita Contemplativa

Thus Cicero stresses the importance of *vita activa* to *vita contemplativa*: "Every duty, therefore, that tends effectively to maintain and safeguard human society should be given the preference over that duty which arises from speculation and science alone." (*De officiis* I, 158) In fact, Cicero somehow warns against the lifestyle of the philosophers who deliberately choose to withdraw from public life in order to pursue their scientific interests. However, Cicero does not totally refuse *the raison d'etre* of a philosophical lifestyle, or a lifestyle in retreat. For example, Cicero's friend and financial adviser, Atticus, has chosen a lifestyle in retreat. In a letter to Atticus, Cicero reflects on the difference in their way of lifestyle: "I have never felt any difference between us except in the modes of life we have chosen. What may be called ambition has led me to seek political advancement, while another and entirely justifiable way of thinking has led you to an honourable independence. In the things that really matter – uprightness, integrity, conscientiousness, fidelity to obligation – I put you second neither to myself nor to any other man, while as to affection towards me, leaving aside my brother and my own home circle, I give you first prize." (*Letters to Atticus*, 17, (I.17) § 5-6, December 5, 61) If, then, a person chooses to live a life withdrawn from the general humdrum of public life, he can avoid the criticism of Cicero, if he by his very person, lifestyle, and approach to life in general stands out to his family and friends, and maybe even to society as a role model in uprightness and reliability. Through *vita contemplativa* a person might even contribute to society with his work after he himself has passed away.

Cicero has a keen eye for the fine balance between work and relaxation, and he knows from experience that being over-stressed takes a toll on every human being. Relaxation of mind is a necessity, and from time to time doing nothing at all is a sign of being a free person. In *De oratore* Cicero lets Crassus tell the charming story about how men of reputation, when on holiday, spent time at the beach at Caieta and Laurentinum collecting "mussels and top-shells." (*De oratore* II, 22-23) As Crassus says: "For to my mind he is no free man, who is not sometimes doing nothing." (*De oratore* II, 24) Although Cicero consequently rejects the hedonistic, or Epicurean lifestyle, he does however leave room for pleasure. From time to time, it is important to relax and to enjoy the charm of doing nothing.

Otium cum Dignitate

Cicero does not approve of an inactive lifestyle and makes ironic remarks about those who give in to laziness, or dwindle off into a luxurious lifestyle. Cicero makes the epitome of such a dishonorable case the target of ridicule and irony in *Brutus*, where a story is told about of a skilled rhetorician who became too lazy to speak, and, in the end, he did not bother to think either. In this way, says Cicero, his skills "waned in proportion to his relaxation of effort." (*Brutus* 247) It is, therefore, very important not to lose the ambition of being active. Even in old age action is important. Cicero writes: "But there is nothing against which old age has to be more on its guard than against surrendering to feebleness and idleness, while luxury, a vice in any time of life, is in old age especially scandalous." (*De officiis* I, 123) Elderly persons might be excused as far as physical labors are concerned, but, says Cicero, "their mental activities should be actually increased." (*De officiis* I, 123) As usual, Cicero gives a number of examples to illuminate his idea of *otium cum dignitate*. In a discussion with his brother, Quintus and his friend Atticus, Cicero depicts a plan of his own retirement in which he still imagines being active: "I have been counting rather upon the leisure to which age entitles one, especially as I should not refuse to sit in the counsellor's chair in accordance with our ancestral custom and advise clients, thus performing the pleasant and honorable duties of a not inactive old age. For under such conditions it would be possible for me to give as much attention as I wished to this task which you require of me and to many other activities even more fruitful and important." (*De Legibus* I, 10) Hence, Cicero's idea of *otium*, is one of action (See *De officiis* I, 69-71) To continue an active lifestyle even in old age, maybe at a slower speed, is with Cicero's words *otium cum dignitate*.

Old age should not turn into a state of disgrace, but elderly persons should instead stand out as role models to the young. Cicero refers to Manius Manilius and others who faithfully offered their service and assistance to the Senate and to anybody else in need of their assistance, be it religious or secular. Every day Manilius appeared at the Forum that people might consult him and get advice on whatever issues might be at stake. (See *De oratore* III, 133) In contrast to Manilius stands the sad example of Cicero's former idol and rival, Hortensius. At the top of his career Hortensius turned his interest into living a life in luxury and thus lost his power. Cicero likens the process to that of colors losing their glow. (See *Brutus* 320) To maintain one's dignity and self-respect is a never-ending project, but to be foolish in old age is more shameful than being a fool when young.

Cicero's ideal is that each person, even in old age, does service to his friends, the young, and to the state. To take active part in the life of society and the state would of course be of benefit to the state, but it also furthers one's own mental and psychological condition. An active lifestyle keeps loneliness from the door. Then, to Cicero *otium* is about being active to the very end. But he also knows that *otium cum dignitate* is only possible in times of peace.

9. The Legacy: The Civilizing Effect of Beauty

Cicero was a brilliant orator, an outstanding lawyer, a man of letters, and an erudite scholar of philosophy and history. In addition, he was acknowledged as an excellent statesman, a dedicated family man, and a faithful friend. These aspects taken as a whole characterize Cicero as a person adding momentum to his pedagogical-philosophical enterprise; he saw the enlightenment of the Roman people as one of his great missions. (See *De divinatione* II, 1-7) But in the aftermath of the murder of Caesar and the following political turmoil Cicero was assassinated on December 7, 43 BC.

When forced into retirement because of political circumstances, Cicero was determined not to bow down to idleness and despair. To the very end, he kept up his spirit. Thus the philosophical work *De officiis* which came to be the last of Cicero's works, is dedicated to his son Marcus who was sent to Athens to study and, as a result of that, was absent from the political scene of atrocities. Thus, *De officiis* functions as a guide or a handbook for the young Marcus, on how to become a gentleman and how to live a decent life. On the last page of *De officiis* Cicero writes:

> Herewith, my son Marcus, you have a present from your father – a generous one, in my humble opinion; but its value will depend upon the spirit in which you receive it. ... please devote as much time as you can to these volumes, for in them my voice will travel with you; and you can devote to

them as much time as you will. ... but as long as you are abroad, I shall converse with you thus at a distance. (*De officiis* III, 121)

Cicero never saw his son Marcus again. But Cicero left a legacy not only to his son and to his contemporaries, but also to posterity. By means of his extensive writings and the fact that the greater part of his *oeuvre* has been delivered to posterity, Cicero's voice has traveled through the centuries, enriching the spirit of one generation after another. In spite of a rather gloomy political atmosphere his writings abound with vitality and charm. Hence, to posterity the influence of Cicero has never ceased to exert itself on a great variety of areas. This continuity is more than anything else due to a certain tenor in Cicero's thinking, namely the love of the natural. For Cicero this meant the inclination to bring into play common sense and the golden mean.

Education

The natural tenor in Cicero's *oeuvre* links with the fact that Cicero follows in the footsteps of a major trend which can be observed in ancient mythology and philosophy, namely the pedagogic attempt to come up with answers to the all-important question: how should I live my life? Cicero himself refers to Aristolte's *dictum* that everybody wants to be happy and live a good life. Then, the crucial question becomes this: how do we approach this goal? These issues are already present in Plato's *Republic*. Socrates muses over the question: "We must now examine ..., whether just people also live better and are happier than unjust ones. I think it's clear already that this is so, but we must look into it further, since the argument concerns no ordinary topic but the way we ought to live." (*Republic* 352d) In fact, the question: how should I live my life? can be traced further back in time. In spite of Plato's famous argument that philosophers are better suited to coming up with proper answers, his esteem for Homer is still high as he is referred to as the poet "who educated Greece." (*Republic* 606e) Hence, the issue of proper education in order to achieve a proper lifestyle is a persistent dimension already in ancient Greek mythology and later in Greek philosophy. Cicero walks in the footsteps of this already long-lasting tradition. And in doing so he sides with Plato on how to further life in the positive. The answer is simply this: people must be educated by means of philosophy. To Cicero, philosophy should deal with life in all its multifarious aspects. (See *De finibus*, I, 11-12) The principles guiding ordinary life is the most important: "The entire end and aim of philosophy is the attainment of happiness; and desire for happiness is the sole motive that has led men to engage in this study. But different thinkers make happiness consist in different things." (*De finibus* II, 86) Philosophy, then, is the tool to guide man in his quest for sound principles and proper advice on how to live. Cicero's whole *oeuvre* can be seen as yet one more powerful contribution to boost this ancient, but universal concern.

Decorum: An All-Embracing Aesthetics

According to ancient Greek thought the beautiful and the good are intertwined. In the day of Cicero this idea was, generally speaking, an accepted doctrine which had gained ground also within Stoic philosophy. With his concept *decorum* Cicero brings the Greek tradition on the beautiful, the good, and the true, and the unity between these one step further. Cicero transforms this high-flown and deeply mystical idea and applies it to the concerns of everyday life.

In conclusion, Cicero's aesthetics embraces not only the contour of an aesthetic theory, but it includes at the same time a system of aesthetical and ethical education. In this sense, Cicero's aesthetics may be held as the ripe fruit of a very long development. From the day of Homer to the philosophical dealings with the beautiful and the ugly, aesthetics has been engaged in answering the practical, aesthetical and ethical questions: how should I perceive the world, how should I conduct myself, and finally, how should I live my life? These interrelated questions are embedded in all profound aesthetic concern. With great stamina Cicero undertakes the task of teaching the Romans in these questions, but the way in which he does so is rather unique, combining *the art of rhetoric* with *the art of life,* and vice versa. The task is done with much life experience and much elegance, so that even today Cicero's advice about how to behave in everyday situations counts as sound counseling, also in a modern context. In particular, the concept of *decorum* is significant because of its universal truth. Hence, the civilizing effect of beauty has a deep impact on life, culture, and society.

Common Sense

According to Quintilian, if one is an ardent admirer of Cicero, it means that no better role model can be found. (See *The Orator's Education,* X, 1.108 ff.) Cicero's thoughts have been absorbed in European culture to the degree that we have come to regard many of his ideas and phrases as natural and, therefore, we do not recognize their origin. As has been my intention, I do hope that the presentation of Cicero's most cherished values have shown the actuality, endurance, and vitality of his thinking. In so many ways Cicero's vocabulary still influences how we face reality, and how we estimate actions of proper human behavior. Cicero's aesthetics is one of distinct preferences, but also one of wise and fair judgements, with a clever eye for nuances and variations. In *De finibus* Cicero writes: "For the virtue known generally as prudence is an attribute as we hold of all arts, and every master crafts-man in each branch of art ought to possess it." (*De finibus*, IV, 76) Then, common sense is the approach that leads to exercising *decorum*.

In his own way Cicero carries out his mission with no less courage and bravery than the Greeks before him did. The idealistic hope to improve human life by molding and refining the values and ideals we live by is indeed an ongoing concern. Cicero called this goal for *humanitas*, that is, the ruling approach in a civilized soci-ety, which would allow the toga to prevail over the sword. In his numerous letters to Atticus, Cicero recapitulates, time and again, what he admires most, namely fine intellect, the charm of manners, kindness, outstanding uprightness, and reliability. That man, sooner or later, might be able to realize these standards, is the great hope nurtured by Cicero. In so many ways Cicero's *oeuvre* embodies a precious source of knowledge and wisdom. Even today, Cicero's counseling in matters of ordinary life is outstanding and may at times outshine much modern coaching.

PART IV

THE MODERN EXILE OF BEAUTY

Repercussions from the Collapse of a Philosophical Tradition

For almost three thousand years the famous triad – *the beautiful, the good, and the true* – was a leading idea that fertilized the field of philosophy and aesthetic theory. Also, this idea has influenced European culture in general. Still today we pay tribute to this highly idealized standard in various ways that add direction and color to our aspirations and hopes, and many of our role models are shaped in accordance to this idea. According to the German philosopher Werner Jaeger, the Greek culture together with Rome invented a whole cosmos of forms that has come to designate European culture and, hence, our values.[1] For example, the repercussion of the Greek ideal of *kalos kagathos* echoes in our ideas of a gentleman; it also lays hidden in various conceptions of general education, and time and again the subtle unity of the beautiful, the good, and the true shows up in our cultural myths of heroes and heroines. In so many ways we still thrive and orientate ourselves according to the vocabulary shaped by our ancestors. The great paradox, however, is that the issue of beauty has been exiled as a proper subject for modern philosophy and aesthetic theory. Theoretically, the concept of beauty has been left behind.

1. Aesthetic Theory in the Twentieth Century

The collapse of the philosophies of beauty, did not occur, of course, overnight, but can be traced as a long-winding process with many stages which finally launches a narrow conception of aesthetics. Today, aesthetics means art theory, or the philosophy of art. The various stages of this complicated historical development cannot be made the subject of discussion here, but a brief outline of the decline, or the collapse of the philosophy of beauty may illustrate the nature of this debate.

---

1   See Werner Jaeger: "Die platonische Philosophie als Paideia" in: Konrad Gaiser (Hrsg.): *Das Platonbild. Zehn Beiträge zum Platonverstandnis.* Hildesheim 1969, pp. 109-24.

Until the eighteenth century aesthetics was a part of the metaphysical and philosophical enterprise. But as the modern paradigm of natural science comes to power, this development puts a certain pressure on the humanities as a general demand for distinct, and almost mathematical, clear-cut definitions. The way in which this demand is dealt with in the ranks of philosophers led to a dramatic change of aesthetics, and finally to the exile of beauty as a proper philosophical concept. For centuries philosophers had struggled to come up with definitions of beauty. But as Johann Wolfgang Goethe saw it, at the end of the day definitions of beauty can only aspire to be *ad hoc* definitions. Indeed, the history of philosophy confirms Goethe's approach. The very heart in all concerns with beauty is this: it is crucial to be aware of beauty and to reflect upon it, but the aspiration to bring home once and for all a clear cut definition will only end in failure. Therefore, to accept the demand for scientific definitions becomes the famous straw on the camel's back that leads to the collapse of a long-standing philosophical tradition. Needless to say, this very harsh approach created huge problems for dealing with the whole field of human existence. Thus terms such as soul, the good, truth, individuality, faith, ethics, death, etc. have suffered in a similar way as did the concept of beauty.

Under influence from the Enlightenment, aesthetics is singled out and established as a field in its own right. In 1750, Alexander Gottlieb Baumgarten, publishes his *Aesthetica* and thus becomes the founding father of modern aesthetics. Later, in *Vorlesungen über die Ästhetik* published in 1806, G.W.F. Hegel clearly states that aesthetics should be understood as the philosophy of art. Therefore, says Hegel, it is rather problematic to publish works on the philosophy of art under titles such as aesthetics. The only reason for doing so, he argues, is the fact that it has become custom to deal with the philosophy of art under this label. To Hegel, the beauty of nature does not belong to the philosophical enterprise anymore. Only the human act of creation counts as a suitable subject for reflection on aesthetic matters.[2] During the nineteenth century philosophers were struggling to come to terms with these modern viewpoints, but with no positive results. At the beginning of the twentieth century the collapse of the philosophy of beauty is a fact. As Georg Lukács has argued in his *Heidelberger Ästhetik (1916-1918)*,[3] it is not really possible to deal with the term beauty without linking somehow to dimensions of metaphysics. According to Lukács, beauty is a genuine metaphysical term, and beauty will, one way or the other, indicate metaphysical assumptions on some level. Such assumptions may

---

2   For discussion, see G.W.F. Hegel: *Vorlesungen über die Ästhetik I/I.* Reclam. Stuttgart 1980, p. 37-39.

3   Georg Lukács: *Heidelberger Ästhetik (1916-18)*. Georg Lukács Werke Bd. 17. Darmstadt; Neuwied 1974.

vary from being distinctly articulated to vaguely hinted at, or they may simply be hovering as unconscious expectations, or background. In effect, concepts of beauty are destined to be all-inclusive, or vague, a fact that in the face of Modernity has paved the road to exile.

In present day scholarship the concept of beauty has become a sort of taboo to the extent that this concept has disappeared from the academic, theoretical, and philosophical discussions. Expressions such as: "Beauty is a blind alley … beauty is a bit of a bore"[4] are symptomatic of the modern approach. Hence, modern aesthetics is heavily influenced by a sceptic and a nihilistic approach. This problem, indeed, links with another problem: namely the separation of the beautiful from the good. Insofar as Modernity takes any notice of the beautiful, the phenomenon is reduced to *pure aesthetics,* which also leaves the good as a *pure* ethical concept with the result that both concepts are deprived of their depths. Today, we have left no aesthetic term to articulate our experience of being as such. In making the aesthetic categories specifically aesthetic or autonomous modern day aesthetics has become one-dimensional compared to, for example, the aesthetics of Antiquity. To monopolize the field of aesthetics to only the philosophy of art has had some very negative consequences. In point of fact, the arts are just a particular dominion of the aesthetical enterprise, and aesthetic experience certainly transgresses such a narrow conceptualization. Hence, today we face a huge gap between aesthetic theory and the experience of the many aspects of beauty. In short, our experiences do not match the curtailed notion of reality like the one, held by modern aesthetics. To crystallize the drama of this historical development, modern aesthetics fails to acknowledge that the aesthetic dimension is a genuine part of the experience of life as such.

One of the negative consequences arising from this historical situation is, with a phrase coined by Michel Foucault, that the "aesthetics of existence" is uncared for.[5] In effect, we have to turn to pre-modern texts to find substantial discussions on the nature of beauty and its significance for human life. The pre-modern discussions on beauty show with great clarity that the reflections on beauty are naturally linked with matters such as *Weltanschauung,* the art of living, and the general education of man. The attempt to understand the nature of beauty is at the same time an attempt to reach an adequate interpretation of existence and reality itself. Therefore, the phenomenon of beauty is a human experience, not to be done away with because of a philosophical taboo. Time and again, the experience of beauty proves itself to be a crucial dimension in our lives.

---

4   Somerset Maugham is quoted for this particular statement, see Wladyslaw Tatarkiewicz: *A History of Six Ideas.* An Essay in Aesthetics. Warszawa 1980, p. 145.

5   See Michel Foucault: *The Use of Pleasure.* The History of Sexuality, Vol. 2. New York 1990, p. 10-11.

The negative repercussions deriving from the contemporary lack of theoretical awareness of the issues of beauty are many. The whole situation as such casts a shadow on our actual awareness of beauty in everyday life. In the academic world the exclusion of the concept of beauty from the field of aesthetics has had an impact not only on the theory of aesthetics and the history of aesthetics, but it spreads to other disciplines too. For example, it appears that the negligence of beauty in modern philosophy has had a negative influence on the very reception of Antiquity. The purpose of the following sections is to give a brief outlook on such repercussions, the genesis of which is the collapse of the philosophies of beauty.

2. Aesthetics as the Philosophy of Art

One of the most conspicuous consequences of the collapse of the philosophy of beauty is, of course, the change of aesthetics, now redefined as the philosophy of art. This shift of paradigm, is, however, veiled by some confusion. As mentioned above, Hegel already warned against the habit of introducing the philosophies of art under wrong labels. Nonetheless, philosophies of art often introduce themselves under the title of aesthetics, but it is indeed rare that they cover the philosophy of beauty, or even touch upon the concept of beauty. In the following we shall examine a few examples.

In his book *Aesthetics. From Classical Greece to The Present* from 1966, Monroe C. Beardsley insists on using the term aesthetics instead of the term philosophy of art. Preferring the former means that Beardsley, in principle, makes room for dealing with a broader range of aesthetic questions, and he even calls attention to the authority of this usage by referring to *The Journal of Aesthetics and Art Criticism* and to *The British Journal of Aesthetics*. But the opening lines of his introduction to Plato reveal his main concern, namely that of art, and of the artist. Similar approaches are to be found in Anne Sheppard's *Aesthetics. An Introduction to the Philosophy of Art*, from 1986, and in Brigitte Scheer's *Einführung in die philosophische Ästhetik*, from 1997. Hence, present-day scholarship in general agrees that aesthetics is identical with the philosophy of art, and thus modern aesthetics travels the path set by Hegel, according to whom the destiny of pre-modern aesthetics is to become completely surpassed by new theories. As a consequence even the study of the history of aesthetics comes to suffer from a lack of interest – a topic to which I shall return later.

As mentioned already, one of the effects of this rigid approach is negligence of the concept of beauty. Compared to the past Modernity is poor in respect of reflections of beauty, and since the nineteenth century the issue of beauty has been treated in an air of iconoclasm. As art is now emancipated from any obligation to serve the idea of the beautiful, the experience of beauty is simply neglected. To Beardsley, for example, the study of the history of aesthetics only serves as a necessary evil, or detour, in order to gain knowledge on what he considers is the prime concern of aesthetics, namely art. The opening lines from his history of aesthetics reads as follows: "Though we cannot say when men first began to reflect philosophically on the arts, we can get some glimpses of the stages that must have preceded the appearance of aesthetics in the full sense."[6] As Beardsley identifies the genuine aesthetic level with only art, he is led to rather capricious arguments. Despite their elaborated finery and household goods, furniture, great architecture, as well as their genuine concern with the ornamentation of tombs, and their belief in substitution by means of representation, the Egyptians, Beardsley argues, did not really take an interest in aesthetic value. Furthermore, the Greeks, according to Beardsley, are somewhat declassified concerning aesthetic issues as they failed to develop distinctive conceptions of fine art.

To get a closer look at one more feature of the modern approach we may, for a moment, return to Anne Sheppard. As for the title of her book, that is, *Aesthetics. An Introduction to the Philosophy of Art*, she is extraordinarily clear in her advertising of perspective and interest. According to Sheppard, aesthetics is all about the philosophy of art, and as a result she avoids contributing to the usual confusion on what to expect from titles such as aesthetics. Like Beardsley and Scheer, Sheppard's main interest is also fine art. However, developing her thesis about art and the experience of it, she occasionally crosses over to discuss our fascination of natural beauty, but with no consequence for her theory.

As her thesis is founded on subjectivity, she returns to the issue of the individual: "We must study ourselves, not nature, if we want an answer to the question why we find certain natural objects expressive. As with works of art, the answer will be partly a matter of psychology."[7] But Sheppard does not take any further steps towards the science of psychology, and also she does not consider the possibilities of it, which might have opened up to discussions of the engagement in aesthetic affairs as an universal concern. Instead, Sheppard backstops her theory on formalistic grounds. In her own words: "The formal study of literature, art, and music is worthwhile not only because it enriches our aesthetic experience but because like any other formal study it provides training in intellectual discipline and rational reflection. Enriching our aesthetic experience goes together with developing our powers of imagination and understanding. Art engages both the emotions and the intellect and the study of art requires a combination of imaginative flexibility and intellectual discipline. If we develop our ability to respond to art we shall develop

---

6   Monroe C. Beardsley: *Aesthetics*. From Classical Greece to The Present. A Short History. Tuscaloosa and London 1975, p. 21.

7   Anne Sheppard: *Aesthetics*. An Introduction to the Philosophy of Art. Oxford and New York 1987, p. 58.

our potential as human beings."[8] Intellectualization and rationalization are the focal points of Sheppard's approach and not in any way unusual. On the contrary, her viewpoints are representative of the paradigm of modern aesthetics.

James Alfred Martin Jr. represents a different type of research. In 1990 he published a book with the title *Beauty and Holiness. The Dialogue between Aesthetics and Religion.*[9] At first this study, lingering on the periphery of the humanities, looks like an undertaking of great promise. Martin's aim is to vitalize aesthetics on the grounds of interdisciplinary and cross-cultural studies. Presenting a sequence of highlights from the history of aesthetic theory, Martin comes across old traditions as well as new attempts to argue for a broad concept of aesthetics, not restricted to art only. To some extent, he even draws attention to non-Western aesthetics, in which art is just one of the many domains, in which the beautiful may be found. Therefore, it comes as a surprise, when also Martin joins the modern approach. Despite his suggestion that the foundation of a new aesthetic theory should be established on "a broad theory of experience,"[10] he fails to leave behind him the straightjacket of contemporary aesthetics.

These brief examples bear witness to the fact that contemporary aesthetics concentrates on the arts. The negative results from this approach are several; the concept of beauty suffers from the lack of theoretical reflection, a vast range of aesthetic phenomena are left unaccounted for by modern theory, and, finally, as I shall discuss later, interest in the very history of aesthetics declines.

3. Wrestling with Plato

The shift of paradigm in aesthetics, declassifying the philosophy of beauty and promoting the philosophy of art instead, has had some devastating consequences for the reception of Platonic tradition. Being the focus of interest for almost three thousand years of aesthetic debate, the concept of beauty vanishes into thin air at the beginning of the twentieth century. When modern philosophers deal with Antiquity, the main focus is on the philosophy of Plato. That both Homer and Cicero, and others, have also contributed substantially to the discussion on aesthetics is a factor that is overlooked. And, finally, when modern philosophy turns to Plato, the ambition is not to discuss his ideas of beauty. The main interest is rather to wrestle with Plato in order to drum up support for the genius of the artist and to rank art above everything else. As the following examples show, these attempts are somehow fated.

---

8   Anne Sheppard 1987, p. 154.
9   James Alfred Martin Jr.: *Beauty and Holiness:* The Dialogue between Aesthetics and Religion. Princeton, New Jersey, and Oxford 1990.
10   James Alfred Martin Jr. 1990, p. 192.

At the beginning of the twentieth century Ernst Cassirer and Erwin Panofsky approached the tension between Platonic tradition and the philosophy of art. Both of them held the view that the philosophy of art is deeply dependent on Platonic tradition, but they also agreed that the philosophy of art must be liberated from this very tradition.

Cassirer, on his part, tries to overcome Platonic tradition by studying the artificial strand in Plato's cosmology, by means of which Platonic tradition is scanned for aspects to support grounds for founding a philosophy on art. In his brilliant essay "Eidos und Eidolon. Das Problem des Schönen und der Kunst in Platons Dialogen" Cassirer contributes to our understanding of the antagonism between the philosophy of beauty and the philosophy of art. As his starting point Cassirer calls attention to a paradoxical fact in the European theories on art. Although Plato's philosophy has no intention to develop a positive concept on art, the philosophies of art nevertheless try to relate, or to found their systems on Platonic tradition.[11] So the philosopher on art as well as the artist have, through centuries, associated their enterprises with the Platonic conceptualization of *eidos*, but *eidos* leaves no room for the artist and his performance. When the theory of art, says Cassirer, is founded in Platonic tradition, it becomes a straightjacket from which it must then escape, as Platonic tradition does not allow for a conception of art as something in its own right. One of the basic problems is that Platonic philosophy develops a profound, yet general concept of form that threatens the concept of form in the arts.[12] In a very concentrated and pointed analysis, Cassirer discusses the paradox of modern art theory roaming about Platonic philosophy, but to no avail. Though the Platonic conceptualization of beauty is concerned with the physical and factual appearance of the world, its definitions of beauty are, nevertheless, metaphysical and cannot be reduced to being a matter of form only. On the contrary, says Cassirer, Plato identifies beauty as a dimension of reality, participating in both a material and a spiritual sphere. In contradiction to the metaphysical reflections of beauty, the aim of art theory is to arrest beauty within the boundaries of artificial form, a strategy cutting off any possible anticipation of transcendence, says Cassirer. After having drawn attention to this crucial strand in Plato's philosophy, which strongly revolts against the doctrine that art should be valued as an authority in itself, Cassirer makes an unexpected U-turn. In fact, he proceeds in the same manner as the traditions he just criticized, squeezing Plato's aesthetics for arguments to restore the field of art philosophy.

To bolster his argumentation Cassirer calls attention to ancient accounts, according to which young Plato, after having met Socrates, burned his artistic works.

---

11   Ernst Cassirer: "Eidos und Eidolon. Das Problem des Schönen und der Kunst in Platons Dialogen." In: *Vorträge der Bibliothek Warburg*. 1922/23 I/II, Liechtenstein 1967, p. 3.

12   Cassirer 1967, p. 4.

Cassirer considers the episode of significance as Plato's treatment of the problems of art does indeed show an inner tension: Plato, the philosopher, was also an excellent artist. One of the best examples of this ambivalence, says Cassirer, is Plato's excellence in visualizing the sphere, where conceptual thinking has no access. Whenever Plato forces his arguments to the limits of what can possibly be known by human beings, he usually advances his argumentation by means of what has traditionally been called the philosophical myths. At this level Plato, the artist, argues by means of images and pictures in order to gain knowledge of what might be the truth. The use of these philosophical myths is a very profound and essential trait of Plato's philosophy which encourages Cassirer to stress the positive valuation of *eidolon*. The positive valuation of *eidolon* is further substantiated by the fact that Plato's whole cosmology rejects the notion of essential negative categories. As Cassirer correctly observes, Plato distinguishes between *eidos* and *eidolon*, but as Plato is also concerned by the relation between the two levels, *eidolon* does indeed anticipate in absolute truth. This aspect is of paramount importance for the interpretation of Plato's cosmology. Though Plato advocates the superiority of *eidos* to *eidolon*, this does not leave the concept of *eidolon* without meaning. Thus *eidolon* still holds a positive dimension. As Cassisrer emphasizes, Plato's philosophy does not contain the idea of something totally negative. Appearance therefore cannot be totally negative since, one way or another, it will always participate in truth.[13]

By emphasizing Plato's use of artificial skill as a very powerful strategic element in his philosophy and the slightly positive evaluation of *eidolon*, which can be derived from Plato's cosmology, Cassirer tries to make room for two viewpoints in order to further the philosophy of art. First, he wants to encourage and confirm the artist in his self-esteem, and, second, with the reference to *eidolon* he tries to argue for the substantiality of artistic skill. So Cassirer claims that the Platonic concept of creative Eros, which strives to procreate by means of beauty, may also include the artist. But when comparing the artist to the Platonic Demiurge in regard to true creation, Cassirer undermines his own critical approach. As discussed in my analysis of Plato's cosmology in Part II, the Platonic Demiurge does indeed contain crucial elements that contradict Cassirer's interpretation. Plato never confuses the concept of the artist with his concept of the Demiurge, as only the latter is considered a true creator, because he is the only one to create real natural living forms. By doing so, the Demiurge states his divine character. Then, in spite of his very clear and sensible interpretation of Plato, Cassirer ends up by joining the very long tradition of art theory that tries to found the doctrines of art on Platonic philosophy.

---

13   Cassirer 1967, p. 10.

Cassirer's study of the origin and development of the philosophy of art has been carried on by Erwin Panofsky, to whom Cassirer refers in a final footnote. In 1924 Panofsky published an article "Idea. Ein Beitrag zur Begriffsgeschichte der älteren Kunsttheorie" in which he contributes to the above-mentioned theme. While Cassirer's approach is a systematic discussion, Panofsky offers a historical research on the reception of Platonic tradition within the field of art theory. Panofsky's work cannot be discussed in this context. But the viewpoint that Plato treated the artist unfairly is repeated, and again, in a slightly reproachful manner. In conclusion, says Panofsky, Plato's aesthetics cannot be described as hostile to art, but it represents an estranged attitude to art.

As a third example of how Plato's philosophy is squeezed in order to deduct from it positive arguments for art, I would like to call attention to Iris Murdoch's interpretation. In her book *The Fire and the Sun. Why Plato banished the Artists* she pinpoints the problem discussed above. Though Murdoch unfolds an inspired reading of Plato's philosophy, she lapses, nevertheless, into the same sort of lack of memory, as did Cassirer. In order to raise the argument for art, she ends up by neglecting crucial aspects of her own observation.

Launching an outlook on Plato's philosophy, Murdoch seeks to create grounds on which to argue for the legitimacy of the artist and for the relevance of good art. As a starting point Murdoch, who herself was a novelist and a philosopher, focuses on the conflict and rivalry between poetry and philosophy. Like Cassirer, Murdoch also considers this clash of skill and orientation to be a common denominator for Plato's creativity. According to Murdoch, Plato suppressed his poetic skill on behalf of a commitment to philosophy and therefore became hostile to the artists. She writes: "… when a man with two talents chooses (or at any rate concentrates upon) one, he may look sourly upon the practitioners of the other."[14] Murdoch's point is this: being a great philosopher Plato is also a great artist, but somewhat undercover. This psychological assumption is further elaborated in analytical detail as Murdoch lists all the grand images with which Plato has illuminated his philosophy. Also Murdoch focuses her interrest on the Demiurge in the *Timaeus,* and she interprets this figure as "an instructive portrait of the artist."[15] The Demiurge, the divine architect in the *Timaeus*, has the power to put the world into order and to create the lesser gods who then in turn create the humans. Murdoch does not overlook this crucial point that the power of the Demiurge is of a specific nature causing him to create only the human soul, and then to delegate to the junior gods to do the rest. If, namely,

---

14 Iris Murdoch: *The Fire and the Sun.* Why Plato banished the Artists. Based upon the Romanes Lecture 1976. Oxford 1978, p. 14.

15 Iris Murdoch 1978, p. 75.

the Demiurge created also the human body, man would not be a mortal creature anymore. But in her effort to argue for the legitimacy of the artist Murdoch pushes her argumentation over the edge and thus confuses the ontological difference between the divine creator and the human artist. Though Murdoch wants to squeeze Plato's writings for "some positive aesthetic touchstone,"[16] she ends up advocating a viewpoint of her own modern making. Murdoch writes: "Art as the great general universal informant is an obvious rival, not necessarily a hostile one, to philosophy and indeed to science, and Plato never did justice to the unique truth-conveying capacities of art."[17]

Since the day of Hegel the philosophical interest has turned dramatically from the concept of beauty to the concept of art and to the legitimation of the artist. When Monroe Beardsley claims that the artist "might deserve from Plato a better treatment," he is indeed in line with several generations of scholars up to the present. In the end, the witty remark by Alfred North Whitehead, who once said "the safest general characterization of the European philosophical tradition is that it consists of a series of footnotes to Plato"[18] has yet again proved its significance.

4. The Concept of Beauty in Modern Receptions of Antiquity

The repercussions from the collapse of the philosophical tradition on beauty appear in numerous ways in the interdisciplinary scholarship on Antiquity. For example, the modern reception of Antiquity is hampered by the strong tendency to overlook the genuine aesthetic nature of ethical categories and thereby the very relation between the beautiful and the good. Also, there is a tendency to battle not with Homer, or Cicero, but with Platonic tradition in order to build up support for the sovereignty of art and the artist. While the aesthetic reflections of Homer and Cicero are not really dealt with, Platonic tradition in particular suffers from the orthodoxy of modern aesthetics.

Needless to say, the reception of Platonic tradition has through the ages undergone many changes, but the changes fuelled by Modernity result in a major shift. Until now the metaphysical worldviews have been the fertile soil upon which the various philosophies of beauty prospered, but as the metaphysical worldviews come under attack by modern philosophy, the concept of beauty is left behind. While Plato's ideas of beauty were still the focus of debate in the nineteenth century, producing a

---

16 Iris Murdoch 1978, p. 73.
17 Iris Murdoch 1978, p. 85.
18 Alfred North Whitehead is quoted from Harry A. Wolfson: "Extradeical and Intradeical Interpretations of Platonic Ideas." IN: *Journal of the History of Ideas*. April-June 1961. Vol. XXII, Number 1, p. 3.

number of monographs on Platonic theory of beauty, the balance now tilts in favor of other themes such as ethics, epistemology, and art theory. To find the theme of beauty as a part of titles, or as the heading of chapters, becomes rare. Luigi Quattrocchi's *L'idea di Bello nel Pensiero di Platone* from 1953 and Seth Benardete's *The Being of the Beautiful*, 1984, are exceptions. Also the comprehensive bibliography, concerning the theme of beauty in Quattrocchi's monograph, reveals that focus of interest in the twentieth century has shifted from studies of Plato's ideas of beauty to his ambiguous views on art.[19] Because of the very character of Plato's works, which in respect of literary form as well as in content are pervaded by a genuine aesthetic approach, Platonic tradition in particular becomes vulnerable to negligence of its unique character.

Though occasionally addressed in various areas of ancient studies such as mythology, history of religion, philology, and hermeneutics, the concept of beauty is badly treated, or even exiled. The theme of beauty simply evaporates in thin air. In the following we shall touch upon approaches showing a number of modern scholars who have considerable problems with beauty.

Academic studies like everything else in this world are subject to tides of fashion and idiosyncrasies. Philological studies are no exception; an example is Julius Jüthner's much quoted work "Kalokagathia"[20] from the thirties. Though a strict philological study, Jüthner, nevertheless, falls under the spell of Modernity in the sense that his main purpose becomes to strip the term *kalokagathia* of any connection with the beautiful and instead launch it as a pure ethical term. Neither Homer nor Plato use the word *kalokagathia,* the Greek term for defining the co-existence of beautiful appearance with inner, ethical responsibility. But both of them give numerous examples of how this idea appears in function. Thus an interpretation of the term is important, and further, it is often used to characterize a particular way of thinking essential to Greek culture.

The habit originating from the ancient Greek aristocracy of describing the *aristoi* as good looking (*kalos*) and good (*agathos*) later gives rise to a new noun, namely *kalokagathia,* which was used to describe the excellence of human beings, their character, societies, things, relationships, and phenomena.[21] According to Jüthner, the term is first to be found in material as late as the fifth century BC, and, here, being subject to trivial as well as philosophical use. However, on the basis of examples

---

19   This topic is discussed in my essay "Dannelsesbegrebets æstetiske Dimension. Et æstetikhistorisk Perspektiv" in Øivind Andersen (ed.) *Dannelse. Humanitas. Paideia.* Oslo 1999, pp. 235-44.

20   Julius Jüthner: "Kalokagathia" in *Charisteria.* Alois Rzach zum Achtzigsten Geburtstag dargebracht. Reichenberg 1930.

21   See Jüthner 1930, p. 112.

from epigraphy, literature, and philosophy, Jüthner concludes that the term refined by men of letters and by philosophers finally escaped its trivial background. For, of course, argues Jüthner, it is not to be believed that the aristocracy itself, as a sign of excellence, would choose a term, allowing for signs of excellence in outer appearance, to which everybody, in principle, could make an effort to achieve. According to Jüthner, it is a kind of naive folklore to unite the notion of beautiful appearance with the upper class, that is, with aristocracy. Therefore,[22] Jüthner considers it a healthy development that the term already in the past was subject to change, being liberated from its naive origin and thus reserved for the ethical aspect only.[23]

Jüthner's interpretation is launched with a lot of examples, but the problem remains that his main view does not spring from the ancient material itself. When summarizing his points, they speak the language of Modernity. For example, he employs the idea of the "aesthetically beautiful," that is, a sort of *pure aesthetics* which he considers suitable to describe only the beauty of youth, young men and females, while the visual appearance of old age, or other forms of beauty, can only be viewed under the perspective of the ethical. By launching the modern idea of the aesthetically beautiful Jüthner breaks up the beautiful in two, one being the aesthetical, the other being the ethical. Therefore, on the background of this very modern division, or compartmentalization, Jüthner can claim that the aesthetically beautiful has never been an element in the term *kalokagathia*.[24] But as the German philosopher and historian of aesthetics, Julius Walter, has emphasized, Greek terms cannot be torn apart in this manner since they are of a very special sort. Greek terms, namely, have about them the character of being what Walter has called "inclusive," that is, all-embracing, a phenomenon to which we shall return later.

Jüthner's work has been restated in a dissertation, *Kalos kai Agathos*, by Hermann Wankel[25] who like his predecessor denies the concept any relevance in terms of aesthetics. Also in works of more general perspectives, like for example Henri Irenée Marrou's comprehensive work *Histoire de L'Education dans L'Antiquité* the concept of *kalokagathia* is treated in a poor fashion. Marrou's work, published shortly after World War II, and translated to several languages, shares the conclusions of Jüthner and Wankel, but Marrou's argumentation unfolds as an indirect counter-attack on Nazi-theoreticians, some of whom took an interest in the concept. Especially Marrou puts an emphasis on claiming that the concept should be understood as pure philosophical imagination and not as a description of reality. To establish this claim Marrou turns to Aristofanes, who is called upon to witness the far-fetched

---

22   See Jüthner 1930, p. 117.
23   See Jüthner 1930, p. 119.
24   See Jüthner 1930, p. 116.
25   Hermann Wankel: *Kalos kai Agathos,* Frankfurt am Main 1961.

ideas of the philosophers. Referred to are the verses from *The Skies*.[26] Why literature should be preferred to philosophy in order to give a precise account of reality, we are not informed. But Marrou's maneuver is obvious. By using Aristofanes, to whom philosophers and ideas of education are objects of ridicule, Marrou wants to convince the reader that physical beauty and intellectual education are worlds apart and have always been. Thus, Marrou does not even allow the concept of *kalokagathia* its rank of being a formative, pedagogical tool and a *desideratum* to cultures in their struggle for improvement. In this way the modern paradigm of aesthetics, claiming the aesthetically beautiful to be emancipated from any ethical implications, puts a negative stance on a vast field of disciplines. Occasionally, this modern approach leads scholars to rather capricious argumentations in which the very sense of interpretation seems to have come under constraint, and thus hampering the understanding of what is indeed an essential trait of Antiquity.

However, the legacy of Antiquity is not always treated in a negative manner. There are indeed scholars who have contributed substantially to our understanding of Antiquity without twisting its main features. Among these scholars is the German philosopher, Werner Jaeger, in whose works the specific aesthetic nature of the Greek perception is in fact considered. Of special interest are his famous works from the period between World War I and World War II, entitled *Paideia*. In three volumes Jaeger gives an extensive analysis of the ideals of Greek culture, and later, in *The Theology of Early Greek Philosophers* from 1947, he contributes to our understanding of Antiquity by arguing, that the natural philosophers should be credited as forerunners, or founding fathers, of classical Greek philosophy. In his introduction to *Paideia* Jaeger carefully stresses that a natural aesthetic sense "based on the simple act of seeing" lies at the core of the organic way of perceiving. In their approach to reality the Greeks celebrate and ennoble the simple and natural impulse of the eye trying to grasp what it sees. Things are not looked upon as isolated units, but are seen, understood, and evaluated in relation to a context, and so the aesthetic dimension is considered a part of perception itself from the very beginning. To Jaeger the "unconscious natural perception," concerned with grasping a comprehensive understanding of the object, does indeed include the aesthetic.

To view the phenomena from the perspective of sight, trying always to look for structure, pattern, order, and wholeness is essential to the Greeks. The tendency of Greek culture to nurture the aesthetic instinct especially by sight also comes through in the field of philosophy. So Werner Jaeger describes the *theoria* of Greek philosophy as follows: "It embodied not only rational thought, the element which

---

26 Aristofanes: *The Skies,* 1002-1019.

we think of first, but also (as the name implies) vision, which apprehends every object as a whole, which sees the idea in everything – namely, the visible pattern."[27] *Theoria*, then, includes an element of aesthetic vision. The intention to see the idea of things is a visual act, an aesthetic act, but it is at the same time also a logical act trying to reduce or formalize this pattern, this order, or wholeness into one single principle, or law, from which the *ratio* of the object can be grasped. Ancient man is impressed by the world of phenomena, and though he projects the aesthetics of his own body and the feelings of his inner life onto the outer world, the world in return seems to become supportive.

But in spite of Jaeger's awareness of the aesthetic questions, his interpretation to some degree also suffers from the decline of the philosophy of beauty. The lack of modern philosophical traditions in which the profound and essential questions of aesthetics are recycled and reconsidered may be the cause why Jaeger leaves his aesthetic points behind as soon as they revealed, and then moves on. Finally, this maneuver leads to some confusion as to why the concepts developed by the Greeks through centuries have had a lasting influence on European culture, manifesting themselves even in present-day culture. Having said that, it must, however, be emphasized that Jaeger at least indirectly has launched an answer to this problem. According to Jaeger, namely, all forms of Greek culture are "the expressions of an anthropocentric attitude to life, which cannot be explained by or derived from anything else, and which pervades everything felt, made, or thought by the Greeks. Other nations made gods, kings, spirits: the Greeks alone made men."[28] In this reflection the enigma of the beautiful, which still continues to arrest our fascination, drops out of focus. Jaeger's main concern is not the field of aesthetics but the issue of education, the central focus of interest for Jaeger's whole scholarship. The aesthetic aspects of education are indeed included in the comprehensive concept of *paideia*, but it varies as to how much attention Jaeger pays to beauty.

The German philosopher, Hans-Georg Gadamer, also acknowledges the genuinely aesthetic manner in which the Greeks approach their world. In *Wahrheit und Methode* he notices that all the efforts taken by the Greeks to produce educational ideals are guided by the quest for beauty.[29] Thus Gadamer's interpretation of the idea of beauty in *Idee und Wirklichkeit in Platos Timaios*, stands out among the studies of this philosophical myth. Throughout the analysis Gadamer keeps his focus fixed on the actions and the nature of the Demiurge in order to illuminate the aesthetic nature of Plato's cosmology, being the ground on which Plato's idea of *paideia* is

---

27   Werner Jaeger: *Paideia*. The Ideals of Greek Culture, Vol. I, Oxford 1965, p. xxi.

28   Jaeger 1965, p. xxiii.

29   See Hans-Georg Gadamer: *Wahrheit und Methode*. Grundzüge einer philosophischen Hermeneutik. Bd. 1, Tübingen 1986, p.481.

cultivated. Also Gadamer has employed the inspiration from the Platonic ideas of beauty in his own attempt to argue the relevance of beauty.[30]

Finally, other scholars of the twentieth century such as, for example Max Pohlenz, Alfred Baeumler, Aby Warburg, Wilhem Perpeet, Jean-Pierre Wils, and Hans Robert Jauss, to mention but a few, have dealt with the legacy of Antiquity. They all share the characterization, once launched by Jauss, in which he emphasizes that the beautiful, the good and the true constitute the triad upon which Antiquity in general built its concept of reality.[31] In principle, moral values in the ancient world are brought to the surface of conscious thinking as part of their concern for the aesthetical dimension of reality.

5. Historians of Ancient Aesthetics

The modern exile of beauty also influences the very writing of the history of aesthetics in a negative manner. While a number of histories of aesthetics were written during the nineteenth century, the focus on this particular field is no longer in the forefront of academic interest. Especially under influence from Hegelian philosophy the theories of pre-modern epochs tend to be either degraded as not being aesthetics in a proper sense, or their profound aesthetic nature is not acknowledged, due to the philosophical interest in ethics and theory of knowledge. As a result comprehensive studies of the aesthetics of pre-modern epochs become somewhat rare, and works on ancient aesthetics are not numerous. According to the Polish philosopher, Wladyslaw Tatarkiewicz, who himself is the author of a three volume history of aesthetics, almost nothing has been produced on the Greek origin of Western traditions on beauty.[32] But scholars such as Tatarkiewicz and others who have shown an interest to study the roots of Western aesthetics

---

30   See Hans-Georg Gadamer: *The Relevance of the Beautiful and other Essays.* Cambridge University Press. 1995.

31   Cf. Hans Robert Jauss, Hrsg.: *Die Nicht mehr schönen Künste.* Grenzphänomene des Ästhetischen, München 1968, p. 590. See also Hans Robert Jauss: *Ästhetische Erfahrung und literarische Hermeneutik I,* München 1977, p. 103 ff. Umberto Eco, in his *Art and Beauty in the Middle Ages,* London 1986, also touches upon the term *kalokagathia,* suggesting a revival of the term. Medieval tradition together with Antiquity might serve as an inspiration for elaborating a new ideal. Though Eco in his analysis reveals a sensibility of medieval aesthetics that transgresses the limitations of fine art, it does not inspire Eco to promote the idea of expanding the very concept of aesthetics. To Eco aesthetics is still considered as art philosophy, a somewhat unexpected conclusion in respect of his analysis. So Eco, though arguing for a revival of the term *kalokagathia* totally neglects its classical content and meaning, namely that of being the ideal guidance for human life in general.

32   See Wladyslav Tatarkiewicz: *Geschichte der Ästhetik.* Erster Band: Die Ästhetik der Antike. Basel/ Stuttgart 1979, p. 16 ff.

are aware of the neglected status of this legacy, and they have addressed various aspects of the shortcomings of Modernity.

In the following we shall briefly introduce some of the scholars who have dealt with the history of aesthetics. Although they deal with ancient aesthetics from various angles, all of them emphasize that pre-modern aesthetics has the ability to add to our knowledge of beauty and to the perception of reality. Hence, *in toto,* the approaches of the historians almost frame a strategy on how to reconsider the concept of beauty and to put this ancient concept on the agenda again.

One of the very few researches on the foundation of ancient aesthetics, paying attention also to its mythological and poetical roots, is Julius Walter's extensive work *Die Geschichte der Ästhetik im Altertum* from 1893. In his introduction Walter emphasizes some crucial points as to why modern aesthetic theory has lost contact with its own historical background.

Essential to ancient aesthetic tradition is that its concepts are double-sided or all-inclusive, containing always both the aesthetic as well as the ethical aspect, but, says Walter, when the ancient aesthetic vocabulary was adopted by Christianity, the aesthetic dimension became strongly oppressed. Nevertheless, the terms, developed by Antiquity, have had the power to influence the European culture. But due to the influence from the Enlightenment, the focus of interest has shifted. While Antiquity took a broad and general interest in aesthetics because of its metaphysical and educational relevance, Modernity addresses the subject of aesthetics in order to investigate on art only. Thus, already in 1893, Walter observes a certain trait of Modernity, namely its one-dimensional interest in technical skill. For example, when Modernity turns to Antiquity, Aristotle is favored at the expense of Plato and Plotinus. This approach, then legitimated itself by claiming positions like Plato, Plotinus and others to be outdated and too mystical. The crucial point in Walter's argument is that the historical shift in interest has led to a certain estrangement from the founding traditions, the result of which is that Modernity is not aware of the inherent significance deriving from ancient aesthetics. Therefore, Walter finds that a historical study of Antiquity is essential in dealing with the nature of aesthetical questions.

While Walter notices how the discipline of aesthetics has become one-dimensional, focusing its theories on art only and leaving all other aesthetical phenomena exiled from the agenda, the German philosopher, Alfred Baeumler, in his *Ästhetik* from 1934, addresses the tension between aesthetics and art. To Baeumler, aesthetics as such originated from two different roots. While the idea of beauty was generated by Plato and later becomes the point of focus of a rich and long-standing Platonic tradition, carried forward especially by Plotinus, Augustine, and the Renaissance, the concept of art, on the other hand, was developed by Aristotle and elaborated by rhetoric and art theory. In the opening lines of his book Baeumler illuminates a fundamental problem when stressing that aesthetic reflection initially did not emerge as a result of the experience of art, but from the confrontation with the beauty of natural beings and phenomena.[33] Hence, at the very beginning of the history of aesthetics we are introduced to the experience of living beauty and not to the experience of art. Aesthetic reflection in its early forms is the outcome of man's encounter with the beauty of living beings. With this approach Baeumler like Walter and Tatarkiewicz addresses the lack of consciousness in modern aesthetics which fails to acknowledge the very roots of aesthetics.

Finally, I would like to call attention to the works of the German historian and philosopher, Wilhelm Perpeet, who among other things has dealt with the aesthetics of Antiquity and the Middle Ages. Like the historians mentioned above, also Perpeet holds a critical approach to modern theory for ignoring a vast field of the phenomena of beauty. To Perpeet, modern aesthetics has lost touch with the concrete experience of beauty and its multifarious historical expressions. Also, Perpeet is critical against the systematic approaches to aesthetics which often fail to discuss the essential features of beauty. Perpeet further emphasizes that the history of the concept of beauty and the history of aesthetics as such should in no way be identified with the history of art, as is the case in the modern approach to aesthetics. And to bring home this argument, Perpeet refers to Alexander Gottlieb Baumgarten – the founding father of modern aesthetics as a discipline – who, in no way gave in to a reductive approach. On the contrary, says Perpeet, Baumgarten introduced a scientific ideal to support a renewed understanding of the discipline in its own right. According to Perpeet aesthetics must take its departure from the rich field of phenomena in order to discover beauty and reflect upon it.[34] Hence, the theory of aesthetics has an obligation to reflect upon beauty, no matter in which province of reality it may manifest itself.

Thus the study of the historical approaches to beauty, says Perpeet, is the most effective protection against dogmatic systems. The aim is not to decide what should be labeled as beautiful, but to pay attention to what is already found to be beautiful and then to reflect upon it. Also, Perpeet finds that pure systematic approaches may easily lead to erroneous results. Such methods Perpeet compares to a frog living in a well, but which in spite of this assumes the authority to speak of the sea.[35] The historical approach may function as a healing remedy against the modern, reductive tendencies and contribute to a more varied and profound concept of beauty.

---

33   Alfred Baeumler: *Ästhetik.* München. Wien 1934, pp. 3-4.
34   Wilhelm Perpeet: *Antike Ästhetik,* Freiburg/München 1988, p. 8.
35   See Wilhelm Perpeet, *Antike Ästhetik,* 1988, pp. 18-19.

Ancient aesthetics continues to be an eye-opener because of its special character. Essential to ancient aesthetics is namely that there is always a close link between the concrete experience of beauty and the reflection upon it. To Perpeet, exactly this approach is a *conditio sine qua non* for all enterprises on aesthetical matters. Perpeet plays upon the Hegelian doctrine of *Anstrennung des Begriffs* by turning this dictum into *die Anstrengung der Anschauung.* This is to say that the roots of all prosperous conceptualization lay hidden in the natural talent *to see.* Hence, the power of conception surely rests upon the passionate and distinctive power of perception. But, says Perpeet, to change the modern attitude to a more balanced approach takes the courage *to wonder* again. Perpeet uses the Greek word "thaumazein."[36] Exactly this attitude, to wonder, has been reduced in value by Modernity which ignores such individual impulse as a starting point. But to understand Nature and the essence of Beauty takes a humble attitude. According to ancient myth and philosophy in general, and to Platonic philosophy in particular, to wonder is indeed the bedrock of all great endeavors.[37]

In conclusion, the historical study of beauty is essential in order to avoid an impoverishment of the discipline itself. The history of aesthetics may in general turn out to be a healing remedy against a narrow understanding of aesthetics. Also scholars such as Umberto Eco, Ernesto Grassi, and Rosario Assunto share the hope that the analyses of epochs, different in attitude and scope from Modernity, may illuminate and heal the crisis of contemporary aesthetics. Hence, in order to renew the philosophy of beauty – to put the question of beauty on the agenda again – we have to trace the history of this very idea. As Perpeet has emphasized, the shortest way of gaining proper knowledge on the beautiful is excactly to set out on a detour that will introduce us to the history of this category.[38] Hence, the aesthetics of Antiquity is a true eye-opener to further a broad discourse of the idea of beauty.

6. The Importance of Reconsidering Beauty

The foundation of the aesthetics in Antiquity is of historical interest to our understanding of Western culture in general, and, in particular, the study of ancient aesthetics is crucial in order to avoid an impoverishment of the discipline itself. Aby Warburg, the founder of the Library of the Warburg Institute, argued that Antiquity has genuinely shaped our Western values in terms of action, orientation, word, and image. Then, the aim of studying the history of aesthetics is not generated from an

---

36   Wilhelm Perpeet 1988, p. 21.

37   See for example the discussion in Plato: *Theaetetus* 155d.

38   In German, the argument is articulated as follows: "Der kürzeste Weg zum Wissen von Schönem ist der Umweg über diese Geschichte." Wilhelm Perpeet 1988, pp. 18-19.

antiquarian interest but from a need to give voice to a more adequate concept of aesthetics, and subsequently to change and broaden our notion of reality.

Hence, the need to reconsider the mythological and philosophical traditions on beauty is produced by the historical development itself. Modern theories, if they address the issue of beauty at all, label beauty as a cliché, as a sort of *trivia*, or as sheer nostalgia. This situation has produced a great discrepancy between modern theories on aesthetics and the individual and personal experience of beauty. In spite of modern theory having abandoned the discussion of beauty, we still use the vocabulary of beauty in our everyday life. Thus the elder aesthetic categories state their own substantiality, archaic or not, by their very presence, but this phenomenon is not acknowledged by modern aesthetics. Historical development does not necessarily transgress, or make false older aesthetic categories. In fact, their persistence in Western tradition and their use in our modern culture and everyday life may originate in their capacity to describe fundamental issues. To quote Bernard Williams: "What is alive from the Greek world is already alive and is helping (often in hidden ways) to keep us alive."[39] By using expressions such as order, beauty, and the shining of beauty we call attention to fundamental experiences of wholeness. Then, not only our emotional makeup, but also our imaginations, symbols, terms, categories, and concepts are intertwined with the past. In numerous ways we still pay tribute to the ancient approach to reality by using a specific aesthetic vocabulary. And the experience of beauty seems to contain some profound elements that boost vital life forces.

Then, to restate my argument, the aim of studying the history of aesthetics is not generated from an antiquarian interest but from a need to define the discipline of aesthetics anew, and subsequently to acknowledge that we are linked with the past in subtle and surprising ways. Any ambition to breathe new life into the discussion on beauty is, of course, fated to challenge the very core in modern ideology. In the following I wish briefly to call attention to some of the main obstacles waiting ahead on this up-hill struggle.

The core of argument in Modernity is this one word: progress. The idea of progress then becomes the very tool by which to put the past behind as dated, including the concept of beauty. But this is an arrogance that leads to a false perception of real life. Herbert Marcuse once argued that some categories such as, for example, reason do not belong to special epochs. Reason, says Marcuse, is a basic category to all philosophical reflection. Also categories such as spirit, morality, knowledge, and happiness do not solely belong to bourgeois, capitalist philosophy but these

---

39   Bernard Williams: *Shame and Necessity.* Berkeley, Los Angeles, and London 1993, p. 7.

categories belong with the destiny of man. As such categories must always, says Marcuse, be redefined, and historical epoch, or class, cannot claim any monopoly on these categories.[40]

Marcuse's argument links with other observations made by Georg Lukács, and later, by Jürgen Habermas, both of whom having argued the existence of a certain asymmetry within historical progress. In other words: in spite of modern ideology, our everyday lives are still imbued with archaic living in a number of ways. While great changes may take place within the social and intellectual level of society, fundamental human feelings may not change at the same speed. Hence, social and intellectual consciousness is one thing, and the nature of human feeling another. Already in 1910 Georg Lukács emphasized that there is a certain conservative dimension at stake in the development of feelings. Anthropologically, the constitution of man is such that for long periods of time basic feelings do not change much in spite of the fact that feelings are somehow always tinted by history. Among other things, Lukács uses this observation to explain why we still today are able to read and understand the works of William Shakespeare. Then, to Lukács basic human feelings are in principle archaic, and in consequence not prone to exploitation and change as is intellectual life.[41] Later, in 1981, Jürgen Habermas gave credit to this view in his book *Theorie des kommunikativen Handelns* by developing a concept of "Lebenswelt" as a field which embodies a different *raison d'etre* than do systems. In other words, we should have the courage to see clearly and to acknowledge to which extent we share experiences with the past and how we carry the past with us.

Then, as argued by Perpeet, the great challenge is finding the courage *to wonder* again. And wonder can hardly avoid subscribing to a celebration of the world which opens up the possibility of embracing a metaphysical outlook of some sort. One of the great contributions of Georg Lukács was exactly to make clear that the concept of beauty, in principle, is a genuine metaphysical concept. Any concept of beauty will, one way or other, contain a metaphysical dimension. But Lukacs' observation leaves open to discussion the question of whether a complete metaphysical framework is needed in order to work with the concept of beauty. Of course, the aesthetic categories developed by Antiquity were supported by various metaphysical systems, which today are not considered valid anymore. Hence, the challenge is to test if and how these classical metaphysical traditions can be of inspiration

---

40   See Jürgen Habermas: *Theorie des kommunikativen Handelns.* Zur Kritik der funktionalistischen Vernunft. Band 2. Frankfurt am Main 1981, pp. 559-560.

41   Georg Lukács first developed these ideas in an article "Zur Theorie der Literaturgeschichte" in *Text + Kritik. Zeitschrift für Literatur.* Heft 39/40 Oktober 1973. Also, this topic is discussed in my book on Lukács, see Inga R. Gammel: *Æstetisk Erfaring.* Temaer i Georg Lukács' Skrifter 1908-1918. Aarhus Universitetsforlag 1987, pp. 27-33.

and guidance to perhaps minor, or fragmented, metaphysical systems in which the question of beauty can be dealt with theoretically and philosophically. The point of departure is of course the very experience of beauty embracing wholeness and value. As Julius Walter and others have stressed, it is crucial to keep in mind that the concept of beauty is an inclusive concept. Accepting these facts might pave the way for new metaphysical attempts to argue for the concept of beauty. At a minimun, the discussion of beauty has to be set free from the ideologies which prevent us to see and realize what is actually there. In the past, as well as in the present, discussions of the phenomena of beauty have always been a challenge. According to Johann Wolfgang von Goethe it is a *condition humaine* that we in many areas of life must be content with *ad hoc* definitions. But *ad hoc* definitions are better than no definitions at all.

Even though modern theories find that the concept of beauty is outdated, the experience of beauty is still a dimension of how we perceive the world and what we value. The phenomena of beauty still fascinate, and the quest to understand the nature of beauty and its importance for human life has not become obsolete. In everyday life we have strong desires to pursue the beautiful in life, and we despise the ugly. In some of his attitudes man is indeed very conservative. But if modern scholarship neglects the traditions that have had a profound influence on our European culture and still have, we are misled. And if we abstain from reflecting on the issue of beauty, we subscribe to an oppressed worldview, destitute of quality, meaning, and joy.

Gilbert Murray once said that for all our progress we cannot get beyond the essential qualities captured and brought to light by the ancients. The question rather, according to Murray, is whether we can rise to them. When it comes to dealing with vital life forces we have not got ahead of our ancestors. Also in common colloquial speech the word beauty has not lost its splendor. The word itself connotes an atmosphere of joy and enthusiasm. When a phenomenon is classified or charaterized as a beauty, we deal with standards of value to man, and to life. Hence, the beautiful is indeed a feature of reality, found in the natural world as well as in human creativity and conduct. All this manifold beauty is displayed to us in great variety. Against the backdrop of the increasing theoretical and philosophical *amnesia* concerning beauty, it becomes meaningful to consider once more the abundance of reflections on beauty offered by ancient mythology, classical philosophy, and rhetoric. Again and again, these texts, handed down to us through the ages offer themselves as eye-openers to that which we have become unaware of, but on which we still can thrive and prosper. Therefore, it is crucial to put the question of beauty on the agenda again.

And, last but not least, we still walk under the same sky as did the ancients!

REFERENCES

Armstrong, Arthur Hilary (Ed.): *Classical Mediterranean Spirituality.* Egyptian, Greek, Roman. Vol. 15 of World Spirituality. An Encyclopedic History of Religious Quest. Routledge & Kegan Paul. London 1986.

Assunto, Rosario: *Die Theorie des schönen im Mittelalter.* DuMont Buchverlag. Köln 1982.

Athanassakis, Apostolos N.: *The Homeric Hymns.* Translation, Introduction, and Notes. The Johns Hopkins University Press. Baltimore and London 1976.

Baeumler, Alfred: *Ästhetik.* Wissenschaftliche Buchgesellschaft, Darmstadt. R. Oldenbourg Verlag. München. Wien 1974.

Barmeyer, Eike: *Die Musen.* Ein Beitrag zur Inspirationstheorie. Wilhelm Fink Verlag. München 1968.

Beardsley, Monroe C.: *Aesthetics.* From Classical Greece to The Present. A Short Story. The University of Alabama Press. Tuscaloosa and London 1975.

Benardete, Seth: *The Being of the Beautiful.* Plato's Theaetetus, Sophist and Statesman. Translated and with Commentary by Seth Benardete. Chicago and London 1984.

The Bible: *The New Jerusalem Bible.* Study Edition. Darton, Longman & Todd. London 1994.

Cassirer, Ernst: "Eidos und Eidolon. Das Problem des Schönen und der Kunst in Platons Dialogen" in *Vorträge der Bibliothek Warburg.* 1922/23 I/II, Lichtenstein 1967.

Christes, Johannes: *Bildung und Gesellschaft.* Die Einschätzung der Bildung und ihrer Vermittler in der griechisch-römischen Antike. Darmstadt 1975.

Cicero: *Works.* In Twenty-Nine Volumes. The Loeb Classical Library. Harvard University Press. Cambridge, Massachusetts. London. 1988 ff.

Cicero: *Letters to Atticus,* Vol I-IV. Ed. and translated by D. R. Shackleton Bailey. The Loeb Classical Library. Harvard University Press. Cambridge, Massachusetts. London 1999.

Cicero: *Letters to Friends,* Vol I-III. Ed. and translated by D. R. Shackleton Bailey. The Loeb Classical Library. Harvard University Press. Cambridge, Massachusetts. London 2001.

Dixon, Robert: *The Baumgarten Corruption.* From Sense to Nonsense in Art and Philosophy. Pluto Press. London, East Haven, Connecticut 1995.

Eckermann, Johann Peter: *Gespräche mit Goethe.* Zu den letzten Jahres seines Lebens. Zürich 1948.

Eco; Umberto: *Art and Beauty in the Middle Ages.* Yale University Press. New Haven and London 1986.

Ehrenspeck, Yvonne: "Aisthesis und Ästhetik. Überlegungen zu einer problematischen Entdifferenzierung" in *Aisthesis/Ästhetik.* Zwischen Wahrnehmung und Bewusstsein. Pädagogische Anthropologie, Band 1. Hrsg. von Klaus Mollenhauer/Christoph Wulf. Deutscher Studien Verlag. Weinheim 1996.

Gadamer, Hans-Georg: *Idee und Wirklichkeit in Platos Timaios*. Sitzungsberichte der Heidelberger Akademie der Wissenschaften, Philosophish-historische Klasse, Jahrgang 1974. Carl Winter Universitätsverlag Heidelberg 1974.

Gadamer, Hans-Georg: *Die Idee des Guten zwischen Plato und Aristoteles*. Sitzungsberichte der Heidelberger Akademie der Wissenschaften, Philosophish-historische klasse, Jahrgang 1978, Carl Winter Universitätsverlag, Heidelberg 1978.

Gadamer, Hans-Georg: *Wahrheit und Methode*. Grundzüge einer philosophischen Hermeneutik. Bd. 1. Tübingen 1986.

Gadamer, Hans-Georg: *The Relevance of the Beautiful and other Essays*. Cambridge 1995.

Gaiser, Konrad (Hrsg.): *Das Platonbild*. Zehn Beiträge zum Platonverständnis. Hildesheim 1969.

Gammel, Inga R.: *Æstetisk Erfaring*. Temaer i Georg Lukács' Skrifter 1908-1918. [=*Aesthetic Experience*. The Writings of Georg Lukács 1908-1018]. With German Summary. Aarhus Universitetsforlag. Aarhus 1987.

Gammel, Inga R.: *Skønhedens Filosofi*. Fra Homer til Hugo Boss. [*The Philosophy of Beauty*. From Homer to Hugo Boss]. With English Summary and 16 Color Plates. Aarhus Universitetsforlag. Aarhus 1994.

Gammel, Inga R.: "Dannelsesbegrebets æstetiske Dimension. Et æstetikhistorisk Perspektiv" in Øivind Andersen (ed.): *Dannelse-Humanitas-Paideia*. Oslo 1999.

Gammel, Inga R.: "The Philosophy of Beauty. From Plato to Modernity – and Back?" in *ANALECTA ROMANA*. Instituti Danici. XXIX. Romae MMIII, pp. 235-245.

Gammel, Inga R.: *The Passion for Order*. Myth and Beauty in the Writings of Plato, Heisenberg, Pauli, Jung, John D. Barrow, and Others. Münchener Schriften zur Design Science, Band 3. Hrsg. Rainer E. Zimmermann und Michael Keller. Shaker Verlag. Aachen 2015.

Graf, Fritz: *Griechische Mythologie*. Eine Einführung. München und Zürich 1991.

Grassi, Ernesto: *Die Theorie des Schönen in der Antike*. DuMont Buchverlag. Köln 1980.

Habermas, Jürgen: *Theorie des kommunikativen Handelns*. Zur Kritik der funktionalistischen Vernunft. Band 1-2. Frankfurt am Main 1981.

Hegel, G.W.F.: *Ästhetik I/II. Vorlesungen über die Ästhetik*. Hrsg. Rüdiger Bubner. Reclam. Stuttgart 1980.

Henckmann, Wolfhart, Hrsg.: *Ästhetik*. Wege der Forschung. Band XXXI. Wissenschaftliche Buchgesellschaft. Darmstadt 1979.

Herodotus: *The Histories*. Translated by George Rawlinson. With an Introduction by Rosalind Thomas. Everyman's Library 234. London 1997.

Hesiod: *Theogony and Works and Days*. Translated with an Introduction and Notes by M. L. West. The World's Classics. Oxford University Press. Oxford, New York 1988.

Homer: *The Iliad of Homer*. Translated with an Introduction by Richmond Lattimore. (1951) The University of Chicago Press. Chicago and London 1961.

Homer: *The Odyssey of Homer*. Translated with an Introduction by Richmond Lattimore. (1965) Harper Perennial. New York 1991.

Jaeger, Werner: *The Theology of the Early Greek Philosophers*. The Gifford Lectures 1936. At The Clarendon Press. Oxford 1947.

Jaeger, Werner (Hrsg.): *Das Problem des Klassischen und die Antike*. Wissenschaftliche Buchgesellschaft. Darmstadt 1961.

Jaeger, Werner: *Paideia*. The Ideals of Greek Culture, Vol. I-III, Oxford 1965.

Jaeger, Werner: "Die Platonische Philosophie als Paideia" in *Das Platonbild. Zehn Beiträge zum Platonverstandnis*. Hrsg. von Konrad Gaiser. Hildesheim 1969.

Jauss, Hans Robert: *Ästhetische Erfahrung und literarische Hermeneutik I*. München 1977.

Jones, Peter V.: *Homer's Odyssey*. A Companion to the English Translation of Richmond Lattimore. Bristol Classical Press. London 1992.

Journal of the History of Ideas. April-June 1961. Vol. XXII, Number 1.

Jüthner, Julius: "Kalokagathia"in *Charisteria*. Alois Rzach zum Achtzigsten Geburtstag dargebracht. Reichenberg 1930.

Kirk, G. S. and J. E. Raven: *The Presocratic Philosophers*. A Critical History with a Selection of Texts. Cambridge University Press. Cambridge 1957.

Klingner, Friedrich: *Römische Geisteswelt*. Verlag Heinrich Ellermann. Hamburg und München 1961.

Krüger, Gerhard: *Einsicht und Leidenschaft*. Das Wesen des platonischen Denkens. Vittorio Klostermann. Frankfurt am Main 1992.

Livingstone, R. W., Ed.: *The Legacy of Greece*. The Clarendon Press. Oxford 1928.

Lukács, Georg: *Heidelberger Philosophie der Kunst (1912-14)*, Georg Lukács Werke, Bd. 16. Darmstadt; Neuwied 1974.

Lukács, Georg: *Heidelberger Ästhetik (1916-18)*, Georg Lukács Werke, Bd. 17. Darmstadt; Neuwied 1974.

MacKendrick, Paul: *The Philosophical Books of Cicero*. Duckworth. London 1989.

Martin, James Alfred Jr.: *Beauty and Holiness*. The Dialogue between Aesthetics and Religion. Princeton University Press. Princeton, New Jersey, Oxford 1990.

Maurach, Gregor, Hrsg.: *Römische Philosophie*. Wege der Forschung 193. Darmstadt 1976.

Meyer, Heinz: *Das Ästhetische Urteil*. Zürich. Georg Olms Verlag Hildesheim. New York 1990.

Moravcsik Julius: *Plato and Platonism*. Plato's Conception of Appearance and Reality in Ontology, Epistemology, and Ethics, and its Modern Echoes. Oxford 1992.

Murdoch, Iris: *The Fire and the Sun*. Why Plato banished the Artists. Based upon the Romanes Lecture 1976. Oxford 1978.

Murrey, Gilbert: "The Value of Greece to the Future of the World" in *The Legacy of Greece*. Ed. by R. W. Levingstone. The Clarendon Press. Oxford 1928.

Ostenfeld, Erik Nis: *Forms, Matter and Mind*. Three Strands in Plato's Metaphysics. Martinus Nijhoff Publishers. The Hague/Boston/London 1982.

Perpeet, Wilhelm: *Ästhetik im Mittelalter*. Verlag Karl Alber. Freiburg/München 1977.

Perpeet, Wilhelm: *Antike Ästhetik*. (1961) Verlag Karl Alber. Freiburg/München 1988.

Plato: *Complete Works.* Edited, with Introduction and Notes, by John M. Cooper. Hackett Publishing Company. Indianapolis/Cambridge 1997.

Plotinus: *The Enneads.* Translated by Stephen MacKenna. Abridged with an Introduction and Notes by John Dillon. Penguin Books 1991.

Plutarch: *Lives.* Bd. VII. The Loeb Classical Library. Harvard University Press. Cambridge. Massachusetts. London 1994.

Pohlenz, Max: *Der hellenische Mensch.* Göttingen 1947.

Quattrocchi, Luigi: *L'Idea di Bello nel Pensiero di Platone.* Roma 1953.

Quintilian: *The Orator's Education.* Books 1-12. Edited and Translated by Donald A. Russell. Loeb Classical Library. Harvard University Press. Cambridge, Massachusetts and London 2001.

Reinhardt, Karl: *Platons Mythen.* Bonn 1927.

Robinson, T. M.: *Plato's Psychology.* University of Toronto Press. Second Edition. Toronto, Buffalo, London 1995.

Rosenkranz Karl: *Äesthetik des Hässlichen.* (1826) Leipzig 1990.

Santayana, George: *The Sense of Beauty. Being an Outline of Aesthetic Theory.* Dover Publications. New York (1896) 1955.

Scheer, Brigitte: *Einführung in die Philosophische Ästhetik.* Wissenschaftliche Buchgesellscaft. Darmstadt 1997.

Schrödinger, Erwin: *What is Life?* Cambridge University Press. Cambridge 2001.

Seneca, the Elder: *Suasoriae.* In *Declamations;* Vol. II. The Loeb Classical Library. Harvard University Press. London 1974.

Sheppard, Anne: *Aesthetics.* An Introduction to the Philosophy of Art. Oxford University Press. Oxford, New York, 1987.

Sontag, Susan: "On Style" in *Partisan Review,* Vol. XXXII, No. 4/1965.

Stenzel, Julius: *Platon, der Erzieher.* Felix Meiner Verlag. Leipzig 1928.

Tatarkiewicz, Wladyslaw: *Geschichte der Ästhetik,* Bd. I: *Die Ästhetik der Antike.* Basel/Stuttgart 1979.

Tatarkiewicz, Wladyslaw: *A History of Six Ideas.* An Essay in Aesthetics. Warszawa 1980.

Vitruvius: *The Ten Books on Architecture.* Translated by Morris Hicky Morgan. Dover Publications. New York 1960.

Vlastos, Gregory: *Plato's Universe.* Parmenides Press. Canada. 2005.

Walter, Julius: *Die Geschichte der Ästhetik im Altertum.* Ihrer Begrifflichen Entwicklung nach Dargestellt. (1893) Georg Olms Verlagsbuchhandlung. Hildesheim 1967.

Wankel, Hermann: *Kalos kai Agathos.* Inaugural Dissertation. Frankfurt am Main 1961.

Wilcock, Malcolm M.: *A Companion to the Iliad.* Based on the Translation by Richard Lattimore. The University of Chicago Press. Chicago and London 1976.

Williams; Bernard: *Shame and Necessity.* University of California Press. Berkeley, Los Angeles, and London, 1993.

Wright, M.R.: *Cosmology in Antiquity.* London 1995.

INDEX OF NAMES

Note: The names Homer, Plato, and Cicero, being ubiquitous in PART I, II, and III, are only indexed when appearing outside their individual sections.

A

Achilleus 29, 34-35, 37-38, 40, 45, 47, 50-53, 55, 59, 61-63, 85, 115, 122
Aeneas 61
Aeschylus 16
Aesop 80
Agamemnon 34, 41-42, 51, 130
Agathon 68-70, 88
Aïdoneus, name of the god Hades 30
Alkibiades 95-96
Alkinoos 55-56, 59, 63
Amalthea, nymph 133
Antinoos 56
Antonius, Marcus 124-126
Aphrodite 26-28, 40, 45-47, 49, 54, 70-71, 88, 114
Apollo 24, 29, 45, 51, 59, 62, 80, 85, 101
Ares 27, 61
Argos, Odysseus' dog 44-45, 48
Aristofanes 156-157
Aristotle 15, 126, 133, 141, 160
Armstrong, Arthur Hilary 11
Assunto, Rosario 162
Astyanax, son of Hektor 41
Athene 27, 29, 40-45, 47, 57, 59, 62
Athenian, the speaker in Plato's Laws 98, 100, 102-103
Atticus, see under Pomponius Atticus, Titus
Augustine 15, 160

B

Baeumler, Alfred 45, 159-161
Barmeyer, Eike 85
Baumgarten, Alexander Gottlieb 146, 161

Beardsley, Monroe C. 148-149, 154
Benardete, Seth 155
Boreas, the North Wind 79
Briareus 24
Brutus, Marcus Junius 115

C

Caesar, see under Julius Caesar
Calliope, one of the nine Muses 87
Cassirer, Ernst 151-153
Cato Uticensis, M. Porcius 136
Charis, goddess and in the *Iliad* wife of Hephaistos 54
Cicero, see under Tullius Cicero
Circe 30, 39, 51, 53, 57-58
Clinias 98
Cooper, John M. 18, 68
Crassus, Lucius Licinus, famous rhetorician 113, 115, 117, 124, 127, 134, 139

D

Demeter 24-25, 31, 46
Demiurge, the mythical figure in Plato's cosmology 31, 79-80, 88-94, 105, 152-154, 158
Demosthenes 108, 111-112, 118-119
Desire, personification of passion 85
Destiny 22-24, 26, 29, 31-32, 39-45, 51, 54, 56, 59, 61-62, 84, 86, 94, 107, 111, 118, 164
Diana 130
Diomedes 55
Dionysos 53, 68, 101
Diotima 68, 70-72, 74-78, 83, 88, 92, 95
Dolon 39, 55, 64

E

Eco, Umberto 159, 162
Eilithuia 71
Elpenor 34
Elysian Field 27-28, 38, 60
Empedocles 12
Eos, goddess of Dawn 27, 36
Ephialtes 24
Epicurus 139
Erebos, abyss of ultimate Darkness 35, 58, 61
Eros, or Love 68-74, 81-82, 88, 152
Eryximachus 68
Euryalos 55-56
Eurykleia 49

F

Foucault, Michel 147

G

Gadamer, Hans-Georg 80, 89-90, 158-159
Gaia 27, 31, 46
Ganymedes 39
Goethe, Johann Wolfgang 146, 165
Graces 41, 44, 85
Graf, Fritz 23
Grassi, Ernesto 162

H

Habermas, Jürgen 164
Hades 23-26, 30-35, 46, 53-54, 60, 130
Hannibal 125
Hegel, G. W. F. 19, 146, 148, 154, 159, 162
Heisenberg, Werner 15
Hektor 29, 41, 45, 52-53, 61-63
Helen 17, 38, 40-41, 51
Helios, the Sun God 24-28, 33, 36-37, 50, 52-53, 59, 65, 130
Hephaistos 26, 28, 37-38, 43, 46, 50-51, 54, 60
Hera 26-27, 30, 40, 46-47, 50, 60, 66
Herakles 24, 27, 32, 34
Hermes 31, 33, 35, 40
Hesiod 22, 46, 67, 69, 84-85, 97, 114
Hesper, evening star 37, 50
Hippias 68
Homer 14-18, 67, 80, 84-85, 97, 103-105, 115, 127, 130, 141-142, 150, 154-155
Hortensius 108, 115, 137, 140
Hyperion, epithet of Helios 26
Hyperion, father of Helios 25, 27

I

Iapetos 26
Ikmalios 52
Iphigeneia 130
Iris 47
Iros 39, 56

J

Jaeger, Werner 97, 145, 157-158
Jauss, Hans Robert 159
Jones, Peter 51
Julius Caesar 120, 125, 135-136, 140
Jung, Carl Gustav 15
Jupiter, Latin name of Zeus 113
Jüthner, Julius 155-156

K

Kalypso 35, 38, 49, 51, 57
Kirk, G. S. 22
Kleitos 39
Kronos 26
Krüger, Gerhard 80, 90
Kythereia, epithet of Aphrodite 43

L

Laertes 45
Lattimore, Richmond 17, 18, 22
Lucullus, Lucius Licinius 131, 136-137
Lukács, Georg 146, 164
Lysias 81-82

M

MacKendrick, Paul 135
Manilius, Manius 140
Marcuse, Herbert 163-164
Marius 109
Mars 133
Marsyas, satyr 95-96
Martin, James Alfred Jr. 150
Maugham, Somerset 147
Megillus 98, 101
Menelaos 28, 37-38, 41-42, 61
Meyer, Heinz 13
Mnemosyne 85-86
Moon, goddess, also Selene 27-28, 37, 50, 52-53
Murdoch, Iris 153-154
Murrey, Gilbert 16, 165
Muses, the nine daughters of Zeus and Mnemosyne 54, 85-87, 101

N

Nastes 50-51
Nausikaa 41, 43
Necessity 26, 59, 69, 89
Night, personification 26, 36
Niobe 62, 65

O

Odysseus 25, 27, 29-30, 33-35, 38-39, 41-45,
    48-49, 51-53, 55-59
Okeanos, nature god and river encircling the
    earth 23, 27, 31, 33, 38, 50
Olympos 22-24, 27-30, 39, 47, 50, 53, 63, 85, 127
Orion 34
Otos 24

P

Pan 79, 82, 96
Panofsky, Erwin 151, 153
Paris 40-41, 62
Patroklos 35, 45, 47, 54, 61-62
Pauli, Wolfgang 15
Peitho, goddess of persuasion 114
Peleus 29, 61
Penelope 41, 43-44, 48-49, 51-53, 56
Perpeet, Wilhelm 14, 159, 161-162, 164
Persephone 24-25, 30-34, 39, 46
Phaedrus 68-69, 71, 79, 81-82, 87, 96-97, 132,
    134
Phaethon, son of Helios 130
Phoenix, master of horses and companion
    of Achilleus 115, 122
Pindar 84-85
Plato 14-16, 18, 31, 41, 44, 55, 63-65, 107, 111-114,
    117, 126, 129, 132-134, 141, 148, 150-155, 158,
    160, 162
Plotinus 15, 129-130, 160
Plutarch 108, 136
Pohlenz, Max 159
Pollio, Asinius 108
Polyphemos, greatest of the Cyclops 56-57
Pompeius, Magnus 126
Pomponius Atticus, Titus, friend and economi-
    cal
    adviser of Cicero 125, 132-133, 135-136,
    138-139, 143
Poseidon 23-25, 27, 30, 40, 57
Posidonius, Stoic philosopher 129
Priam 40-42, 45, 52, 58, 62
Procrustes 13
Protagoras 102
Proteus 38

Q

Quattrocchi, Luigi 155
Quintilian 18, 114, 142

R

Rhadamanthys 38
Robinson, T. M. 93
Roscius Amerinus, Sextus 109
Roscius, Q., actor 118, 123-124
Rosenkranz, Karl 12

S

Scheer, Brigitte 148-149
Schrödinger, Erwin 15
Selene, see under Moon
Seneca, the Elder 108
Shakespeare, William 164
Sheppard, Anne 148-150
Silenus, head of satyrs 95
Sirens, female monsters 57
Sirius, or Orion's Dog, autumn star 37, 50
Sisyphos 35
Skamandros, a river, see also under Xanthos 32,
    60, 63
Skylla, female monster 57-58
Socrates 63, 67-71, 73-74, 77, 79-84, 86-88, 93,
    95-97, 129, 132, 134, 141, 151
Sontag, Susan 13
Stenzel, Julius 97
Sulla 109, 131

T

Tartaros, abyss 23, 25-27, 30, 35
Tatarkiewicz, Wladyslaw 17, 147, 159, 161
Teiresias 34
Telemachos, son of Odysseus and Penelope 28,
    43, 51
Thersites 39, 55, 64
Thetis 24, 29, 38, 45, 50, 53
Timaeus, natural philosopher 91
Tithonos 36
Tullius Cicero, Marcus 14-16, 18, 65, 88, 150, 154
Tullius Cicero, Marcus, Cicero's son 140-141
Tullius Cicero, Quintus, Cicero's brother 114,
    132, 139
Tyro, fabulous queen 27

U

Urania, one of the nine Muses 87

V

Varro 110, 126
Vitruvius 134
Vlastos, Gregory 103

W

Walter, Julius 156, 160-161, 165
Wankel, Hermann 156
Warburg, Aby 159, 162
Whitehead, Alfred North 15, 154
Wilcock, Malcolm M. 62
Williams, Bernard 10, 17, 163
Wils, Jean-Pierre 159
Winds 47, 54

X

Xanthos, name of one of Achilleus' immortal
    horses 62
Xanthos, the gods name for the river Skaman-
    dros 32, 60

Z

Zephyros, the West Wind 47-48
Zeus 22-31, 36, 38, 41, 43, 45-47, 50, 53-54,
    58-60, 70, 84-86, 92, 98, 130, 132-133

INDEX LOCORUM

References to ancient sources are followed by the relevant page numbers in this book.

Homer:

Iliad

1.400:	24	8.13-16:	23, 30	19.37-39:	45
1.423-25:	28	8.15:	26	19.223:	59
1.595-96:	46	8.46:	37	19.362-63:	50
1.601-04:	85	8.69-70:	59	19.374:	50
2.48-49:	36	8.478-79:	30	19.382-83:	50
2.101-09:	51	8.480-81:	26, 30	19.398:	50
2.169:	41	8.555-59:	37	19.416-17:	62
2.217-19:	55	9.159:	32	20.61-67:	30
2.407:	41	9.200:	53	20.233:	39
2.467:	60	9.393-400:	61	20.498-503:	61
2.636:	41	9.400-02:	61	21.349-52:	60
2.872:	51	9.443:	115, 122	21.379-80:	60
3.126:	53	10.495:	22	22.71-76:	45
3.156-60:	41	11.1-2:	36	22.209-12:	59
3.158:	41	11.52-55:	60	22.220-21:	29
3.168-70:	42	11.54:	53	22.270:	62
3.194:	42	13.71-72:	40	22.359:	62
3.220-24:	42	13.355:	24	22.317-19:	50
3.277:	24	13.639:	61	22.318:	37
3.396-97:	40	14.173:	28	22.371-72:	45
4.1 ff:	59	14.174:	47	23.70-74:	35
4.76-79:	40	14.199:	47	23.184-91:	45
4.450-51:	60	14.200 ff:	23	23.203:	47
5.5-6:	37	14.259:	26, 36	23.212-18:	47
5.394 ff:	24	14.342-45:	26	23.226:	36
5.394-97:	32	14.350-51:	28	24.18-21:	45
5.426-27:	46	15.193:	24	24.28-30:	40
5.426-30:	26	17.547-51:	53	24.60-64:	29
5.561:	61	18.107-10:	62	24.94:	53
6.401:	41	18.239-41:	27	24.229-34:	52
7.58-59:	59	18.403-05:	26, 38	24.375-77:	40
7.428-31:	60	18.416-20:	51	24.525-26:	29
		18.423-27:	50	24.526:	59
		18.462-67:	50	24.602-03:	62
		18.548-49:	51	24.796:	53

Odyssey

1.32-34:	92
3.2:	26
3.213:	42
4.45:	28
4.71-75:	28
4.115:	53
4.154:	53
4.305:	51
4.563-68:	38
5.73-74:	38
5.184 ff.:	22
5.184-86:	35
5.230-32:	51
6.15-18:	41
6.44:	127
6.44-45:	28
6.229-37:	43
6.306:	53
8.84-85:	53
8.167-77:	55
8.271:	24
8.579-80:	59
9.276:	57
9.513-16:	57
10.120:	57
10.352:	53
10.460-65:	39
10.510:	34
10.543-45:	51
11.5:	33
11.14-19:	33
11.32-33:	31
11.43:	34
11.109:	24
11.156:	33
11.249-50:	27
11.305-20:	24
11.488-91:	34
11.498:	37
11.619 ff.:	34
12.39-46:	57
12.87-88:	58
12.118:	58
12.159:	57
12.184:	57
12.354:	25
12.381-83:	25
13.32:	52
13.108:	52
13.330:	44
13.398 ff.:	44
15.108:	51

16.174-76:	43
17.306-23:	45
17.454-55:	56
17.518-19:	48
18.1-10:	56
18.192-96:	44
18.210:	51
18.296:	51
19.53-54:	41
19.56:	52
19.107 ff.:	48
19.204-09:	48
19.211-12:	48
19.225-27:	53
19.225-34:	49
19.233-34:	53
19.255-56:	53
19.255-57:	53
20.88-90:	49
20.194:	44
23.156-63:	43
23.181ff.:	44
23.200:	52
23.201:	53
23.205-07:	49
23.207-08:	49
23.231-32:	49
23.233-40:	49
23.241-46:	27
23.341:	52
24.6-10:	33
24.12-13:	29
24.13:	33
24.60-64:	85
24.148:	52
24.252-55:	45
24.371:	45

The Homeric Hymns:

To Aphrodite

45-60:	26
141-142:	28

To Demeter

10-14:	46
10-16:	31
62 ff.:	24
75-87:	25

To Selene

3-13:	37

Plato:

Phaedo

60e:	80

Cratylus

409a-b:	37

Theaetetus

152:	102
176:	93
155d:	162

Symposium

177c:	69
178d:	69, 97
179e:	69
188d:	69
189d:	69
197b-c:	88
199b:	70
201a:	88
201c:	71
203:	70
203d:	70
206c-e:	71-72
210e-211a:	74
210d:	88
211a-b:	74
211d:	77
211e-212a:	76
215b:	95
221e:	96

Phaedrus

229e:	79
229e-230a:	79
230c-d:	81
246a:	83
246d-e:	83
246e-248:	84
247c-d:	84
247d:	84
250d-e:	86-87
252d:	84
255c-d:	87
259b-c:	87
259d:	87
259e:	88
270c:	83
270e:	82
273e:	87
279b-c:	96

Greater Hippias
286e: 67-68

Republic
352d: 141
402c-d: 95
444d ff.:   93
606e: 63, 114
620a-d: 97
620c: 55

Timaeus
29a: 93
29c-d: 76, 80
29e-30:   89
30b: 80
33a: 93
37c-d: 91
40:      90, 91
41a-b: 94
42c: 94
86e: 97
87c: 94

Laws
624:      98
625b: 98
625c: 98
636e: 102
643a: 101
645:      101
654:      101
664a-b: 100
665c: 100
700b: 99
716c: 102
728a-b: 99
792c-793b: 101
800a: 99
803d-e: 103
803d: 102
817b: 99
896e-899a: 93
903b: 100
920d-e: 102

Cicero:

De inventione
I, 1:   114

De oratore
I, 17-18:   121

I, 27:   134
I, 28-29:   134
I, 116-117:   118
I, 131-132:   117
I, 132-133:   124
I, 134:   117
I, 199:   138
I, 224:   112
I, 251:   118
II, 22-23:   139
II, 24:   139
II, 34:   116
II, 357 ff.:   129
III, 24:   115
III, 28:   120
III, 29:   122
III, 32 ff.:   119
III, 44:   113
III, 57:   122
III, 76:   115
III, 95:   113
III, 129:   113
III, 133:   140
III, 171:   122
III 178:   120-121
III, 178:   127
III, 179:   126-127
III, 179-180:   127
III, 181-182:   129

De re publica
I, 10:   110

De legibus
I, 10:   138
I, 10:   139
II, 3:   132
II, 17 ff.:   114
III, 1:   132

Brutus
24:      133
117:      117
120-121:   113
121:      111
142:      118
247:      139
252:      120
320:      140
330:      115

De optimo
I, 3:   116

Orator
46:      112
70:      119, 123
120:      117
125:      112
126:      112

Academica
I, 11:   110
I, 19:   110

De finibus
I, 6:   114
I, 11-12:   141
II, 86:   141
III, 7:   136
IV, 76:   143
V, 58:   138
V, 59 ff.:   121

Tusculanae disputationes
I, 22:   132
I, 119:   134
II, 9:   133
III, 7:   133

De natura
I, 6:   111

De divinatione
II, 1:   110
II, 2:   111
II, 4:   110
II, 5-6:   111
II, 7:   110
II, 1-7:   140
II, 96:   118

De officiis
I, 69-71:   139
I, 93:   124
I, 98:   123
I, 99:   124
I, 100:   128
I, 103:   122
I. 110:   128
I, 121:   128
I, 123:   139
I, 125:   128
I, 139:   131
I, 146:   124
I, 156:   112
I, 158:   138

I, 159: 159
II, 4: III
II, 64: 135
III, 94-95: 130
III, 105-106: 129
III, 121: 140-141

Pro Sextus Roscius:
154: 109

The Philippics
II, 43: 125
II, 63: 125
II, 66-67: 126
II, 105: 126
III, 10: 126
IV, 11-12: 126
V, 12: 126
V, 25: 125

Letters to Atticus
205 (X. 13): 125
1 (1.5) § 7: 132
2 (1.6) § 2: 132
414 (XVI) § 2: 133
16 (I.16) § 18: 133
414 (XVI.6) § 1: 135
353 (XIII. 52) § 1-2: 135-136
17 (I, 17) § 5-6: 138

Letters to Friends
22 (V.12) § 1-9: 133

Other Authors

Aristofanes:

The Skies
1002-1019: 157

Aristotle:

Metaphysics
XIII, iii 8iv: 15

Hesiod:

Theogony
62-63: 85
62-65: 85
69-70: 85
331-365: 114

Plotinus:

The Enneads
I, 8: 129-130

Plutarch:

Bd. VII, Lives.
      Demosthenes and Cicero
I, 1-4: 108
I, 4-6: 108

Quintilian:

The Orator's Education
XIII, Prooem. § 3:18
X, 2.25-26: 18
X, 1.108 ff.: 142

Seneca, the Elder:

Suasoriae
VI, 24: 108

Vitruvius:

The Ten Books
      on Architecture
VII 5.2: 134